The Literature of Suburban Change

Modern American Literature and the New Twentieth Century
Series Editors: Martin Halliwell and Mark Whalan

Published Titles

Writing Nature in Cold War American Literature
Sarah Daw

F. Scott Fitzgerald's Short Fiction and American Popular Culture: From Ragtime to Swing Time
Jade Broughton Adams

The Labour of Laziness in Twentieth-Century American Literature
Zuzanna Ladyga

The Literature of Suburban Change: Narrating Spatial Complexity in Metropolitan America
Martin Dines

The Literary Afterlife of Raymond Carver: Influence and Craftsmanship in the Neoliberal Era
Jonathan Pountney

Living Jim Crow: The Segregated Town in Mid-Century Southern Fiction
Gavan Lennon

The Little Art Colony and US Modernism: Carmel, Provincetown, Taos
Geneva M. Gano

Forthcoming Titles

The Big Red Little Magazine: New Masses, 1926–1948
Susan Currell

The Reproductive Politics of American Literature and Film, 1959–1973
Sophie Jones

Ordinary Pursuits in American Writing after Modernism
Rachel Malkin

Sensing Willa Cather: The Writer and the Body in Transition
Guy Reynolds

The Plastic Theatre of Tennessee Williams: Expressionist Drama and the Visual Arts
Henry I. Schvey

Class, Culture and the Making of US Modernism
Michael Collins

Black Childhood in Modern African American Fiction
Nicole King

Visit our website at www.edinburghuniversitypress.com/series/MALTNTC

The Literature of Suburban Change

Narrating Spatial Complexity in Metropolitan America

MARTIN DINES

EDINBURGH
University Press

Edinburgh University Press is one of the leading university presses in the UK. We publish academic books and journals in our selected subject areas across the humanities and social sciences, combining cutting-edge scholarship with high editorial and production values to produce academic works of lasting importance. For more information visit our website: edinburghuniversitypress.com

Edinburgh University Press Ltd
The Tun – Holyrood Road
12(2f) Jackson's Entry
Edinburgh EH8 8PJ

First published in hardback by Edinburgh University Press 2020

Typeset in 10/13 ITC Giovanni Std Book by
Servis Filmsetting Ltd, Stockport, Cheshire,
and printed and bound by CPI Group (UK) Ltd,
Croydon, CR0 4YY

A CIP record for this book is available from the British Library

ISBN 978 1 4744 2648 0 (hardback)
ISBN 978 1 4744 2649 7 (paperback)
ISBN 978 1 4744 2650 3 (webready PDF)
ISBN 978 1 4744 2651 0 (epub)

CONTENTS

LIST OF ILLUSTRATIONS

ACKNOWLEDGEMENTS

This book grew out of ideas and arguments I began to assemble at conferences organised by fellow partners of the Leverhulme Trust-funded Cultures of the Suburbs International Research Network between 2011 and 2014. I would like to thank everyone involved – and in particular Jo Gill, Timotheus Vermeulen, Chris Niedt and Mary Corcoran – for making these events so stimulating and genial. I have also benefited from opportunities to present papers and receive valuable feedback at recent conferences organised by the British Association of American Studies, the Association of Literary Urban Studies, the Canadian Association of American Studies, and the John Updike Society, as well as symposia held at the Universities of Exeter, Leeds, Westminster and Roehampton.

I am grateful to Kingston University's School of Arts, Culture and Communication for granting me a research sabbatical in early 2016 – which allowed me to begin writing the book in earnest – and for providing financial support that enabled me to attend several conferences in the UK and the US. Kingston's Race/Gender Matters Research Cluster made a generous contribution towards permissions expenses, for which I am thankful. To my colleagues in the Department of Humanities, and in particular Éadaoin Agnew, Matthew Birchwood, Fred Botting, Tina Chanter, Meg Jensen, Jane Jordan, Helen Palmer, Patricia Phillippy and Selene Scarsi: thank you for helping build a genuinely supportive intellectual community whose outlook has managed to remain both critical and playful in these straitened times. The Race/Gender Matters research seminars, which began in autumn 2017, have been productive and convivial forums for engaging with colleagues' work-in-progress; I really appreciated and benefitted from the many thoughtful responses to draft material from this book. I have also learnt a great deal from undergraduate and postgraduate students who took my special study module 'America Dreaming: Suburbia, Literature, Culture', on which I have taught at least one text discussed in each chapter of this book. Thanks to all of you for making our investigations in those classes such fun.

Several people kindly reviewed chapter drafts: Sergio Rigoletto, Lisa Robertson, Diarmuid Hester, Paul Williams and Meg Jensen. My sincere thanks to each of you for your keen eyes and smart advice. I would also like to thank the anonymous reviewers for their intelligent responses to my project proposal and draft material. Series editors Martin Halliwell and Mark Whelan provided helpful guidance throughout the process, and I am especially grateful for their comments following their final review of my manuscript. The enthusiasm and resourcefulness of Michelle Houston, Commissioning Editor at Edinburgh University Press, has helped make preparing the manuscript a more straightforward and pleasant task than it otherwise might have been. I kindly thank D. J. Waldie for his generous comments about my work, and for agreeing to take me on a guided tour of Lakewood; like *Holy Land*, it was revelatory. I am also indebted to Heide Solbrig: thank you for your rich responses to all my queries about your practice.

Some final thanks are due. Helen Palmer: our looking out for each other over this last challenging year has meant a lot to me. Sam Solomon: for being an eager fellow-explorer of the ordinary, and for your extraordinary kindness. Lastly, writing this book would neither have been possible, nor particularly meaningful, without the love of friends and family in Brighton and beyond.

Permissions

An earlier version of the section in Chapter 2 titled 'Out of Time: Suburban Gothic and White Ethnicity in Jeffrey Eugenides's *The Virgin Suicides*' originally appeared as 'Suburban Gothic and the Ethnic Uncanny in Jeffrey Eugenides's *The Virgin Suicides*', in

Journal of American Studies, 46(4) (2012), 959–75, copyright © 2012 University of Cambridge Press, reprinted with permission.

An earlier version of the section in Chapter 5 titled 'Vernacular Adaptations: Commemorating Suburban Change' originally appeared as 'Metaburbia: The Evolving Suburb in Contemporary Fiction', in *Making Suburbia: New Histories of Everyday America*, ed. John Archer, Paul J. P. Sandul and Katherine Solomonson, Minneapolis: University of Minnesota Press, 81–90, copyright © 2015 University of Minnesota Press, reprinted with permission.

Four photographs by William A. Garnett – 'Grading, Lakewood, California', 1950; 'Foundations and Slabs, Lakewood, California', 1950; 'Framing, Lakewood, California', 1950; and 'Finished Housing, Lakewood, California' 1950 – are published with permission from the Jay M. Garnett and Nancy J. Garnett Revocable Trust, and from the J. Paul Getty Museum, Los Angeles.

Illustrations – including that used on this volume's cover – from *Here*, by Richard McGuire, copyright © 2014 by Richard McGuire, are used by permission of The Wylie Agency (UK) Limited, and of Pantheon Books, an imprint of the Knopf Doubleday Publishing Group, a division of Penguin Random House LLC. All rights reserved.

Illustration from *Jimmy Corrigan, The Smartest Kid on Earth* by Chris Ware, copyright © 2000, 2003 by Chris Ware (published in the UK by Jonathan Cape and in the US by Pantheon Books), is reproduced by permission of The Random House Group Ltd © 2001, and of Pantheon Books, an imprint of the Knopf Doubleday Publishing Group, a division of Penguin Random House LLC. All rights reserved.

Illustration from *Building Stories* by Chris Ware, copyright © 2012 by Chris Ware (published in the UK by Jonathan Cape and in the US by Pantheon Books), is reproduced by permission of The Random House Group Ltd © 2012, and of Pantheon Books, an imprint of the Knopf Doubleday Publishing Group, a division of Penguin Random House LLC. All rights reserved.

Illustrations from *The Dandelion King: Love and Loss Waiting in the Gas Line: A Graphic Memoir* by Heide Solbrig, are reproduced with kind permission of Heide Solbrig.

Introduction:
The Time of the Suburb

The American suburbs are not what they were. Since the late 1960s, economic deregulation, the decentralisation of employment and shifts in immigration policy have been reshaping the nation's metropolitan areas. Demographic and social change, from African American suburbanisation to the rise of dual-income households, has made anachronisms of many commonplace assumptions about the suburbs. Much of suburbia today resembles a vast, bewildering patchwork. Closer scrutiny of its quotidian operations, however, reveals complexes of nodes, conduits and territories, and interactions taking place at local, regional and global scales. The dynamism and diversity of suburban spatiality has licensed a neologising zeal: terms such as 'technoburbs', 'edge cities' and 'ethnoburbs' jostle for attention as commentators attempt to make sense of emergent forms and processes. This proliferating nomenclature arguably describes a post-suburban – or even post-metropolitan – present in which the traditional polarities of city and suburb no longer serve as useful paradigms, whether for planners and developers or activists for social justice.[1]

Several official metrics, however, continue to recognise 'suburban' as a category, and register that an ever-increasing proportion of the nation's population live and work in suburbs.[2] Further, in the US, suburbs usually designate discrete political entities that are fiscally independent from nearby urban municipalities. Authoritative definitions of place, of course, do not always correspond with local perceptions and practices. Nevertheless, the boundaries between

cities and suburbs, as well as an appreciation of the distinct qualities of different kinds of settlement, undoubtedly inform the everyday stories that people tell about the places they inhabit. Such
stories, in turn, help reify place. Where there is social conflict, rival
claims to places generate competing stories. Thus in metropolitan
areas in the US, place-making is so often predicated on a sense of
the suburban, though both within particular and across different
communities that sense is rarely unitary. One thing, though, is
certain: no one trying to narrate a broader story about the American
suburbs will be able to make much sense of these places without
first appreciating their composite, interconnected, evolving and
contested nature.

This book examines literary and cultural material produced after
1960 which responds to the socio-spatial transformations that
have been taking place across metropolitan America. Despite the
repeated claims of geographers, economists and environmentalists
about its obsolescence both as a concept and as a way of life,
the suburb continues to provide American literature a principal
setting and narrative framework. Suburbia's enduring interest has
much to do with its unabating proliferation and diversification.
The suburban story is still being told because the suburb is still
coming into being. This book is not, however, primarily a study
of recent literary engagements with newly emergent spatial forms.
Neither am I trying to argue, as some scholars have, that a single
epochal event has altered the course of a literary tradition by pre-
cipitating a radically different approach to narrating the American
suburbs.[3] Rather, *The Literature of Suburban Change* focuses on the
ongoing attempts by authors to articulate the temporal dimensions of suburbia. The suburbs, I contend, are conceptualised in
late twentieth-century writing both as being in process across time
and as places which have accumulated significant histories. The
attention paid by writers to the ongoing development of places and
to their continually evolving histories has reshaped the suburban
story. Further, over the last half century it has proliferated across a
range of forms and genres, exploiting and adapting those narrative
modes that are most clearly defined by sequentiality or historicity: the novel sequence, Gothic fiction, the short story cycle, the
memoir and comics. By examining a range of literary and cultural

modes, this book asserts the formal diversity and innovation of suburban stories, which, I argue, advance a more complex and productive understanding of suburbs – and spatiality more broadly – as incomplete, as networked, as plural. Such complexity contrasts with prevailing constructions of the American suburbs as standing outside of time and of history. A re-temporalised suburbia, I further contend, has the potential to interrupt and even disable narratives whose relative simplicity disguises structures of middle-class white privilege and obscures the causes and consequences of environmental change. By attending to the temporalities of suburbs across diverse narrative forms, this book not only revises the established literary history of late twentieth-century American suburbia but also enables more responsible reflection on the contemporary challenges and potential futures of metropolitan America.

From Instant Suburbs to Suburban Histories

My opening sketch of suburbia and its representations in literature as heterogeneous, interconnected and in flux may seem fantastic to some readers. It is certainly true that some American suburbs are less diverse than others. Much the same thing, however, could be said of urban and rural areas. Moreover, recent scholarship has shown American suburbia to be an increasingly diverse region overall by a variety of measures.[4] But there are reasons for why it is still difficult to conceive of the suburbs as changing and for why it is hard to see them as having meaningful histories. Within the 'suburban imaginary' – the discursive domain in which images of and stories about the suburbs circulate – a decidedly narrow and static set of tropes prevails.

Such stereotypes are easily observed. Entering the terms 'suburban novel' or 'movie suburbs' into an online search engine gives a good illustration of not only what seem to be the main preoccupations of cultural texts with suburban settings, but also the dominant frames through which such texts are appraised. Topping the results pages of my own recent searches were lists proclaiming the '10 Classic Stories of Suburban Ennui', '9 Novels of Suburban Desolation', '21 Novels about Being Trapped in Suburbia', '10 great dark suburbia films' and '10 Ridiculously Hellish Suburbs in Movies'.[5] Although it is hard to measure exactly how influential such sites are, their salience in the results pages is a consequence of the search engine's algorithms, which determine a site's relevance by, among other things, the number of other pages that link to it. The sites I have curated here, then, are likely to be among the most frequently visited by browsers intent on discovering more about suburban representation.

Like so many of the innumerable lists online and elsewhere that compile canons of cultural texts, my examples bespeak the pleasures of cataloguing, of distinguishing generic patterns and of creating hierarchies. But the broadly shared themes across the lists I have collated evince also a connoisseurship of malaise. Evidently, disorder and disaffection are the principal themes through which narratives set in suburbs are made intelligible as suburban stories. Although of course each was produced separately and independently, taken together the lists do seem also to discern a tradition, with recognisably 'classic stories' and a more recent self-conscious turn in which the suburban milieu has become 'ridiculously hellish'. But right across the generic cycle these texts are understood to be telling the same story again and again. Moreover, these lists indicate that ennui, entrapment and other kinds of suffering provide the situations and affects that make these texts so enjoyable. My point here is not to provide sanctimonious prescriptions for more suitable responses to the pain of others. Rather, I mean to query what kind of cultural work is being done by suburban stories and the ways that they are routinely codified, and, further, to speculate on the significance of the disjunction between this narrowly defined tradition and the dramatic transformations that have been taking place across metropolitan America over the last half century. Might it be that the predictability of these stories provides a soothing distraction from the complexities of and responsibilities to the present? Might they represent strategies of 'spatial purification'? Or, to put it another way, could it be that the endless re-telling of the tribulations of conformist, inhibited or neurotic suburbanites is the simplest way of keeping white middle-class people centre stage?

This singular, pessimistic narrative persists in part because few if any competing stories are recognised to exist. Indeed, usually suburbs are presumed to have no other history, or really any history worth speaking of at all. Their apparent depthlessness is demon-strated over and over by the ersatz historicity of so much suburban architecture, despite the long tradition in the US of using revival styles in residential building.[6] Further, suburbanites seem a rootless lot. In *Place and Placelessness* (1976) the humanistic geographer Edward Relph notes the interchangeability of 'home' for modern Americans, who move on average every three years. While he acknowledges that transience does not inevitably lead to placeless-ness, Relph contends that mobility has a corrosive effect on people's capacity to feel strong attachments to place. Indeed, he links the radical mobility of people, products and ideas to the spread of a homogenising mass-culture that promotes inauthentic attitudes to place. Such attitudes are defined as 'involving no awareness of the deep and symbolic significances of places and no appreciation of their identities'. Such inauthenticity is the hallmark of life in the suburbs, for their uniformity precludes the very possibility of 'deep or symbolic significance'.[7] A lack of authentic involvement, moreo-ver, leads to places becoming de-temporalised. For Relph, 'this does not mean just that there is no awareness of history, but also, and more profoundly, that places can become almost independent of time'.[8] Thus, in Relph's view, suburban rootlessness leads directly to an equally disconcerting timelessness.

Fellow humanist Yi-Fu Tuan is more sanguine about the potential for place-attachment in suburbs, in part because he acknowledges suburban diversity. He also recognises the inevitability of subur-ban change. However, Tuan understands a suburb to be merely a stage in the process of urbanisation: 'The suburb is at the frontier of metropolitan expansion. It is a society coming into being, a society undergoing change, at the end of which is urban culture.'[9] In other words, suburbs do not usually stay suburbs for long. The arrival of people not usually associated with suburban settlement – African Americans, say, or lesbians and gay men – is often taken as indicative of a suburb's urbanisation.[10] Thus, suburbs cannot change; they can only change into something else. Indeed, Tuan's account leaves almost no scope for any meaningful understanding of suburban history. Suburbs constitute at most a brief window of space–time within a wholly predictable developmental trajectory.

Given that geographers are liable to portray modern suburbs as being detached from temporal processes, it should come as no surprise that more readily accessible representations do just the same. The suburban imaginary from the post-war years to the present has been dominated by a narrow and unchanging repertoire of images that present uniform, static landscapes. Were I to repeat my previous internet search, this time limiting its remit to just visual depictions of suburbs, I would be confronted with page after page of photographs with mostly the same perspective: bird's-eye views revealing highly patterned but entirely depopulated arrangements of uniform streets and houses.[11] The writer D. J. Waldie, whose work I discuss at length in Chapter 3, has drawn attention to the role of aerial photography in shaping the way American suburbs are conceived. The abstract renderings of the first planned residential suburbs, such as Lakewood, California, depict their subjects in various stages of incompletion and always before anyone has moved in. Ironically, although these photographs 'were factually out of date as soon as the prints were dry, the anxieties they evoked became perfectly timeless'. Indeed, Waldie contends, this small stock of images informs so much anti-suburban criticism. More than sixty years after they were taken, the same photographs 'still serve as a model for how the "no place" of suburbia is to be simultaneously imagined and rejected'.[12]

What has helped sustain these images' currency is their confirmation of a sense of the suburb's instantaneity. In the early post-war years, mass-produced units of housing were often described as having appeared simultaneously out of nowhere. In one of the most influential books of the 1950s, *The Organization Man*, William H. Whyte describes the emergence of a conformist 'other-directed' culture linked to 'the great package suburbs that have *sprung up* outside our cities since the war'.[13] Two decades later Tuan would observe that 'the most singular feature in modern metropolitan expansion is its speed and scale. Suburbs appeared "overnight." They have the character of a "rush."'[14] His quotation marks indicate the hardening of commentary into commonplace. There is no doubting that suburban growth was in fact more rapid and extensive during the post-war years than at any previous time. At the close of World War II the US was ill-prepared for the sudden demand for housing in the wake of demobilisation and the baby boom. The crisis was mitigated by the endeavours of large builders, the most famous being the Levitts, who pioneered mass-production techniques in the development of three huge subdivisions in the Northeast. Simplicity of design, industrial methods of construction and massive federal subsidies yielded housing that was irresistibly affordable.[15] But the language of instantaneity serves to dematerialise the processes of production and denies these places any capacity for future change.

Indeed, many of the early critics who castigated the post-war suburbs for their dulling uniformity and oppressive conformism presumed that the object of their derision had reached its full and final form. For example, in his magnum opus *The City in History* (1961), Lewis Mumford tells the long story of suburbanisation and suggests that suburbs have always served 'as an experimental field for the development of a new type of open plan and a new distribution of urban functions'. But the post-war mass-produced suburb is denounced as 'a multitude of uniform, unidentifiable houses, lined up inflexibly, at uniform distances, on uniform roads, in a treeless communal waste'.[16] Mumford's much-quoted caricature, which rather obviously takes its cue from the bleak panoramas of aerial photography, forecloses any possibility of the suburbs providing 'an experimental field'. They are a fully formed, massified excrescence, and a betrayal of the autonomy that suburbanisation once promised to the select few. His infamous dismissal of Levittown, New York as an 'instant slum' is an even starker example of the mass-produced suburbs' de-temporalisation by an elite, city-dwelling critic.[17] This quality of instantaneity not only denies the suburbs any historicity, it also absolves the critic from any requirement to be sensitive to historical context. Hence the repeated deployment of the perspective of the aerial photographer across six decades of criticism.[18] Instantaneity is an eminently portable motif. The timelessness that critics insist is the product of mass-produced suburbs in fact provides the very basis for their attacks. One of the main aims of this book, then, is to try to give time back to the suburbs by examining the ways writers have exploited different narrative forms to articulate more complex stories that demonstrate how suburbs, and their pasts, are still in production. By doing so, *The Literature of Suburban Change* dismantles a critical platform whose familiar contours have facilitated decades of selective, complacent discourse. One of my central aims, therefore, is to 'reactivate' the suburbs, to present them as urgent, living sites whose spatial and temporal dimensions are still being explored.

For sure, the innumerable excoriations of the post-war suburbs did not go uncontested. As early as 1961, the sociologist Bennett Berger took issue with the 'myth of suburbia', which he argued had become established through the repeated characterisation of suburban settlement as 'a new way of life' defined by transience and homogeneity. For Berger, the insistent focus on the trials of commuting and the kinds of hyperactive socialising that were presumed to lead to surveillance, conformity and a rightward shift of political allegiances did not constitute falsification so much as highly selective reporting. A small number of studies of planned residential developments settled by white-collar populations had come to represent a nationwide phenomenon. Thus the considerable heterogeneity of suburbs was overlooked. Certainly, there was no attempt to appraise the conditions of blue-collar suburbs, which was Berger's principal interest.[19] The myth of suburbia flourished in large part because it confirmed the general outlook of various schools of opinion, most notably that of 'not-quite-completely-critical' left-wing intellectuals for whom, declares Bennett, the suburb provided a relatively safe target. It is a stance that places the (presumed-male) critic 'comfortably in the great tradition of social criticism', rendering him both 'respectable and harmless' – harmless because his critique is cultural rather than political and economic, and threatens no entrenched interests and contains 'no direct implications for agitation or concerted action'.[20]

In his landmark participant-observer study of the residents of the third Levittown to be built, in New Jersey, Herbert Gans similarly takes critics to task for depicting suburbanites as 'mindless conformers' who have 'allowed themselves to be swayed by builders, the mass media, and their neighbours'. For Gans, these prejudices are primarily a product of class: the likes of Lewis Mumford believe in the universality of their own upper-middle-class urban cosmopolitanism while 'refus[ing] to acknowledge the existence of lower-middle-class and working-class ways of living'.[21] Gans's conclusions were far more nuanced than of those who peddled the myth of suburbia. Hyperactive socialising, he determined, was not an unknown phenomenon in Levittown, but it was a phase which occurred out of necessity during the earliest stages of settlement. Conformity indeed prevailed, 'though less as malicious or passive copying than as sharing of useful ideas'.[22] And while Levittown was homogenous in terms of race, age and income, such homogeneity was 'more statistical than real'. In fact, by ethnic and religious criteria, Levittown was more diverse than many urban neighbourhoods; meanwhile, the population's narrow income range disguised many permutations of occupational and educational status.[23] Lastly, Gans acknowledges that people's lives were changed by the move to suburbia, though only in degree. In any case, the changes were usually both anticipated and desired, and were 'only expressions of more widespread societal changes and national cultural goals'.[24]

Despite the interventions of Bennett, Gans and others, the conventional critical view of the suburbs – an extensive but narrow body of commentary that the historian Paul H. Mattingly calls the 'suburban canon' – takes for granted their homogeneity and their timelessness.[25] Yet there exists a rich historiography of suburbanisation, of which Mumford's contribution is an early highlight, and from which *The Literature of Suburban Change* draws inspiration.[26] Pioneering studies published in the 1980s, most notably Kenneth T. Jackson's *Crabgrass Frontier* (1985), offer particularly detailed accounts of suburban development in mid-twentieth-century America. The many sprawling post-war subdivisions, whose progress has been frozen in innumerable aerial photographs, largely owe their existence, these histories show, to a series of initiatives in federal housing policy that commenced during the Great Depression. By far the most important of these was the establishment in 1934 of the Federal Housing Administration (FHA), whose purpose was to generate employment by stimulating the moribund construction industry. The FHA transformed home finance, principally by indemnifying private lenders against losses on new mortgages. With home loans subsequently posing little financial risk to lenders, interest rates tumbled. With new financial instruments such as fully amortised loans helping to further slash premiums and down payments, homeownership came within the grasp of many for whom it had previously been an unrealisable dream. Indeed, in most instances buying was a more affordable option than renting, and housing starts accelerated throughout the late 1930s. The Serviceman's Readjustment Act of 1944, popularly known as the GI Bill, established the Veterans Administration. The VA, whose purpose was to help returning military personnel purchase homes, mostly employed the same procedures as the FHA. According to Jackson, between 1934 and 1968 'both the FHA and the VA (since 1944) have had a remarkable record of accomplishment'. Over roughly the same period, rates of owner-occupation in the US rose from 44 to 63 per cent.[27]

The FHA programme spurred suburbanisation in part through its establishment of minimum standards for home construction. By the end of the 1930s these requirements had become closely modelled on newly built, free-standing suburban homes, which, according to Jackson, eliminated whole categories of dwelling, such as the traditional narrow row houses of eastern cities, from eligibility for loan guarantees.[28] More significant, though, was the FHA's wholesale adoption of a geography of risk articulated first and foremost by residential security maps. These documents were the innovation of another New Deal institution, the Home Owners' Loan Corporation (HOLC), which had been set up in 1933 to offer relief to homeowners threatened with foreclosure. The infamous HOLC maps offered a granular assessment of the long-term value of real estate in several US metropolitan areas. Individual neighbourhoods were categorised according to how likely property was judged to hold its value. Newly built, higher-income, entirely white and architecturally homogenous neighbourhoods – typically suburban in location – received the highest security grades. Areas with older, denser and more diverse housing stock and with poorer and ethnically mixed or predominantly black populations – almost always located in central cities – were much more likely to be considered 'declining' or 'hazardous'. The refusal of the FHA to back mortgages for property in low-grade areas encouraged further decentralisation, and stripped cities of their middle-class residents. African Americans and immigrants were largely prevented from joining the outflux by racially restrictive covenants and zoning laws designed to prevent the infiltration of wealthier residential neighbourhoods by poorer people. Consequently working-class, black and ethnic minority populations were pinned in rapidly declining cities, where redlining precluded them from obtaining loans to purchase homes.

In these ways federal intervention both encouraged racial and class segregation through suburbanisation and led to disinvestment in increasingly non-white cities. The privileges of suburban living were further subsidised through the development of infrastructure. A massive nationwide, federally funded programme of highway construction ensued in 1956. The biggest beneficiaries, naturally, were automobile manufacturers and operators in attendant industries. But those who owned or who were able to purchase cars and homes in the suburbs certainly benefited from government actions far more than their materially less-fortunate counterparts, and all too frequently the new highways that connected suburbs to central cities bifurcated or obliterated neighbourhoods settled by people of colour.[29]

According to Jackson, federal housing policies were not however a necessary condition for the post-war suburban explosion: 'the dominant residential drift in American cities had been toward the periphery for at least a century before the New Deal, and there is no reason to assume the suburban trend would not have continued in the absence of direct federal assistance'.[30] Indeed, historians such as Jackson, Robert Fishman and John Stilgoe have each attempted to take a much longer view of suburbanisation, and focus on the ways public policy, technological innovation, entrepreneurial desire and cultural change have combined across two centuries to transform the geography of metropolitan America.[31] Typically these histories distinguish a number of successive stages to suburbanisation. Writing in 2003, Delores Hayden identifies the evolution of seven vernacular patterns:

> Building in the borderlands began in 1820. Picturesque enclaves started around 1850 and streetcar buildout around 1870. Mail-order and self-built suburbs arrived in 1900. Mass-produced, urban-scale 'sitcom' suburbs appeared around 1940. Edge nodes coalesced around 1960. Rural fringes intensified around 1980. All of these patterns survive in the metropolitan areas of 2003. Many continue to be constructed.[32]

Hayden, however, distinguishes her study from earlier suburban historiography. Instead of focusing on developments to transport technology, her own work concentrates on the relations between real estate entrepreneurs and suburban residents and workers. An emphasis on commuting, she argues, has allowed the experience of middle- and upper-middle-class male breadwinners to eclipse that of women and children, and has also obscured the cross-class constituency of many suburbs. Indeed, Hayden's analysis helps to expose a problem with the earlier or 'classic' histories: they, like the post-war critiques of the suburbs, suffer from being selective. As the title of Fishman's 1987 book, *Bourgeois Utopias*, suggests, the focus once again is on middle- and upper-middle-class suburbs. Despite attending to the multiple forces driving the de-concentration of American cities, these histories hardly register suburban diversity. The presumption that suburbanisation in the US is a story solely about white middle-class residential settlement strikes out the development of industrial and working-class suburbs from history.

In fact, suburbs have also long harboured enclaves of people who service wealthier suburbanites. While Jackson helpfully explicates how federal policies and local initiatives led to the exclusion of ethnic and racial minorities from suburbs, he rather assumes these strategies worked flawlessly. Indeed, as Andrew Wiese has it, 'historians have done a better job excluding African Americans from the suburbs than even white suburbanites'.[33] In his 2005 study *Places of Their Own*, Wiese argues that black suburbanisation between 1960 and 2000 is as significant a demographic shift as the Great Migration. African American settlement on the urban periphery in the post-war years marks the emergence of a new black middle class, but Wiese also illuminates earlier histories of pioneering working-class African Americans whose communities provided a foundation for subsequent migration. Wiese explores how, regardless of their economic circumstances, 'across the US suburbanisation was a cumulative process linked through time and space by contested racial struggle and the desire of black families to create places of their own'.[34]

A further criticism of the early histories is their tendency to present suburbs as self-contained spaces. While offering persuasively detailed accounts of suburbs' internal social and physical characteristics, the first wave of historiography largely ignores the relations between suburbs and cities and between different settlements on the periphery. Kevin M. Kruse and Thomas J. Sugrue insist that a proper understanding of suburban development is only possible with a 'metropolitan outlook': that is, one which recognises that 'the histories of cities and suburbs are fundamentally intertwined, even as municipal boundaries kept them separate', and which pays particular attention to the 'contests for power taking place in the struggles over policy, money and the law', and the ways these conflicts have shaped modern America.[35]

The interventions of Hayden, Wiese, and Kruse and Sugrue are then each explicitly revisionist. Together they contribute to a second wave of historiography sometimes referred to as the 'New Suburban History'.[36] *The Literature of Suburban Change* takes a leaf from the New Suburban History to the extent that it insistently focuses on how writers have appraised the relationships between suburbs and other spaces. While most of the works I address were written by white authors and focus on middle- and upper-middle-class communities, they nevertheless range across a diversity of experience: of men and women, children and the elderly, and the upwardly mobile and the déclassé; but also, of drivers and pedestrians, writers and realtors, and recent immigrants and perennial outsiders. These stories even conceive of non-human agencies normally beyond the scope of historiography, including animals and buildings. Further, I show how these narratives are preoccupied by the ways suburban sites are contested through competing histories. Thus *The Literature of Suburban Change* demonstrates not only that the settings of suburban stories are, in vital ways, in process, but also that suburban pasts are being continually redefined and redeployed in order to make claims about the present and future. Who gets to author and narrate history and how they are enabled to do so are key concerns in this book. This should come as no surprise: the history of suburbanisation in the US is after all a history of the unequal distribution of resources; narrative, arguably, is just another resource. But I am equally exercised by how certain narrative modes help to legitimise and delegitimise specific voices and positions. Indeed, the book's first three chapters examine texts whose form enables them to interrogate and even problematise the presumed universality – and therefore the authority – of white middle-class male perspectives that continue to dominate the suburban story.

By contrast, the fourth and fifth chapters and the book's conclusion focus mainly on texts whose arrangement serves to articulate not only diverse voices but also multiple temporalities. Broadly, then, *The Literature of Suburban Change* is shaped by a trajectory towards increasingly complex narrative forms and complex renderings of suburban spatiality.

Theorising Suburban Complexity

To view places not as static enclaves defined by singular identities but instead as conjunctures of multiple trajectories has important and far-reaching consequences, and not only for conceptualising suburbs and the stories we tell about them. The supposedly more intuitive perspective, which sees space as merely inert or purely abstract and which presumes places to be detached and fully formed unities, can limit the political imagination in potentially harmful ways. Such attitudes are liable to mystify the larger forces and flows that produce space, and obscure continuing conflicts over place and the possibilities of spatial change. Worse, they can enable a retreat into isolationism and give credence to chauvinist, exceptionalist narratives about situated communities imagined on both local and national scales. As Doreen Massey argues, to emphasise that space is instead the product of interrelations, is shaped by multiplicity, and is always unfinished, in development, helps elucidate a 'range of connections between the imagination of the spatial and the imagination of the political'.[37] For sure, the task of explicating the political dimensions of space and place has been a central objective of thinkers who have participated in the 'spatial turn' in the humanities and social sciences. Attending to the ongoing assemblages of space and of place, however, helps to clarify the ways a progressive politics of spatiality coordinates with the principal campaigns of late twentieth-century critical theory: the rejection of grand narratives; an insistence on the genuine openness of the future; a commitment to anti-essentialism; and a focus on difference and heterogeneity.[38]

Massey has probably been more determined than any other theorist in demanding that space be conceived in ways which foreground its multiplicity, its ongoing production, and its interactions across various scales. Other thinkers, however – whether their work emerges out of the tradition of humanistic geography, which focuses on the subjective experience of place and the ways that places provide loci of meaning for humankind, or from the more radical tradition, in which Massey is situated, with its commitment to appraising how the production of space is defined by relations of power – have come to broadly similar conclusions. For instance, in his phenomenologically oriented treatise *Place and Experience* of 1999, Jeff Malpas insists on the complexity of place, which he holds to be, among other things, bounded yet permeable, nested and networked, and spatio-temporal in nature.[39] As Eric Prieto observes, despite their very different starting points and priorities – respectively, the social-political dimensions of space, and the inseparability of individuals from their experience of place – Henri Lefebvre shares with Malpas a sense of place/space as a ramified formation that both shapes and is shaped by human agency.[40] Throughout *The Literature of Suburban Change*, I engage with the arguments of humanistic as well as radical geographers, not only because articulations of spatiality's complexity are forthcoming from both traditions, but also because of their mutual interest in narrative. For humanistic geographers such as Nicholas Entrikin, it is narrative that produces a logical grasping together of elements, which in turn transforms a mere site into a meaningful place.[41] Radical geographers, as ever, are more concerned with dynamics of power. So, when Michel de Certeau discusses 'spatial stories', he is exercised by the question of which narratives get to be authorised as well as what forms of behaviour are sanctioned by official narratives and which are delegitimised.[42] I understand the texts that I examine in this book to be narratives that make meaningful the very idea of suburban space and place. Further, these texts, whether traditionally realist or explicitly metafictional, continually draw attention to the role of narrative in the creation and contestation of place-based identities. Such self-reflexivity, I contend, provides scope for a much more politicised understanding of suburban stories and suburban spatiality.

Attentive readers will have noticed the careful alignment in the previous paragraph of the term 'place' with the concerns of humanistic geographers and 'space' with their radical counterparts. The differentiation is intentional and registers the distinct intellectual trajectory of each tradition, as well as divergent assumptions about methodology and politics. Theoretical interest in 'place' in the anglophone academy gained ground from the 1970s and marked a reaction against a hegemonic scientism which presumed that only positivistic modes of enquiry could produce reliable and useful forms of geographical knowledge. Bolstered by their engagement with a continental European tradition of phenomenological thought, humanistic geographers re-asserted subjective experience of place as a worthwhile object of intellectual scrutiny. Moreover, places were understood to constitute, in Edward Relph's words, 'the profound centers of human experience'; the intentionality that defines being in place comprises the very essence of what it is to be human.[43] Further, for humanistic geographers a keen sense of place both encourages greater moral accountability, by generating what Yi-Fu Tuan calls 'fields of care', and provides a bulwark against the homogenising forces of global modernity.[44] By contrast, for radical geographers the scientific associations of 'space' have been welcome. The term's more abstract cast is suggestive of mobility, freedom and political possibility. 'Place', on the other hand, is either denigrated or avoided altogether: it suffers from associations with tradition, nostalgia and, worse, an atavistic territorialism. Further, the presumed connection between Heidegger's valorisation of rooted place and his Nazism has prompted a reciprocal turning away from phenomenology by radical geographers. I, however, am not motivated to elevate one term over the other, largely because I understand both space and place to be socially produced and therefore similarly complex. For sure, 'space' better facilitates generalisation about geographical arrangements and relationships, whereas 'place' helps to particularise them. 'Place' designates a location and material setting made meaningful by people through various kinds of practice, though these meanings are rarely if ever stable or fully shared. 'Spatiality' substitutes 'space and place', providing a superordinate term that also helpfully connotes the complexities that I have been foregrounding.

Another dyad that is invoked again and again by cultural geographers is that of space and representation. Despite their interest in the politics of narrative, many radical geographers evince a deeply felt

suspicion about the representation, as opposed to the lived experience, of space. The concerns have a similar basis to those that motivate the repudiation of place: representation tames, stabilises the
spatial. For Lefebvre and especially de Certeau, the representation
of space is closely associated with the tools of technocratic management: maps, plans, scientific writing and other abstractions. For de
Certeau, the abstract panoramic projections of architects, planners
and cartographers are 'a way of keeping aloof' from everyday life;
the condition of possibility of these 'facsimile[s] is an oblivion and
a misunderstanding of practice'.[45] Such mapping deadens, denies
real life its dynamism and flow, and thus prevents true becoming.
As Massey observes, these repudiations of representation reveal
a presumption that time can be 'captured' by space. Thus, space
constitutes an inferior dimension; the liveliness of the world is ultimately defined by temporality. De Certeau's implicit denigration of
space would appear to be a residual formation, a hangover from the
'epoch of history', during which temporality provided the principal
frame for appraising human endeavour.[46]

Of course, not all representations of space constitute technologies of control. Lefebvre considers certain kinds of artistic practice
as capable of harnessing the complex symbolisms of 'bodily lived
experience' to resist authoritative representational frameworks
designed to regulate social life. However, these interventions are
conceived not so much as mimetic (and hence stabilising) than
as ongoing practices, continuous productions that are part of and
engaged with the world.[47] As such these practices transcend the
traditional binary of space and representation; they are constitutive
of what Edward Soja refers to as 'thirdspace', or 'real-and-imagined
space'.[48] Massey contends that all kinds of representation, even
the scientific, might reasonably be conceived of as 'productive
and experimental, rather than simply mimetic, and an embodied
knowledge rather than a mediation'. What would be even more
useful, she suggests, is to appreciate that representations do not
merely capture the temporality of human life; rather, they articulate
its spatio-temporality.[49] This would appear to be at the heart of
Bertrand Westphal's 'geo-critical' approach. Harnessing the ideas
of Soja and other postmodern spatial theorists, Westphal insists on
the usefulness of engaging with 'literature and the mimetic arts'.

Indeed, he says, 'the space-time revealed at the intersections of various mimetic representations is this third space that geocriticism proposes to explore. Geocriticism will work to map possible worlds, to create plural and paradoxical maps, because it embraces space in its mobile heterogeneity.'[50]

How might suburban representation constitute an ongoing production of embodied knowledge that registers its spatial as well as its temporal dimensions? In *Sprawling Places* (2008), the philosopher David Kolb makes some useful suggestions for reconfiguring the ways in which we conceptualise and represent suburban space. Kolb notes that the American suburbs are typically measured against traditional standards of space which privilege unity, centredness and symmetry. That these are obviously aesthetic categories begins to explain why the harshest critics of suburbs are preoccupied by their aesthetic shortcomings. Kolb, however, is not concerned to make a case for sprawl being an under-appreciated architectural marvel, and he acknowledges many of manifest problems associated with suburbanisation, from environmental despoliation to the unequal distribution of the social costs of low-density living. Kolb insists, though, that the frequently expressed contempt for suburbs and many other contemporary places in the US is misguided because it fails to register their complexity. Typically, critics do not appreciate sprawling places' interconnections – or potential connections – with other locations and wider processes; neither do they register how such environments change over time. Perceiving this complexity is necessary but not easy, for it 'demands a sensitivity to contours and links that are more than spatial'.[51] What is required are ways of enhancing this complexity, and strategies for making these connections more obvious. The practice of making suburbs more self-aware can take place at several levels. Architects, designers and planners can both reveal and compound the structural complexity of suburbs by emphasising borders, linkages and routes of action. Residents themselves might foreground the temporal processes of living in place through the small acts of modification to their own homes; indeed, says Kolb, 'the cumulative effects of such bricolage could change the sense of the whole'.[52] While wary of the fact that public art is all too often commissioned to celebrate a narrowly defined *genius loci*, Kolb suggests that artists too can contribute to the cause of making suburban places more self-aware. For instance, Tobias Armborst's redesign of an 'absolutely ordinary' strip mall outside Cambridge, Massachusetts is commended as an attempt to clarify 'the simultaneous presence of multiple temporalities'. By emphasising the different temporal activities of different groups of people the project successfully extends and makes visible 'all these multiple and co-existing interpretations of this place' without prettifying or transforming the mall into another kind of place. Indeed, by intensifying what is already there, Armborst's work 'enhances everyday experience, building in a kind of ordinary magic that was absent in [the] mall's previous everyday life'.[53]

Kolb does not directly countenance an equivalent role for literature, but he does conclude suggestively with the claim that a more complex suburbia will be 'reread and remade without ever coming together hierarchically. As a shared story, its narrative form [. . .] will be a joining of episodes where each has more than one focus as it moves and links in many directions at once'.[54] The novels, short stories, memoirs, comics and plays examined in this book accord with Kolb's suggestions insofar as these materials are centrally concerned with suburban complexity and typically are shaped by multiple focuses and movements. Most of the literary texts I discuss are indeed interested in the idea of suburbia's being a 'shared story'. Sometimes this story is imagined as being singular and collective: a national narrative. More often – and perhaps more usefully – it is conceived of as being composite and plural. And, once again, these texts are preoccupied by the politics of narrating space: with the matter of who gets to tell whose story, with conflicting accounts of changing circumstances, and with contested histories. At the same time, this literature employs old forms with long histories to tell new stories. I ask then what kinds of formal innovation are required to make sense of the historicity of the suburbs, and what kinds of pressures these literary traditions bring to bear on attempts to articulate spatial change.

Forms of the Suburban Story

Alongside the New Suburban History, a flourishing body of scholarship has taken up the task of reckoning with cultural representations of the American suburbs. One of the most important literary studies in this new field remains Catherine Jurca's *White Diaspora* (2001). In this path-breaking book, Jurca argues that the suburban novel has long provided a vehicle for expressing the anguish of a white middle class that feels itself to be inauthentic and dispossessed despite, and sometimes because of, its evident affluence and security. Jurca calls such discursive chicanery 'sentimental dispossession' and argues that suburban-set fiction promulgates a 'fantasy of victimisation'.[55] Certainly, anything which makes clear how class and racial privileges come to be disavowed is enormously useful, and I draw on some of Jurca's key observations on several occasions throughout this book. What is perhaps less helpful about Jurca's argument is her assumption that the suburban story in the late twentieth century remains the 'same as it ever was', recycling the same clichéd imagery and manifesting the same self-pity.[56] The likes of John Updike and Richard Ford are, in her view, merely inheritors of a tradition, rather than innovators. Jurca acknowledges that such writers have been 'dedicated to charting the fluid contours and complex social and spatial geographies' of an increasingly 'polymorphous' suburbia. But their appreciation of this new terrain is mere window dressing as they plough on with stories of suffering suburbanites.[57] If this conclusion disappoints it is perhaps because it merely confirms what is already well known. As the online lists that I previously mentioned showed, suburban stories are not only recognised but also celebrated for their singular focus on middle-class distress. The historical flatness of Jurca's study is also homologous to the repetitious deployments of aerial photography in anti-suburban criticism. My readings of Updike's and Ford's fiction, which I turn to in the next chapter, suggest that Jurca's brief engagements with literary material published after 1960 are selective; I demonstrate instead how such writers keenly explore how suburbs have evolved as lived places and have provided scope for multiple though frequently contested place-based attachments.

Kathy Knapp takes a different view to Jurca insofar as she identifies 9/11 as having had a galvanising and transformative effect on the literature of the American suburbs. In the 1990s authors of suburban-set fiction revelled in an orgy of destruction: novel after novel saw suburban homes razed by fire and flood; suburban families were routinely ripped apart by brutal acts of violence. That these tropes intensified almost beyond bearing underscore for Knapp how the suburbs and the suburban story were deemed by writers to be well past their sell-by date. In the aftermath of 9/11, however, such fantasies of devastation became unseemly. Moreover, the deadliest-ever single terrorist attack on US soil (and indeed the world) shattered any sense of security previously afforded by the suburbs. Indeed, contends Knapp, 'the cohort of writers who have returned to this beat do not offer the postwar suburb as a retreat from the larger world but suggest that the world has come to the suburbs'.[58] Post-9/11 novels, she argues, approach the suburbs through an aesthetic of contingency, fragility and open-endedness. Meanwhile, their white middle-class male protagonists demonstrate a willingness to hold themselves accountable for their past failures and, generally, twenty-first-century narratives advance a more ethical model for middle-class life that emphasises interdependence over independence. Knapp's readings of her selected novels are, like Jurca's, truly compelling and illuminating. But there is an obvious risk in loading one historical juncture with so much explanatory power. For, just as the laying waste to suburban houses is a habit that extends beyond 1990s fiction, a great many narratives published prior to 9/11 demonstrate the contingent nature of suburban communities.[59]

Indeed, as Joseph George shows in his excellent study of post-war American fiction, all manner of writers, from Richard Yates in the early 1960s to Gish Jen in the mid-1990s, have been concerned with the dynamics of what he terms 'critical hospitality', that is, the face-to-face interactions that go beyond the contractual requirements imposed by planning and law. A great many suburban stories published since World War II, George argues, in fact 'highlight the messy and contingent results of infinite individuals sharing space with one another, making fractured and non-determining communities together'.[60] Thus, transitions of the kind that Knapp identifies can easily be overstated. Like George's, my approach is predominantly revisionist; I too seek to re-evaluate a narrative tradition that has persistently been understood in narrow terms. George, however, admits that the suburbs, in his reading, are 'surprisingly static': he understands that their most important role is to provide imaginary 'stages' for playing out scenarios that explore how people might better live with one another and with difference.[61] George's project of reimagining community and intersubjectivity is a vital one, though in *The Literature of Suburban Change* I am not content to read the suburbs as an inert backdrop. Where I focus on imagined communities in suburban narrative – in Chapter 3 in particular – I see them as always interacting with an understanding of the changing material circumstances and with the evolving histories of suburban spatiality.

The studies of Jurca, Knapp and George each deal solely with novels. There are perhaps good reasons for presuming, as these and other scholars do, that the novel is the primary cultural vehicle for engaging with suburban life throughout the twentieth and twenty-first centuries. The tradition is as long as the corpus is extensive. But the novel's dominion over the suburban imaginary has been abetted by the critical standards by which other literary modes are evaluated. In her important study, *The Poetics of the American Suburbs* (2011), Jo Gill suggests that the reason why poetry that addresses suburban themes and readerships has been largely ignored is a consequence of the failure of this material – much of it exhibiting characteristics of light verse – to meet 'the perceived standard for recognition as "poetry"'. Hence the widespread but false assumption that poetry has nothing to say about suburbia.[62] Gill argues to the contrary that, across the mid-twentieth century, poetry 'devises a language, structure and voice appropriate to the physical and social formations of the contemporary suburbs'. The very best examples, indeed, display 'an awareness of [poetry's] own processes of perception, reflection and meaning production'.[63] Those who have taken the novel as their focus have been noticeably less assiduous than Gill in attending to the formal and generic dimensions of suburban representation. Indeed, while they do give account of their own interpretive strategies, critics rarely see the novel as much more than a transparent receptacle, a container of stories, representations and so on.

By contrast, questions about form are at the forefront of Timotheus Vermeulen's innovative study of suburban space in film and television, *Scenes from the Suburbs* (2014). Vermeulen notes that suburban stories have been valued in popular criticism above all for their sociological insights, for their accurate depictions of Americans at home and at work. Meanwhile, academic engagements with the same material are driven by a historicising impulse; typically, scholars are preoccupied with the development of a distinct chronotope over time.[64] For Vermeulen, neither approach adequately addresses the crucial matter of aesthetics. He contends that only careful analysis of rhythm, tone, stylistic register and so on can disclose how texts cohere as suburban stories, how suburbs not only feature in but also structure the stories in which they feature. In other words, paying attention to aesthetics can help elucidate the ways that suburban representation and suburban spatiality are mutually constitutive, or as Vermeulen – echoing Lefebvre – puts it, how 'the space of the US suburb is produced in the stories it produces'.[65] To this end, Vermeulen sidelines historical concerns and selects material that he considers representative of leading generic trends in contemporary film and television. Focusing on the contemporary of course does not, and indeed should not, necessarily preclude historicism, but I applaud Vermeulen's commitment to exploring how aesthetic elements combine to produce a sense of the suburbs.

In similar fashion to Vermeulen's study, each of my book's five chapters examines a discrete literary form or genre: the novel sequence, the Gothic novel, memoir, comics and the short story cycle; in addition, my conclusion reflects on some recent two-act plays. Each chapter investigates how these modes have shaped, and have been shaped by, a concern with suburban spatiality. Unlike Vermeulen, however, I consider it necessary to appraise the historical development of each form. There are two main reasons for this. First, many of the texts I discuss are innovative in various ways. Their adaptations of specific forms of writing are responses to, and help make meaningful, the complex processes of suburban change. An appreciation of the innovativeness of the texts under examination necessitates a longer view of the literary traditions in which they participate. Second, each mode has a particularly long and close association with the suburban and the domestic. Despite this latter fact, little critical attention has been paid to any of them as vehicles for the suburban story; once again, a consideration of novels – and, specifically, their narrative content – has dominated scholarship. As for my choice of particular texts, I do not presume that a single case study can represent an entire literary mode. Each chapter therefore examines multiple examples. I draw attention to the divergences and well as the similarities between texts operating within particular formal and generic traditions. Indeed, the aim of this book, which I hope is clear by this stage, is not to achieve the kind of spatial purification that popular reports and some scholarly studies presume is the function of suburban stories; a certain messiness, or complexity, befits my subject.

The earliest text that I examine in detail is John Updike's breakthrough novel *Rabbit, Run*, which was first published in 1960. The most recent, Heide Solbrig's transmedia project *Dandelion King*, is still in progress. What these very different texts have in common with each other and with the numerous others that I discuss in this book is the way they attend to developing suburban forms, which often originate from earlier in the twentieth century. Indeed, I contend that the late twentieth- and twenty-first-century suburban story is defined by an appreciation of the historicity of its setting. Inevitably, however, this historicity is produced differently across different literary forms, with varying implications for present-day suburbia and for future developments.

In Chapter 1, which focuses on novel sequences, I describe this sense of the past as 'metropolitan memory', as its province is congruent with entire city regions. I argue that a metropolitan perspective – enabled by innumerable commuting journeys – better facilitates an appreciation of suburban complexity, from the dynamic relationships between centre and periphery to the ramifications of economic and demographic change. This mode of remembering is revisionary, in two senses of the word. On the one hand, the perspectives employed by the protagonists of novel sequences are continually subject to revision: successive novels develop new, improved optics for countenancing and engaging with metropolitan change. On the other hand, far from producing a solidification of space, the protagonists' repetitive journeys reveal its contingency and incompleteness. If all novel sequences are shaped by provisionality thanks to the multiple beginnings and endings supplied across their many instalments, I suggest that suburban novel sequences are further defined by a tension between the production of progressivist and deconstructive narratives, between revisions that refine and revisions that dismantle.

Chapter 2 considers novels that employ a distinctly Gothic mode in order to situate their suburban locations within histories defined by class- and race-based exclusion. If uncertainty and anxiety are the troubling but potentially radical qualities of Gothic narrative, suburban Gothic has typically been understood in terms of a banal unhomeliness which merely confirms reassuring commonplaces about the post-war American suburbs. In such readings, the suburbs are supposed to embody a desire to stand outside of history: either they are places in which people seek refuge from their own pasts, or they represent an idealised past removed from the challenges of the present. I argue that if suburban Gothic has any power to disturb it is when it registers the historicity of the suburbs while confounding a desire to put the past in its place, that is, to contain it, to keep it from touching the present.

Chapter 3 situates the emergence of suburban memoir within the broader 'memoir boom' that gathered pace in the 1990s – itself partly an outcome of the maturation of the post-war baby boom generation. I consider how memoirists of suburban experience have countered persistent criticisms of both the suburbs and memoir as low-grade, mass-produced and self-indulgent cultural forms, through their articulation of the complexity of suburban history and their narration of collective stories. Indeed, while it has been claimed that memoir as a genre is rooted in the way ordinary people narrate their lives, I contend that memoirists of suburban experience employ more specialist narrative modes – from autoethnography to prosopography – in order to historicise everyday life and to foreground the interconnections between suburban localities and other times and places.

Chapter 4 examines material that combines visual and textual elements: graphic narrative, or comics as they are more commonly known. I consider the ways graphic narratives situate suburban homes within broader environmental, economic and social histories. I focus in particular on the ways comics artists have innovated with framing techniques to produce what I call 'narrative ecologies': complex assemblages of ongoing stories about particular sites which emphasise their connectedness with other spaces, processes and histories. I argue some graphic narratives articulate 'anticipatory histories', which foreground process rather than permanence and thereby enable more responsible consideration of future change. In doing so this material helps to combat a very particular but widespread form of cultural amnesia, 'shifting baseline syndrome'.

Chapter 5 considers short story cycles, whose multipartite structure provides a useful narrative vehicle for articulating diverse perspectives on, and the complex temporalities of, suburban localities. I examine cycles that reflect on the significance of suburbs – and their histories – for diasporic communities. I also reflect on the use of metafictional techniques to engage with the changing form of US suburbs. This self-reflexivity distances these cycles from suburban literature's traditional insistence on dispossession, and instead demonstrates how writing can performatively create home attachments, and how nostalgia might be harnessed in productive ways. Moreover, this material suggests the need for a sophisticated kind of spatial literacy, as well as collaborative, insurgent narrative interventions on the part of suburbanites themselves.

The book's conclusion examines the significance of narrating suburban historicity at a time of frequent and vocal proclamations of the end of the suburban era, a period repeatedly judged to have been historically anomalous. I consider recent theatrical productions which dwell on the changing social and material conditions and the always-ambivalent and contested historic value of housing constructed in the mid-twentieth century. I argue that these plays challenge the out-and-out pessimism of contemporary experts by foregrounding both the need and ability of ordinary suburban residents to dispute the histories of their own environments. In so doing these plays provide critical perspectives on the intersecting processes of suburbanisation and the preservation and gentrification of residential neighbourhoods. Thus the book concludes by reasserting one of its central premises: that the twentieth-century suburbs were not a peculiar, and now closed, chapter in American history. Across its many forms the suburban story is neither singular nor complete. Indeed, as the following chapters demonstrate, the time of the suburb is neither over nor easily locatable in the past. Rather, its temporality is complex and contested; just as the histories of suburbia are ongoing, its legacies remain live, unresolved issues in metropolitan America.

CHAPTER 1

The Everyman and his Car: Metropolitan Memory and the Novel Sequence

The novel sequence is perhaps the most obvious subject with which to commence a study of narratives that attempt to bring a sense of history to the suburbs. The two sequences examined in this opening chapter, John Updike's Rabbit novels and Richard Ford's Frank Bascombe books, have after all come to occupy a central place within the literature of the late twentieth-century American suburbs. The prominence of both sequences, moreover, owes much to their long form. After the publication of *Rabbit Run* in 1960, Updike returned to the ordinary exploits of Harry Angstrom at roughly ten-year intervals: a further three novels followed – *Rabbit Redux* (1971), *Rabbit is Rich* (1981) and *Rabbit at Rest* (1990) – with the novella 'Rabbit Remembered' (2001) providing the sequence a reflective coda. Ford's Bascombe tetralogy – *The Sportswriter* (1986), *Independence Day* (1995), *The Lay of the Land* (2005) and *Let Me Be Frank with You* (2014) – whose publication history overlaps that of the Rabbit stories, has helped confirm the novel sequence as the pre-eminent form for examining metropolitan change in the US. The regular appearance over many decades of the two sequences' protagonists, their ageing in real time, and the books' attendance to the impact of social, economic and political transformations on their protagonists' everyday lives, have further served to consolidate Harry 'Rabbit' Angstrom's and Frank Bascombe's status as white American Everyman figures. The two characters are thus not only the most familiar of literary suburbanites, they are also widely perceived to be the most representative. In any literary history of the American suburbs, they are going to have to feature.

Yet both sequences appear ambivalent about the usefulness of a historical perspective. Both, for one, are narrated in the present tense. In his afterword to the fourth Rabbit novel, Updike declared that his decision to employ a present-tense narrative voice in *Rabbit Run* felt 'rebellious and liberating in 1959'.[1] Updike contends that the formal device, which enables author and reader 'to move in a purged space, on the travelling edge of the future', constituted a break with a literary tradition bound to the past tense's 'subtly dead, muffling hand'.[2] But present-tense narration also provided a suitable mode with which to articulate the disquiet of a young male subject born during the Depression years who has come to feel uneasy about his social inheritance. In *The Sportswriter* Frank is dismissive of the significance usually invested in personal histories. He announces on more than one occasion that 'we are all released to the rest of our lives'. (Though, ironically enough, he understands this sense of liberation to be a consequence of historical circumstances, of his having been born in the dawn of the post-war period.)

As the sequences progress, however, the volumes inevitably develop a historical perspective in spite of their present-tense articulation and their protagonists' professed ambivalence towards the past. Predictably, as Harry and Frank age, they become increasingly engaged in retrospection, whether as nostalgists, amateur historians or as homeowners keenly aware of how the long story of their property impacts on its market value. This historical awareness – sometimes critical, sometimes complacent – owes greatly to the protagonists' embeddedness within and commitment to their localities. Frank at one point speaks of the importance for suburbanites to develop a 'municipal memory', but his own facility for responding to spatial change noticeably takes on a regional dimension. The 'metropolitan memory' that Harry and Frank develop across each novel sequence is dependent on the repeated journeys taken by car across their respective territories: the declining industrial city region of Brewer in east Pennsylvania and the affluent commuter town of Haddam and the surrounding sprawl of mid New Jersey.[3] Crucially, their perspective is revisionary: rather than passively perceiving a piling up of history while being propelled along by it – in the manner of Walter Benjamin's famous account of the Angel of History – the repetition of narrated journeys, which promotes both a deep familiarity with habitat and an acute sensitivity to change, serves to underscore the impermanence of local arrangements as well as their interconnectedness with the wider world. The sense of the contingency of placed-based conditions that these traversals engender in turn fosters a critical historical consciousness rather than a blind faith in progress. In other words, the ongoing development of these sequences, their continual revising of apparently stable spatial structures, suggests that cities and suburbs might have been – and may yet be – organised very differently. Thus the perspectives of the Rabbit and Bascombe novels are not so remote from Benjamin's ambitions, which are to 'explode' the 'homogenous and empty time' of a hegemonic, progressivist historicism.[4]

Playing off Updike's and Ford's protagonists against Benjamin's Angel of History may seem an absurdly overblown bit of rhetoric. It is bad enough that Harry Angstrom and Frank Bascombe have acquired the status of representative 'Everyman' figures; now it seems I am suggesting they are messianic. The concerns of the novels of Updike and Ford are in any case remote from not only a European continent ripped apart by war but also Benjamin's preoccupation with how the 'suppressed past' might be revisioned to galvanise and help realise utopian ambitions. Updike – famously jittery about the social upheavals of the 1960s – is an especially unlikely candidate for revolutionary writer. Ford's vision, meanwhile, is entirely secular; his protagonist has little time for metaphysics, let alone angels. Certainly, there is limited correspondence between Ford's fiction and Benjamin's allegory, which meditates on, among other things, how theology and historical materialism might inform one another in potentially hopeful, productive ways. It is true that Updike similarly wavers between materialist and religious registers. He declared that his preoccupation with conveying 'the quality of existence itself that hovers beneath the quotidian details' – a project that is most apparent in the first Rabbit novel – constituted an artistic project akin to 'religious faith'.[5] While Harry is shown to be a visionary of sorts, his special powers of perception have to do with his affinity with his habitat and a heightened appreciation of its materiality. Frank's approach is more democratic: he insists that attending carefully to one's environment is not the preserve of the especially capable; all might benefit from doing so. But each novel sequence shows over its course how close engagement with place can enable a revisioning of the past that disabuses their main actors of a faith in an original paradise. Like Benjamin, then, Ford and Updike engage in a memory-based politics and hold to a belief in the past's incompleteness; unlike Benjamin, they also engage in a place-based politics.[6] In this chapter I explore how Updike's and Ford's novel sequences attempt to integrate these two modes. I argue that a sense of the past's openness – that is, both its present-ness and its openness to revision – is enabled by, on the one hand, the ongoing nature of spatial engagements in these narratives and, on the other, the ambivalent qualities of the novel sequence, which, perhaps more than any other form, oscillates between repetition and progression and between continuation and closure.

A Short History of a Long Form

There are literary precedents for the preoccupations and techniques that shape the Rabbit and Frank Bascombe books. Indeed, the novel sequence is a form long associated with an appreciation of the quotidian rhythms of a distinct locality and with charting historical change across fictional lives. The English novelist Anthony Trollope, author of the Chronicles of Barsetshire (1855–67) and the Palliser novels (1864–79), insisted that a principal objective of his fiction was 'the tracing of changes in characters over a lifetime'.[7] As a modernist Henry James was more enamoured with Trollope's attentiveness to the ordinary: the 'inestimable merit' of Trollope, James declared, was his 'complete appreciation of the usual', his ability to feel 'all daily and immediate things as well as s[ee] them'.[8] Actually, the compliment was backhanded; for James, Trollope's sprawling stories suffered from being too focused on the domestic, a tendency which revealed their author's limited, feminine imagination. By contrast, Honoré de Balzac's incomplete La Comédie humaine (1799–1850), though significantly more voluminous than Trollope's two series combined, operated under more scientific principles, which for James confirmed the French author's superior, masculine artistic vision. In the twentieth century, whether they operated within established realist paradigms or engaged in modernist experimentation, novel sequences tended to be more tightly organised around the experience of an individual or extended family. Consider for instance the Forsyte clan of John Galsworthy's *The Forsyte Chronicles* (1906–35), which satirises its eponymous family's exploits and anxieties in the wake of its recent elevation into the urban upper-middle classes; or Miriam Henderson of Dorothy Richardson's *Pilgrimage* sequence, a modernist *roman-a-clèf* in twelve parts (1915–38; an incomplete manuscript of a thirteenth instalment was published posthumously) that traces the development of a distinctly feminine consciousness; or Lewis Eliot, the principal character of C. P. Snow's *Strangers and Brothers* series (1940–70), who narrates his progress across the various professional milieus he occupies throughout his working life.

A property shared by novel sequences produced in both the nineteenth and twentieth centuries, though, is their ambivalence in relation to some of the novel's constitutive narrative elements and, consequently, their equivocal engagement with history. Lynette Felber argues that while the stand-alone novel privileges closure, the novel sequence exhibits a proliferation of endings. Given that 'each volume supplies both a new beginning and a provisional ending', the novel sequence is inevitably shaped by a tension between unity and continuity, and between continuation and termination.[9] Felber notes how this tension is articulated by the French term for the novel sequence, *roman-fleuve* ('river novel'): 'fleuve designates the matter, dynamic and unrestricted, whereas roman provides the frame that contains and restricts the driving force'.[10] Steven Connor identifies a similar tension expressed by the English term, and finds suggestive its uncertainty, poised as it is 'between the idea of a sequence of novels and the idea of a single novel lengthened and diversified into a sequence'.[11] For Connor, this ambiguity enables the novel sequence to harness different modes of historiography simultaneously:

> If sequences allow the production and renewal of a closed and self-consistent world, they also mimic the unpredictable looseness and contingency of lived historical time, in which the senses of process,

interruption and discontinuity are as necessary a part as the principles of recurrence, resumption and repetition. The sequence novel can therefore be closed off from the historical real and also responsive to it; it has the packed inclusiveness of the historical novel and the porousness to its exterior of the chronicle.[12]

In post-war Britain the proliferation of the novel sequence, which coincided with Trollope's return to popularity, might easily be put down to the shadow cast by World War II and the threat of nuclear conflagration. In other words, the novel sequence's continual reincarnation of closely observed worlds and the sense of familiarity accrued by readers from these repeated returns helped satisfy a desire for stability and continuity. Connor suggests, however, that circumstances did not allow for such comforts: novel sequences responded to a world in which the local and the global were 'both incompatible and oppressively, confusingly interdependent'. Consequently, the form became driven by contradictory impulses: 'to integrate the fragmented and to maintain dissolved distinctions.'[13]

The above literary and critical examples are all European in their provenance or focus. Felber's and Connor's observations about the novel sequence's formal ambiguities are nonetheless pertinent to equivalent American materials. In addition, Connor's comments relating to the post-war British novel sequence's ambivalent historicising voice and its contorted negotiations of the micro- and macroscopic are cognate with Updike's and Ford's equivocations. But the novel sequence's relative rarity in the US is conspicuous. Perhaps only Phillip Roth's Zuckerman novels (1974–2007) could be said to constellate with the Rabbit and Frank Bascombe books to comprise a narrowly based post-war American literary tradition, although Roth's sequence traverses a much broader range of territories and temporalities than do either Updike's or Ford's. Actually, the novel sequence has long been a staple of US publishing but, operating largely within the realms of genre fiction, in particular science fiction and fantasy, it has evaded significant scrutiny. As Felber notes, the relative lack of critical attention directed at novel sequences qua sequences has had as much to do with their association with popular genres and with female audiences as it has had with their trying length and looseness. Indeed, it is noticeable that the likes of Armistead Maupin's San Francisco-set *Tales of the City* novels (1978–2014) are usually referred to as series, as are most fantasy and science fiction sequences. In the case of Maupin's fiction, presumably the slightly less impressive designation owes to his novels' ensemble cast of characters – predominantly women and gay men – and to the earliest titles having first appeared in serialised form in local newspapers. 'Novel sequence', then, is an appellation reserved for narratives with a certain literary pedigree.

However, where Roth and Updike have faced criticism about their baggiest monsters, it is not because they have been seen to be operating in a feminised mode, as James once suggested of Trollope. Indeed, notoriously, David Foster Wallace referred to both writers, along with Thomas Pynchon, as the 'Great Male Narcissists'. According to Wallace, 'no U.S. novelist has mapped the solipsist's terrain better than John Updike, whose rise in the 60's and 70's established him as both chronicler and voice of probably the single most self-absorbed generation since Louis XIV'.[14] Despite the epithets of 'phallocrat' and 'G. M. N.', Wallace considered himself still to be an admirer of Updike; indeed, the caustic terms are presumed to articulate the frustration and contempt for established male authors felt by a younger generation for whom the self-expression and sexual freedom that Updike once wrote about 'so beautifully' has deteriorated into 'the joyless and anomic self-indulgence of the Me Generation'.[15] Wallace's defence of Updike, however, risks presenting any criticism of the dominance of literary culture by a masculine coterie as evidence of cultural malaise, of a fall from grace.

Taking her cue from Wallace, Kathy Knapp – who would appear to be the only scholar to have previously considered the significance of novel sequence in the US – has argued that the later Zuckerman and Rabbit novels in fact interrogate the historical bases for white masculine privilege. Knapp contends that 'from the vantage point of the 1980s, Roth and Updike's protagonists survey their past to intuit that the value they placed on individual autonomy, increased choices, and meritocratic advancement helped build a free-market society that has buoyed them but left people of color adrift'.[16] In other words, the Reagan era is not understood, in the conventional fashion, to constitute a break with the past, but instead as an extension of sixties-era liberation, 'by way of restless white characters endlessly fascinated by the novel and the new'.[17] Actually, the younger Harry of the first two Rabbit novels is not quite the freewheeling, experience-seeking individualist that Knapp (and Wallace) suggests. *Rabbit, Run* was after all conceived in response to the radical dislocations of *On the Road*. Updike has declared that he resented Kerouac's 'apparent instruction to cut loose; *Rabbit, Run* was meant to be a realistic demonstration of what happens when a young American family man goes on the road – the people left behind get hurt'.[18] *Rabbit Redux*, meanwhile, centres on Harry's attempts to construct an alternative household that crosses race and class divides, and demonstrates a willingness to learn about the social and political realities of others. Otherwise, however, Knapp's argument accords with my own with respect to the effects of the novel sequence:

> The long form that [Roth and Updike] use – the novel sequence – undercuts the logic of inevitability and the infinite promise of the future that are neoliberalism's helpmeets. These novels, released intermittently over several years, do not unfold teleologically but instead stop, start, and circle back in a discontinuous, haphazard fashion determined by chance and the unforeseen consequences of their protagonist's choices before concluding unceremoniously and with the only inevitability we can count on. It is only when taken as a whole and with the benefit of hindsight that they – and we – can see clearly a recent history that might have followed a different path that follows interdependence over independence.[19]

My reading of the sequences' stop-starting, though, is as much spatial as it is temporal, and sees these movements not as haphazard but rather as governed by routine. Indeed, my discussion of both novel sequences outlines a series of modes of engagement with everyday spatiality which work towards opening up both past and place, which are revealed to be neither fixed nor final. In the Rabbit novels, these modes take the form of a series of figures which I label as the sector, the transect, and rhythmic nostalgia; each one is more dynamic than the last and more capable of appraising spatio-temporality in critical ways. Ford's protagonist, by contrast, is appreciative of the spatio-temporal dimensions of his environment from the off. Nevertheless, the Bascombe novels also propose a succession of techniques for engaging with the world. Each corresponds to a distinct phase in the life of the protagonist but also to different ethical standards. Noticeably, at various stages, the sequence calls into question the very qualities that Knapp valorises, namely, chance and discontinuity. For what, after all, constitutes a more perfect helpmeet to neo-liberalism than an ethic that normalises disruption and contingency? Many critics – including Knapp – read Ford's novel sequence as having a progressive trajectory, with its protagonist coming increasingly to appreciate interdependence over independence as he ages.[20] On the surface, this is a reasonable assessment. But it downplays how Frank's modes of engagement are perpetually in crisis. Indeed, the books switch continually between such strategies, sometimes even reinstalling ones that have been previously discarded. More than the Rabbit novels, then, the Bascombe books exploit the ambivalence of the form. I suggest that the fluctuations and equivocations of Ford's novel sequence are first and foremost a response to the vagaries of market forces that continually reconstitute spatiality. Frank's never-ending attempts to acclimatise himself to shifting circumstances rather demonstrate that individual actions – even the kind that fosters interdependence – are inadequate to the task of ameliorating the conditions of late capitalism. Indeed, Frank's very resourcefulness – or, rather, his preparedness to constantly reconstitute himself and his relationships with both place and the past – demonstrates how thoroughly conditioned he is by the demands of neo-liberalism. Thus Ford's novel sequence gestures towards the limitations of both its own form and its white suburban Everyman narrator.

A Rabbit's-Eye View: Sectors, Transects and Rhythmic Nostalgia in John Updike's Rabbit Novels

Sectors

I call the first of the Rabbit tetralogy's recurrent figures the 'sector'. It consists of visions of, if not the entire urban region, then large sections of it, from vantage points that are usually removed and static – for instance, when a character is looking down from high ground or out of the window of a house or an apartment. Urban and suburban landscapes, from these perspectives, typically take on a uniform character and, in Updike's writing, are defined by qualities that are comfortingly familiar. Near the beginning of *Rabbit, Run*, for instance, Harry envisages looking out over Brewer from the top of Mt Judge, from where the city appears 'spread out like a carpet', entirely 'flowerpot red'. Such uniform, domestic imagery is well-worn; one of Brewer's nicknames is the 'flowerpot city'. Harry recognises that his is an unworldly, even immature perception of urbanity: the brick-red blush of Brewer is 'unlike the color of any city in the world yet to the children of the county is the only color of cities, the color all cities are'.[21] These comforting, universalising descriptions encourage claims of ownership over sectors of the metropolis: 'my valley, my home' Harry thinks as he looks 'straight out the windows' of his house, across the town and 'into the wide farm valley' (127). There is certainly also something compensatory about such visions, which afford a sense of orderliness and calm that contrasts with the 'continual crisscrossing mess' (9) of Harry's domestic life and the disagreeable 'unconnectedness' (8) of the body of his frequently drunk wife Janice. One is reminded of the contrast made by Michel de Certeau (about whom I say more in Chapter 3) between the all-seeing but disembodied perspective elevated high over the city, which historically has informed urban planning and governance, and the corporeal confusions, the 'blind mobility' of inhabitants of the streets and buildings below.[22] Updike's rendering of the optic would seem, too, to clarify its gendered dimensions. For certain, this immobilising gaze is a requisite feature of the kinds of conventional anti-suburban commentary I outlined in the introduction. In the Rabbit novels sectors enable similar kinds of criticism, at least at first; I will argue Updike first problematises and then abandons the sectorial perspective for more dynamic modes of interacting with metropolitan spatiality that serve to undercut traditional suburban critique.

The panoramas in *Rabbit, Run* are of course enabled by the locality's distinct topography and, coming so early in the narrative, provide something akin to the establishing shots of cinema and television. These vistas are not merely narrative devices, however;

they reflect newly spectacularised metropolitan environments. In her 2001 book on popular media and the post-war suburbs, *Welcome to the Dreamhouse*, Lynn Spigel asserts that 'increasingly in the postwar period the domestic environment was filled with visual spectacles previously associated with public life, and the home itself was designed as a space for looking': 'the new tract homes of the mass-produced suburbs featured sliding-glass doors, bay windows and open plans that were designed to maximise the visual field'.[23] In the post-war years this 'visibility principle', to use sociologist William Dobriner's term, became a dominant trope in criticisms of a suburban society characterised by vulgar display, conformity and self-delusion.[24] More than any other architectural feature, the picture window became the exemplar of these failings. Responding to the picture window as a debased consumer product, Daniel Boorstin argues, in his 1961 book *The Image*, that 'we are deceived and obstructed by the very machines we make to enlarge our vision'.[25] As its earlier modernist advocates had claimed, the picture window was supposed to facilitate a view onto nature and bring the outside world into the home. In mass-produced housing, however, the only view it was likely to afford was into the home of a neighbour. In reality this was no view at all, merely a reflection, a vision of a catalogue-ordered interior altogether like one's own.[26]

In *Rabbit, Run*, Harry and Janice endure pinched domestic circumstances; they are yet to experience the benefits and disappointments of new suburban housing. However, Harry's initial panoramic view of his home town captures in its sweeping gaze newly built subdivisions and their countless picture windows. His response, which emphasises repetitive, vapid reflection, is entirely conventional: 'twin rows of ranch-houses blare from their picture windows the reflection of the setting sun. One by one, as suddenly as lamps, these windows dim as the sunlight ebbs, drawing across the development and the across the tan fenced land waiting for planting' (11). Later, the narrative voice describes a similar housing development – comprised of 'half-wood half-brick one-and-a-half stories in little flat bulldozed yards with tricycles and spindly three-year-old trees' – as 'the un-grandest landscape in the world' (74). Harry admits to his churchman interlocuter that he feels certain that behind this unprepossessing facade lies something that is worth looking for and, perhaps also, somebody who wants him to find it. Manifestly, these new suburban spaces, underdeveloped and wholly open to scrutiny, can hold no personal or spiritual significance in and of themselves.

A more extended interrogation of the expansion to the visual field in post-war suburbia can be found in the tetralogy's second novel *Rabbit Redux*. Harry's stint in the still-raw subdivision of Penn Villas seems to reiterate the concerns Boorstin et al. regarding the massification of technological and architectural innovation. Like so many suburban toponyms, Harry's street is named after something the development has destroyed. Vista Crescent no longer affords a vista. Or rather it does, only the vision it enables is merely diffractive: 'the view from any window now is as into a fragmented mirror'; extending all around his house 'unpopulated stretches of similar houses hold unbroken the intensity of duplication'.[27] The picture window of Harry's suburban home appears to operate in precisely the manner suggested by contemporary commentators: 'four flawless transparencies permit outdoors to come indoors, other houses enter yours. The mirror is two-way' (357). The contradictory implication of both trespass and surveillance is almost certainly purposeful. Additionally, *Rabbit Redux* reflects on the appearance of suburban interiors. Harry's estrangement from the domestic details of his life stems from their insubstantiality. His Penn Villas home is furnished with objects fabricated from new and unfamiliar synthetic materials, and whose design prioritises visual appeal rather than functionality. Interior space is rendered unhomely by the play of natural and artificial light on its strange surfaces: everywhere in his house Harry 'sees a slippery disposable gloss' (194); 'The furniture that frames his life looks Martian in the morning light: [. . .] furniture Rabbit has lived among but has never known' (221). Inside as well as out, then, the new suburbs' excessive spectacularity is unsettling because it is antithetical to several of the requisite components of the conventional subject: integrity, autonomy, authenticity. However, as I will go on to show, the novel's focus on new technologies, specifically those to do with printing and photography, problematises the very optics through which the new suburbs were typically viewed.

Literary critics have acknowledged Updike's engagement with the new suburbs' distinctive visuality, but have tended to focus on how the replications of the suburban landscape correspond to a putative crisis of masculinity. Robert Beuka, for example, argues that 'Updike's description of Harry's housing development underscores the collapse of the pastoral dream of the suburbs into an unsettling space of homogenous facelessness.'[28] Harry's 'alienation' from this environment directly correlates with his emasculation, his replaceability and also, therefore, his representativeness. Further, as 'a foreigner even to himself', the fractured Harry 'emerges as a fitting emblem of the contradictions of suburban masculinity'.[29] It is true that much about Harry's situation – cuckolded, abandoned and carless in a bleak and distant suburb – confirms his emasculation and alienation. That Harry feels the suburbs to be unmanning is most obvious from his dreams. In one that distils a welter of insecurities, Harry is driving on a 'superhighway' accompanied by the man with whom his wife Janice is having an affair, the Greek-American Charlie Stavros. In the dream Charlie has been invited by Lyndon Johnson to be his Vice-President and has negotiated moving the White House to Brewer on a part-time basis; Harry wonders whether this might be his chance to get into a white-collar job. His feelings of inadequacy are manifest – 'Services and software are where the future lies. He tells Stavros hopefully, "I can lick stamps." He shows him his tongue' (220) – and these anxieties are evidently entwined with ones to do with his own sexual prowess ('the gear shift is very thin, a mere pencil, and he is afraid of breaking it as it shifts') and the advancement of blacks and white ethnics ('a strange white city materialises beside the highway; hill after hill of tall row houses white as bedsheets, crowding to the horizon'). The dream concludes with Harry being dumped in 'a suburban region' with a map he can't make much sense of; confirming his troubled sense of his own masculinity, Harry wakes from the 'unpleasant' dream with an erection that feels 'glassily thin' (220). Even while the dream's hyperbole renders Harry's anxieties somewhat ridiculous, the text indeed clearly equates suburbanisation with masculine crisis.

Causing even more anxiety than sexual inadequacy, though, is Harry's loss of economic competitiveness. Indeed, Harry's feelings of being both left behind and out of place are accentuated by the circumstances of his employment. Unlike many of his neighbours whose suburbanisation appears to have been enabled by jobs in new industries flourishing beyond the city limits, Harry's blue-collar role – he is a linotype operator in a printshop located in the 'stagnant' downtown of Brewer (181) – relies on outmoded technology: hot metal typesetting. Harry finds both the masculine camaraderie of the shop floor and his close engagement with solid, predictable mechanical processes enormously reassuring; his place of work certainly compares favourably with the impersonal environment of Penn Villas and the flimsy, ersatz furnishings of his home. There is an obvious irony in that the first story presented to the reader for which Harry sets type reports on local industrial innovation: a Brewer-based electronics firm, whose anonymous building and 'highly modern, light-green office' occupies the site of a former hosiery factory, has contributed crucial components to the Apollo missions (196). The story thus points to wider technological developments and economic transformations that will shortly put him out of a job.

But there is a further, more complex irony in the fact that the photographic technologies that threaten Harry with obsolescence also underpin his critical view of the suburbs. Verity Press, Harry's employer, is liable to fold as it cannot afford to invest in new printing technologies. The narrator declares: 'over Verity hangs a future that belongs to cool processes, to photo-offset and beyond that to photo-composition, computerized television that throws thousands of letters a second onto film with never the kiss of metal' (195). The photographic eye and photographic reproduction, as I outlined in this book's introduction, defined anti-suburban criticism in the post-war period. One of the most frequently referenced reactions was that of Lewis Mumford, who expressed revulsion over the debasement of the original suburban impulse predicated on self-realisation and independence; suburbanites, now too numerous to be properly accommodated, have become entrapped within the replications of a cheap, prefabricated landscape. But Mumford was merely reiterating an already well-established repertoire of images. Don Kindler's illustrations for John Keats's 1956 anti-suburban screed *The Crack in the Picture Window* depict the same, albeit more drolly. And, as I will discuss further in Chapter 3, Mumford draws heavily on the perspectives of aerial photography. In fact, this sort of recycling is precisely what Updike's text seems to be engaging in. *Rabbit Redux* redeploys images that had already come to metonymise anti-suburban critique. Penn Villas' fragmented mirror replicates the titular conceit of Keats's book as well as other images of fracturing, such as the crack in the living room wall that so torments the Raths in Sloan Wilson's 1955 novel *The Man in the Grey Flannel Suit*. Then there is all the recycled imagery of space flight and the moon landing, whose coverage on TV Updike indicates has reached saturation point. Harry's house is likened to a spacecraft, isolated and adrift, and the immediate environment to a lunar landscape – a lifeless, colourless world that appears like 'a flat, stiff, cold photograph'. (Noticeably, although writing a few years before the Apollo 11 mission of 1969, Mumford uses the same spacecraft simile to describe the 'encapsulated life' of the suburbs.)[30] Updike's foregrounding of the photographic quality of the image tellingly suggests both mediation and reproduction.

It would seem then that it is not so much the machine – in this case, the mass-produced suburban home – that deceives and obstructs, but the critique itself, which is shown to be as repetitive and superficial as its object. There are several instances in the novel where Harry breaks through the codified facade. For instance, Harry wonders if 'anybody mails a letter' in the mailbox nearest his Penn Villas home: 'he passes it every day and it seems mysterious as a fire hydrant, waiting for its moment that may never come. He never hears it clang.' In Mt Judge, by contrast, 'people were always mailing Valentines'. Then, quite on cue, a mailman in his van arrives, opens the mailbox and out pour hundreds of letters (347). Harry also often comments on the meagre saplings that seem weakly tethered to Penn Villas' poor soil. Later in the novel, however, he realises that some of his neighbours' trees have in fact become as tall as housetops. In the same scene where he notices the trees' growth, he realises belatedly that one of his neighbours has built an extension to his house, and that children are playing outside. An appreciation of these developments finally renders the suburb as inhabited place, not just a vision of desolation. Manifestly, it is a certain way of looking at new suburbs that is the principal problem; the narrator declares that Harry 'really only looks at Penn Villas enough to see that it isn't Mt Judge: that is, it is nowhere' (345).

Only after the conventional perspective is discarded can the suburb be understood as being a place, that is, a location possessing both an identifiably temporal dimension and relationships with other places. These qualities enable Harry to imagine a future for himself in Penn Villas, and even to conceive how the suburb might provide his son with the foundations for significant memories: 'Someday, Nelson may come back to this, his childhood neighbourhood, and find it strangely dark, buried in shade, the lawns opulent, the home venerable' (355). Harry's conclusion, 'this could be a nice place if you gave it a chance', is followed by yet another image of duplication: 'And around the other houses men with rakes and mowers mirror him.' It seems that being an undistinguished and indistinguishable suburbanite is not so bad after all, so long as you are prepared to be more attentive to your surroundings.

Nelson's anticipated return to a gracefully aged suburb plumped with fond memories is but a daydream, however. Things go from bad to worse for Harry in Penn Villas after he takes in Jill, an upper-class runaway, and Skeeter, a black radical and Vietnam veteran, who provides his white housemates with a crash-course seminar in the history of American injustice. The household's eccentric set up is too outrageous and transgressive for Penn Villas, especially after Harry, Skeeter and Jill are witnessed having sex in their living room. A confrontation with minatory neighbours is the prelude to an arson attack on Harry's home, which is left a smoking ruin. Jill perishes in the fire; Skeeter takes flight. Nonetheless, the text cuts across those post-war critiques of the suburbs which rely on detached viewpoints that draw very heavily on aerial photography of newly built but as yet uninhabited suburbs, and which presume that these places have reached their final form: an 'instant slum', or a 'treeless waste', to use two of Mumford's much-echoed phrases. Harry then seems to be experiencing cognitive dissonance between received visions of the suburbs and his experiences on the ground. Despite its violent conclusion, the novel communicates how such places are connected to the outside world, how they are undergoing change, and hence how they can contain the promise of a future, or other possible worlds.

Admittedly, these revelations do not lead to any significant or lasting change to Harry's outlook. Self-interest prevails after he learns that he has profited considerably from the house's destruction. Harry is surprised that the property has become so valuable. Janice informs him that the area has become fashionable; the insurance money and the sale of the lot stand to make them a small fortune. This quick-fire exchange confirms Harry's belated achievement of upward mobility:

> 'I thought Brewer was dying.'
> 'Only in the middle.'
> 'Let's sell the bastard.'
> 'Let's.' (408)

Harry's rapid calculation – regarding personal finance based on a recalibrated understanding of the distribution of wealth across the metropolitan area – serves to undercut his earlier litany of grievances. It becomes suddenly clear that the suburban house was making him money all along. Moreover, the scene serves to demonstrate that suburban 'suffering' enables upward mobility. As Catherine Jurca has it, 'thinking of oneself as a victim may be the necessary condition for not becoming one'.[31] In other words, discontentment is crucial for maintaining or reasserting the privileges of class and race. Perhaps then what is needed is a different way of looking at places altogether.

Transects

A sense of the fortunes of central Brewer and its new suburbs being tied to one another is crucial to the second figure I wish to outline. This figure, the transect, differs from the sector in so far as it implies a mobile rather than a static perspective. The concept is drawn from the work of Carl Abbott, a historian of planning who has taken his hand to literary and cultural criticism. In his recent book *Imagined Frontiers* (2015), Abbott argues that the Rabbit novels narrate 'transects', that is, linear routes taken by individuals through the fabric of metropolitan Brewer. These transects, importantly, register the historicity, or 'placeness', of specific localities and the metropolis as a whole. Abbott takes as exemplary the passage at the opening of *Rabbit Redux* where Harry travels by bus from the decrepit environs of downtown Brewer and through various suburban landscapes, a journey which terminates in Harry's Penn Villas tract home. It is a bus ride that relates Harry's disquiet about Brewer's racial diversification. It begins: 'The bus has too many Negroes. Rabbit notices them more and more. They've been here all along [. . .] but now they're noisier' (186). But it is also a journey that registers other, similarly disquieting forms of metropolitan change. On the route the bus passes 'tired five-and-dimes [. . .] and then the empty dusty windows where stores have been starved by the suburban shopping malls and the sad narrow places that come and go called Go-Go or Boutique', and so forth. Brewer gives way to the shinier commercialism of the car-dominated suburb of West Brewer,

> a gappy imitation of the city, the same domino-thin houses of brick painted red, but spaced here and there by the twirlers of a car lot, the pumps and blazoned overhang of a gas station, the lakelike depth of a supermarket parking lot crammed with shimmering fins. (187)

Further on, 'the bus growing lighter, the Negroes vanishing', Harry 'moves towards a dream of spaciousness' (ibid.). As Weiser Street curves and becomes a highway, his ride 'dips into green suburbs where in the Twenties little knights of industry built half-timbered dream-houses, pebbled mortar and clinker brink, stucco flaky as pie crust, witches' houses of candy and hardened cookie dough with two-car garages and curved driveways' (ibid.). Almost nothing in the County eclipses these genteel Penn Park residences in terms of desirability; they represent the pinnacle of white bourgeois accomplishment. Then finally, bathetically, Harry arrives at Penn Villas, a place name that echoes optimistically its upscale neighbour's. It is a typical unincorporated development built by speculative developers with little interest in the settlement's long-term fortunes: the local township's 'single sheriff can hardly cope with this ranch-house village of muddy lawns and potholed macadam and sub-code sewers the developers suddenly left in its care' (ibid.).

Abbott claims the transect is distinct to depictions of eastern cities, and identifies similar structures in Richard Ford's Bascombe tetralogy, of which more below, and in the title sequence of the

TV show *The Sopranos*. The latter depicts its modern mafioso protagonist's homeward commute, which begins with his exiting the
Lincoln Tunnel and joining the New Jersey turnpike, with the
Manhattan skyline receding in his car's wing mirror, followed by
his traversing various, clearly differentiated suburban landscapes,
industrial, commercial and residential. In this manner the show's
intro presents a radial slice through a metropolitan region that
reveals an arrangement of concentric cultural and socio-economic
landscapes. By contrast, Abbott suggests, linear routes taken
through more radically decentred western metropolises do not help
to render them legible, and cannot evince meaningful histories. As
evidence, Abbott points to Edward Soja's breathless accounts of
fragmented 'exopolitan' Orange County, or the free-floating suburban settings of Douglas Coupland's fiction.[32]

According to Abbott, 'a full transect from [peri-urban] edge to
[urban] center to edge' is 'just as an ecological scientist might catalogue the landscape from ridgeline to valley floor to opposite
ridgeline'.[33] The comparison is potentially helpful if one wishes
to respond to planner Patrick Geddes's dictum that human settlement ought always to be analysed within the context of its natural
region.[34] But to me Abbott's simile suggests that the transect is too
linear and too static a figure to fit Updike's project, or, more broadly,
to provide a useful optic for appraising literary geographies. The
example Abbott provides from *Rabbit Redux* is in any case one of
few linear trajectories in the tetralogy that runs straightforwardly
from centre to periphery. This is not to say that Abbott is insensitive
to the ways the tetralogy's protagonist responds to urban change.
Indeed, he contends:

> Harry's life is a transect through both the space and the history of met-
> ropolitan Brewer [. . .] Updike traces neighborhood change through
> Harry's own life and uses neighborhoods to exemplify that history [. . .]
> By moving Rabbit from one suburban neighbourhood to another, Updike
> lets [Harry's] very life trace transects.[35]

But what Abbott does not address is how the tetralogy's multiple
and various journeys continually criss-cross the same sites. It is
precisely these re-crossings, I would argue, that both facilitate and

emphasise Rabbit's sense of the shifting nature of these places, and their changing relationships with other localities. Frequently an individual site appraised in one novel is revisited in the next. Consider for instance the conclusion of *Rabbit, Run*, where Harry imagines slipping free from his habits and his responsibilities to others by fleeing the city. His exit would take him 'down Summer Street to where the city ends. He tries to picture how it will end, with an empty baseball field, a dark factory, and then over a brook into a dirt road, he doesn't know' (177). That he cannot fully conceive of the path ahead speaks volumes of the strength of his current attachments, though the novel's ending – in which Harry runs in 'a sweet panic', direction undisclosed – is purposefully ambiguous. The same location punctuates the conclusion of *Rabbit, Redux*, though Harry's vision of a pastoral idyll beyond the fringe of the city is intruded upon by the humdrum reality of peri-urban commercial development:

> At the end of Summer Street he thinks there will be a brook, and then a dirt road and open pastures; but instead the city street broadens into a highway lined with hamburger diners, and drive-in sub shops, and a miniature golf course with big plaster dinosaurs, and food-stamp stores and motels and gas stations that are changing their names, Humble to Getty, Atlantic to Arco. He has been here before. (409)

The last sentence is ambiguous: it seems to refer to the end of the previous novel, but the 'here' is not what it once was. Or perhaps it is familiar only because it looks like someplace else. But whatever – or wherever – here is, it has changed; moreover, it is 'changing'. The highway strip's temporariness, however, does not inspire Harry's contempt or provoke feelings of disassociation. Indeed, it offers Harry and Janice a place of respite and the opportunity to reconnect with one another. Noticeably, the establishment they briefly check into calls itself *Safe Haven Motel* (410).

Moreover, these spatial formations will subsequently sustain Harry, who is destined to inherit part-ownership of a Toyota franchise out on Route 111. *Rabbit is Rich* opens under the precarious conditions of the second oil crisis of 1979, and throughout the novel Harry reflects on the depleted resources of a global economy seemingly on the brink of exhaustion. However, his opening gambit – 'the fucking world is running out of gas'; 'the people out there are getting frantic, they know the great American ride is ending' (417) – is merely a sales pitch: Harry has the good fortune to be dealing in fuel-efficient Japanese cars.[36] As the novel's title indicates, Harry is living comfortably; it is the 'world's wasting' that helps him to 'feel rich' (422). Harry's self-satisfaction is made clear in the first few pages with a blanketing of phrases: he 'speaks tranquilly' and feels 'cosy', 'serene in his middle years' and 'simply happy to be alive' (420–1). His complacency is exacerbated by his encapsulation within the cars he owns and sells. The Harry that was prepared to cohabit with and learn from people of different classes and races is in the past: 'I love everybody, especially with my car window locked' (465), is his flippant but honest account of his present moral modus operandi. Driving seems to affect the experience of the metropolitan transect. Now, 'as he sits snug in his sealed and well-assembled car the venerable city of Brewer unrolls like a silent sideways movie past his closed windows' (435). This journey more or less reverses the centrifugal route that Harry took at the beginning of *Rabbit Redux*, but now, even the very mode of viewing the city seems quaint ('a silent sideways movie'). Less is revealed from the car's cabin: certain vistas are obscured by tree growth, and Harry is distracted by the radio.

And yet Harry is still able to reflect on change and absences, as well as memories evoked by certain sites. Consecutive drives to and from the lot render it utterly familiar: the staggered roadside signs that mark Harry's approach – 'DISCO, DATSUN, FUEL ECONOMY' (543) – become an automatic litany. Updike's rendering of the peri-urban commercial strip here is reminiscent of observations of Robert Venturi, Denise Scott Brown and Steven Izenour about the highway desert town: 'If you take the signs away, there is no place.'[37] Like the authors of *Learning from Las Vegas*, Updike is not unsympathetic towards 'commercial vernacular' architecture.[38] Indeed, Harry's habitual journeys demonstrate that, contra the likes of Peter Blake, who rage against the desecration of the American landscape by the excrescences of commerce, road signs can engender a sense of place, and even of peace.[39] Venturi et al. note that 'the most unique, most monumental parts of the [Las Vegas] Strip, the signs [. . .], are also the most changeable'. The roadside is after all a highly competitive environment, and leasing systems operated by sign companies and the possibility of total tax write-offs accelerate the signs' rate of obsolescence.[40] For Harry, the very changeability of road signs is what yields a sense of the past, and he frequently rumi-nates on the complex histories of certain signs. The one proclaim-ing DISCO, for instance, evolved improbably out of a 'Mr Peanut' sign that once gestured towards a salted nut emporium. Route 111 is not simply a blank, monotonous landscape without historical depth. Harry is sensitive to the roadside's intricate variations as well as to changes and their implications ('A new industry, gas pump shrouds' (427)). Indeed, its continually changing conditions even gives rise to a connoisseurship of the highway strip: 'Route 111 has a certain beauty in the rain, the colours and the banners and the bluish asphalt of the parking lots all run together through the swish of traffic, the beat of wipers' (543). What Venturi et al. learned from their brief visit to Las Vegas was how to appraise the system and order of the roadside strip; by contrast Updike illustrates how the strip only yields its meanings – and, indeed, its beauty – over time and through habitual use.

Towards the end of Updike's tetralogy, while Harry continues to appraise spatial change in metropolitan Brewer, he increasingly feels the weight of history. Indeed, in *Rabbit at Rest*, the 56-year-old Harry has taken to reading history books, which constitute a change from the diet of consumer reports that sustained him during his forties. The extent to which his new habit is edifying, however, is moot: 'The beautiful thing about history is it puts you right to sleep', he declares.[41] Harry seems to appreciate the comfort-ing heft of history rather than its detail. Certainly, most of Florida, where he now overwinters with Janice, seems as insubstantial as the suburban landscapes around Brewer in which he once lived. 'The whole state is brittle', Harry reflects; in Florida, 'even friendship has a thin, provisional quality, since people might at any minute buy another condominium and move to it, or else up and die' (65). By contrast, 'in Pennsylvania, at least in Diamond County, everything has been paved solid by memory and in any direction you go you've already been there' (79). But actually, in a changing landscape repeat journeys serve to foreground the contingency of place. For example, later in *Rabbit at Rest* Harry muses on the real estate developments that have steadily been taking over the agricultural landscape beyond Brewer's north-western fringe: 'Rabbit as these recent years have gone by has watched the bulldozed land lose its raw look and trees and bushes grow up so it almost seems houses have always been here' (173). That 'almost' suggests how, far from being 'paved solid by memory', places may be rendered indeterminate and incomplete by everyday encounter.

In her review of *Rabbit at Rest* Hermione Lee asserts that while Updike presents a 'solid and "real"' portrait of late twentieth-century middle America, his ageing protagonist remains 'oddly ambivalent' about it.[42] The disconcerting strangeness of Rabbit's environment might be explained by what Stacey Olster has suggested is Updike's tendency to establish 'connections among unlike things', which exceeds mere mimesis, and which, in Updike's words, 'corresponds with the intricacy and opacity of the real world'.[43] I would add that the often-strange connections between various localities and temporalities across the Rabbit tetralogy have very much to do with the unpredictable interactions between memory, desire and place. In *Rabbit is Rich*, on yet another car journey, Summer Street is recalled again, though this time it is Nelson, riding in the passenger seat, who experiences déjà vu – his sudden recollection is 'like when you feel you've been someplace before, only it must have been in a dream' (515). As they proceed through the tetralogy, readers may well be feeling something similar. But even the most securely familiar of places produces all kinds of inversions and uncanny connections. One landmark that Harry continually repasses across the four novels is a war memorial in the form of a tank. In *Rabbit at Rest*, Harry complains that the memorial has been repainted so often so as to forestall corrosion that it has lost its original military green colour. The implication seems to be that familiarity has led to the tank losing its memorial function. Yet driving past the tank, Harry feels himself to be 'under the barrage of streetlights bombarded, and Brewer seems empty of life like those bombed-out cities after the war' (226). On the same car journey – towards Mt Judge – Harry and Janice enter 'territory bred into their bones, streets they crossed and recrossed in all seasons as children, Central, Jackson, Joseph, the hydrants and mailboxes of the borough of Mt.

Judge like buttons fastening down their lives, their real lives'. It is precisely this expectation of familiarity which produces strange and discomforting associations, 'everything drained of color at this nadir of the night, the streets under the burning blue mercury lights looking rounded like bread-loaves [. . .] the brick-pillared porches treacherous like emplacements up behind their little flat laps of lawn' (227). Indeed this nocturnal journey back to what was once their home is dominating by lunar imagery, which inevitably recalls the second novel, and the turbulent part of Harry's life that he declares he has left firmly in the past. Thus the repetitive and peripatetic nature of the Rabbit novels suggest that the 'transect', at least on its own, is too simplistic a device to capture the narration of the metropolitan everyday. This is not a mode of narrative that ignores history, which is a charge that has been levelled at Updike. His repost, 'my fiction about the daily doings of ordinary people has more history in it than history books', is certainly hyperbolic.[44] Yet the Rabbit tetralogy's cumulative recording of the everyday encounters between people and places, between people in place, undeniably constitutes a mode of historiography.

Rhythmic Nostalgia

By way of conclusion I want to suggest how the two figures I have outlined so far, the sector and transect, might well be more illuminating when considered in combination. For a synthesis of the two better enables not only a sense that places are changing in the present, but also that they have always been undergoing change. For sure, Updike shows how experience of spatial change fuels nostalgia, that is, how disturbing developments motivate an investment in comforting images of a lost time and place. Yet, the uncanny connections produced by everyday movements across the metropolis serve also to undermine the security of nostalgic imagery. This process might reasonably be called rhythmic or fluctuating nostalgia. Harry declares in the final novel that he is 'too old for flux' (362), but repeatedly his experiences suggest otherwise. We witness a continual oscillation between nostalgic memories in the wake of spatial change, and a realisation – stemming from such changes – that past places were never as one would prefer to remember them, were not fixed but also in flux. So, this is a nostalgia propelled by change but also undone by it.

My proposed figure of rhythmic nostalgia suggests that the trajectory taken by the Rabbit novels is more complex and self-reflexive than that described by many readers. Between the publication of the second and fourth instalments of the Rabbit sequence – the middle period of Updike's literary career – many critics identified the Rabbit novels as articulating a loss of faith in the American way of life. Anita Brookner, for instance, saw the sequence as a closely observed study of the country's fall from grace, and for Joyce Carol Oates it constituted 'Updike's surpassingly eloquent elegy for his country'.[45] For Josh Getlin, the novels paint 'a dark picture of the American middle class in decline' and are best understood as a social comedy about the 'treachery of the American Dream'.[46] Many, like Richard Todd writing in 1972, observed that Updike had a perennial interest in 'the ironic contrast between history and the present moment' even while the author evinces an abiding attachment to the 1950s and their 'precarious cosiness'.[47] Such nostalgia for pre-Civil Rights-era provincial security is quite reasonably held to blunt the novels' critical appraisal of contemporary disappointments. In more recent years, however, critics have come to see Updike's later work as resisting and critiquing this nostalgic impulse. Stacey Olster, for instance, sees Updike's later writing as continually in dialogue with his earlier material. Moreover, despite his fond feelings for the 1950s, Updike's writing works to deny both the myth of American consensus, but also of American exceptionalism.[48] Donald Greiner concurs, determining that, rather than charting a 'straight line toward confirmation of an ideal', Updike's *oeuvre* constitutes 'a receding curve toward questioning a once assured certainty'.[49] And, as Kathy Knapp has noted, the Rabbit series' long form facilitates the continual revision of apparently secure past verities.

I am suggesting, however, the challenge to nostalgia in fact begins relatively early in the sequence. For instance, towards the end of *Rabbit Redux*, after the destruction of his Penn Villas home, Harry's immediate family reassemble in Mt Judge. But while Harry has escaped from a deracinated suburbia, he is prevented by others from falling into comforting reminiscence. With his sister Mim and their mother, Harry drives out to a nearby quarry and derelict cement works where they used to walk and he and his sister once played among the 'Oz-like tower of sheds and chutes' and daisy- and goldenrod-studded fields. The fabulous ruins and the flowers have, inevitably, given way to housing tracts, but Harry's ailing mother has no truck with her children's fond memories of the place: 'Awful things. Used to happen there. Men and boys' (393). When meeting Janice outside the smouldering wreck of their home, Harry notes how his property sticks out, rendering the surround- ing houses even more unreal: it looks like 'black coal in a row of candies'. But once again, he is barred from nostalgic retreat. With the fire having destroyed most of his possessions, he is wearing his old high school athletics jacket recovered from a trunk in his parents' attic. Janice's response – 'I'd forgotten what awful school colours we had. Ick. Like one of those fake ice creams' – cannot help but invoke their ersatz surroundings. Harry concedes that 'it was an ice cream world he made his mark in' (406); the past, then, is not really a better place, and no less fake, than the present. The destruction of the Penn Villas home also has the effect of rendering his own past contingent. Meditating on the 'homely street' where he grew up – which even several years after his departure 'excited Rabbit with the magic of its own existence', 'each downtwirling maple seed of more account than galaxies' – Harry is finally able to countenance its alteration, even its demolition. These reflections enable a breakthrough that is anti-nostalgic at its base: 'Time is our element, not a mistaken invader. How stupid, it has taken him thirty-six years to begin to believe that' (395).

This realisation does not cure Harry of nostalgia. But it shows him to possess the intellectual and emotional resources to question nostalgic impulses, which are derived from comparisons made across the metropolitan landscape. Some of Harry's most power- ful nostalgic memories centre on his childhood experiences of the commercial downtown of Brewer, and in particular the department stores, which he remembers as a 'wonderland'. From *Rabbit, Run* onwards, Harry attributes central Brewer's decline to the pressures of deindustrialisation and suburbanisation. (Indeed, so attached does he become to the image of a desolated downtown that he is some- times unable to read the effects of regeneration and gentrification.)

In his later forays beyond the city limits, though, Brewer's newly built suburban peripheries become increasingly alluring. In *Rabbit is Rich* their attraction is couched in terms of space and light: fitting the novel's inflationary theme, property and wealth are increasingly understood as abstractions, as divorced from materiality. Yet as well as articulating opportunity to the belatedly upwardly mobile Harry, these visions of space and light reactivate memory. Driving back from the Murketts' house in the new development of Brewer Heights, Harry notes that 'six hours ago when they drove up this road each house was lit in its bower of unbulldozed woods like displays in the façade of a long gray department store.' As well as reasserting the imbrication of city and suburbs, the simile invokes change – it is after all already a remembered image. The street is now dark; 'the seasons catch up with you' (604), remarks Harry. It seems to foreshadow the final closure of Kroll's, the department store that had 'stood in the center of Brewer all these years, bigger than a church, older than the courthouse' (419). On his final car journey, to Florida, Harry meditates on his feelings of betrayal in the wake of the store's closure: 'He was reared in a world where war was not strange but change was: the world stood still so you could grow up in it.' But his memories of working behind the scenes 'witnessing the hiring and firing, the panicky gamble of merchandising' simultaneously foreground Kroll's contingency, and precipitate Harry's terminal judgement, that 'the world was not solid and benign, it was a shabby set of temporary arrangements rigged up for the time being, all for the sake of money', and 'if Kroll's could go, the courthouse could go, the banks could go' (419).

Thus, my understanding of Harry's nostalgia as rhythmic and his movements across metropolitan space as flux rather than flight, clarifies the tetralogy's capacity for critique. Further, my re-framing of the tetralogy in this manner challenges established literary histories of the American suburbs which hold that, first, the Rabbit novels merely perpetuate a mid-twentieth-century emphasis on the malaise of a disconnected, dispossessed white middle class and, second, that suburban-set fiction has developed a more sophisticated spatial awareness – which correlates to a more ethically responsible outlook – only in the wake of 9/11. Noticeably, however, Updike's final Rabbit instalment – published in 2001 and set during the dying moments of the twentieth century – is predicated on a nostalgia for the very kinds of intimate geographical knowledge that Harry once embodied. 'Rabbit Remembered' describes the navigations across metropolitan Brewer by Janice, now remarried and making a success of her earlier career change into real estate, and by a much more civic-minded Nelson, who has taken up caring for the most disadvantaged residents of Brewer. Their journeys provide updates on the status of the many locales made familiar by Harry's repeated passage. After decades of stagnation and decline the 1990s property boom has finally made central Brewer an attractive proposition. 'Inner city is *in* now', Janice reminds some finicky clients who seem little interested in the city's identity, its past and its prospects.[50] But real estate can only provide a narrow, self-interested perspective on the history of a place: Janice recalls being told in a realty class that 'nineteenth-century industrial cities [. . .] made a big mistake by turning their backs on their waterfronts' (207).

The interests of private property are shown also to erode public space. Driving home, Brewer pours by Janice's car, 'a river of bricks and signage', 'a stream of sights deepened by a lifetime's familiarity'. Janice notes that 'signage' is a word used in 'planning-board hearings as to whether or not there is too much of it; real-estate values shoot up when a community cuts down on signage' (206). The removal of signs – which have such a presence throughout the Rabbit saga – is felt as loss. Old store signs in the centre of the city remain only as after-images – Updike renders them typographically distinct – of a bustling urban past. The tank war memorial is finally taken away, replaced by a graffiti-attracting bandstand in yet another ill-advised urban-renewal project. Predictably enough, their loss leads also to a loss of direction. Nelson fondly recalls his father 'delivering his son somewhere in this urban area that he knew block by block, intersection by intersection' (252), but during the sequence's very last journey – on the night of Y2K – Nelson loses his way and misses the party. Moreover, he is only able to navigate his way back into Brewer by way of his father's old haunts. On passing the site of the former Springer Motors one last account of the signage along Route 111 is provided. Yet the history of the sign that originally promoted a Planters Peanut store predates Nelson's experience: the narrative thus reinstalls Harry's memories. Shortly after completing the sequence's final novel, Updike explained 'Why Rabbit had to go': he was wholly defined by an era that had passed; 'he was always justified, at the back of his mind, by a concept of freedom, of America, that took sharpness from contrast with Communism'.[51] In the sequence's coda, Janice declares she can 'scarcely believe so much is gone and she is still here to remember it' (208); Updike's text, it seems, can scarcely believe that Rabbit is gone and cannot quite relinquish a mode of remembering predicated on spatial change.

'All About Development': Periodicity and Suburban Change in Ford's Bascombe Books

Richard Ford's sequence of novels featuring the protagonist Frank Bascombe – *The Sportswriter* (1986), *Independence Day* (1995), *The Lay of the Land* (2005), and *Let Me Be Frank with You* (2014) – is a literary creation that, superficially at least, has much in common with Updike's Rabbit saga. Both series, which share a present-tense articulation, are principally focused on the more-or-less ordinary travails of a white, suburban male whose situation is revisited and updated at roughly ten-year intervals. Harry and Frank are afforded by their authors an equally intimate knowledge of and deep regard for their material surroundings and the metropolitan landscapes they inhabit. Further, both characters, thanks to their attentiveness to their environments, continually register change, both physical and social. It would be wrong, however, to conclude that Harry constitutes a prototype for Frank, or that the Bascombe sequence is inspired by, and directly modelled on, the Rabbit novels. For while Ford has declared his enormous admiration for Updike's writing, he admits to having read only one of the Rabbit novels all the way through. However, Ford has acknowledged that, at the very least, the success of the Rabbit novels showed that there was scope to return to his own literary creation in the same fashion.[52]

In any case, there are numerous, significant differences between the two series. The most obvious is Frank's first-person narration, which forecloses the possibility of discrete authorial commentary about the books' characters and their habitats. In the Rabbit novels, by contrast, it is frequently difficult to attribute some of the

third-person narration to Updike's protagonist. The perceptions
of historical change during Harry's many routine journeys sometimes seem supplementary. Consider, for instance, these comments
during one of his drives into Brewer:

> Eisenhower Avenue climbs steeply through tight-built neighborhoods
> of row houses built by solid German workingmen's savings and loans
> associations, only fanlights of stained glass immune to the later layers of
> aluminum awning and Permastone siding, the Polacks and Italians being
> squeezed out by the blacks and Hispanics that in Harry's youth were held
> to the low blocks down by the river.[53]

Similar summaries of the economic bases and subsequent development of Brewer's housing stock, and of ethnic and racial succession, appear, suitably updated, across the sequence. But as the
formal-sounding allusion to 'Harry's youth' indicates, these material histories are less a record of Harry's conscious processing of
his environment than they are a foundation for them. Further, the
levels of lyricism and insight in Updike's prose often seem beyond
the imaginative resources of a man whose reading diet is at one
stage restricted to consumer reports.[54] The informed and eloquent
commentaries on space and place in the Bascombe books though
are, indubitably, entirely Frank's own.

Some critics, however, have refused to take the introspections
of Ford's protagonist at face value. Edward Depuy and Matthew
Guinn, for instance, are both disbelieving that New Jersey's banal-
scapes warrant such interpretive fireworks; Frank's sophisticated
responses to his factitious environs must therefore be seen either as
an extended ironic performance or as evidence that Ford is sending
up his protagonist.[55] Such enactments could conceivably comprise
a mode of critique of sorts. Frank, after all, remains a Democrat-
voting liberal in a solidly Republican town. Frank though is clearly
dubious about this kind of operating-behind-enemy-lines routine.
His son Paul, who has trumped his father's avowed commitment
to life in the mainstream by moving to Kansas City to work for
the venerable, family-owned corporation Hallmark, embodies this
strategy, and is all the more unpleasant for it. Paul justifies his
actions thus: 'I reflect society . . . I understand myself as a comic

figure. I'm fucking normal. You oughta try it.'[56] But Frank has no patience for this kind of posturing, wishing only 'that he was leagues away from my son [. . .] who had somehow become an asshole'.[57] Catherine Jurca meanwhile reacts with obvious irritation to the narrator-protagonist's unrelenting sensitivity, which she reads as condescension and a strategy through which Frank maintains a sense of his superiority over his suburban milieu following the failure of his literary career.[58] These critics' responses all demonstrate incredulity that the suburban everyday can attract generous scrutiny lacking in instrumentality. As Tim Foster notes, however, in several interviews Ford has professed that he thought an unironic stance would enable 'a more interesting surgery on the suburbs'.[59] I would add that interpretations of Frank as an ironic or even insincere narrator mostly emerged before the later instalments in the series were published. It is certainly harder to sustain such readings over the course of the sequence, not least because Frank's engagements with his environment are continually affected by socio-economic change, obliging him to interrogate and revise the very bases for his own world view. A more accurate account then would be that across the four books Ford's protagonist vacillates between sincerity and cynicism, and between commitment and complacency. What follows is in part an appraisal of the conditions and processes that enable and propel these shifts.

Some of the sophistication of Frank's engagements with his surroundings owes to the very complexity of those places. This constitutes another important difference between Updike's and Ford's creations. I am not contending that the Haddam area is more complex than metropolitan Brewer, or that a similar contrast can be made between the real settlements on which these imaginary locales are respectively loosely based. Frank after all remarks that Haddam is 'not a hard town to understand'.[60] However, the wider landscape of New Jersey sprawl is frequently ambiguous and complex. Abbot's model of the linear transect – which relies on clearly differentiated centres and peripheries – has little purchase here. Indeed, New Jersey sprawl is oriented not to one but to many centres: it is not clear, remarks Frank, whether Haddam is a suburb of Philadelphia or New York City; latterly, following the 1990s property boom, Haddam itself becomes a commuting destination.[61]

Further, while individual places in New Jersey typically feel familiar – reminiscent of 'the other places you've been in your life' – they are arranged like 'squares in a puzzle'.[62] This richly variegated and ever-changing landscape is heterotopic in the sense that (almost) all American places can be found here: 'Suddenly it is a high pale sky like Florida, but a mile further on, it is the Mississippi delta [...] Beyond that lies Maine.'[63] Yet Frank rejects the notion that he has a special mastery over this landscape and, by extension, is in possession of a unique critical handle on the state of the nation. Instead, he contends, New Jersey is 'the most diverting and readable of landscapes, and the language is always American'.[64] Once again, then, far from seeing himself as a sophisticate whose connoisseurship of New Jersey sprawl is unrivalled, Frank firmly believes in a democratic mode of spatial knowledge that merely requires one to be a 'conscientious observer', a 'citizen scientist'.[65] Such an attitude tallies with Frank's scepticism – bordering on contempt – for academics (which also tallies with Princeton's re-inscription as the university-free Haddam). In this respect Frank differs from Updike's putative Everyman, whose special aptitude for embodied knowledge of place – the product of a particular, now-degraded, spatial formation – has been lost, and can only be mourned.

Both series do, however, demonstrate periodic self-consciousness in order to contemplate the implications of their long form and sequentiality. Near the end of *Rabbit is Rich*, for example, the novel's predominant theme of exhaustion accrues a drolly self-reflexive attitude. Harry asks, ostensibly in response to the movie *Jaws II*, 'D'you ever get the feeling everything these days is sequels?' – 'Like people are running out of ideas' (662). In the fourth and last story of the final instalment of the Bascombe series, Frank is in dialogue with a former acquaintance, who is close to death. The bedridden Eddie Medley asks the ex-writer: 'I always wonder. I was an engineer [...] when you write a book, how do you know when you've finished it? Do you know ahead of time? Is that always clear? It baffles me. Nothing I did had an end.'[66] Frank rejects Eddie's assumption that narrative conclusions warrant special consideration, declaring 'endings always seemed arbitrary to me'. He goes on to report: 'if I'd gotten myself fully expressed [...] I stopped. You bet. But if I didn't, I kept on putting words down.'[67] Frank's comments delineate a sort of literary functionalism, a belief that fiction should be shaped by its purpose, must fit experience. The explanation fails to impress Frank's interlocutor; evidently, Frank's aesthetics provide little consolation to the dying. But only sentimental or disingenuous forms of writing can do this; fiction's proper purpose, according to Frank, is to achieve a close measure of lived life. There is a rather obvious irony that so much material gets to be written about a man who gave up his literary career long before the narrative present of the sequence's opening novel. Defined by human mortality and narrative termination, the bedside discussion can perhaps be seen as a more prolix equivalent of the exhausted declaration that closes the final novel in the Rabbit sequence and which performatively lays Harry to rest: 'Enough' (466). But typically for Frank – and as the punning title of the final Bascombe book underscores – his observations about the limits of literature are not achieved by personal fiat but are reached through dialogue with a near stranger, through engagement with the very world that sustains the kind of fiction he finds most meaningful.[68] Here, though, the encounter demonstrates a failure, or the limits of empathy – which, as we shall see, is the first of many such failures for Frank.

Turning from Literature Back to Life: *The Sportswriter*

In *The Sportswriter*, Frank repeatedly considers his truncated literary career, which he abandoned shortly after his arrival in Haddam in the late 1960s. These reflections draw attention to the relationship between the suburbs and writing, and situate the sequence within a longer tradition of suburban-set realist fiction. Frank's move into the suburbs is for sure facilitated by his successful engagement in the literary marketplace. His first house purchase – an ample mock-Tudor on leafy Hoving Road – was funded from the proceeds of selling the movie rights of his first and only published literary work, a slender volume of short stories. The move, though, is not understood as a cashing in of his artistic credentials. Rather, it is rationalised, initially at least, as an aid to Frank's writing: 'unexpectant and unprepossessing' New Jersey and 'neutral' Haddam are presumed to make few demands on an author, leaving him suitably anonymous and autonomous.[69] These arguments have a literary precedent. Frank follows in the footsteps of his name-sake Frank Wheeler, the protagonist of Richard Yates's 1961 novel *Revolutionary Road*, whose literary ambitions similarly founder on the shoals of suburban ordinariness. Unlike Frank Wheeler, how-ever, Frank Bascombe soon comes to terms with the modest extent of his talents and recognises his previous justifications for his own suburbanisation for what they were: acts of self-aggrandisement and self-deception. Frank perceives that, as well as being 'stuck in bad stereotypes' (43), his writing strained at achieving universal significance. The latter tendency was particularly unfortunate since, as Frank admits, he had nothing meaningful to say about the wider world. He notes, for instance, how his stories were always set in places he had never been to and knew nothing about, but which seemed suitable locations for staging significant human dramas such as 'searching for history'. In other words, by turning away from the particular, his writing succumbs to pretentiousness, or what Frank terms 'gross seriousness' (44).

The antidote to all this lazy universalising is 'to turn from litera-ture back to life' (44), which, he determines, is ultimately 'unconju-gatable' (363), merely 'the thing that happens' (366). Frank pledges himself to his suburban surroundings and determines to say yes to as much as he can: 'yes to my town, my neighbourhood, my neigh-bour, yes to his car, her lawn and hedge and rain gutters' (49). He is aware that this sort of commitment to everyday life 'isn't enough for literature', but he is past caring. His declaration is an instance of dramatic irony of course, another of the series' self-reflexive moves in which the protagonist unwittingly participates. It helps delineate the mode of writing about suburbia that is to be pursued by Ford: one that is self-consciously yet fully engaged with changing sub-urban space and lives, and which succumbs neither to smugness nor self-pity. For Frank, sportswriting constitutes a more sustain-able and responsible mode of engagement with the world than high-minded literary endeavour. Athletes after all demand from themselves complete focus and commitment, and a self-assurance – being 'more within oneself' (4) – that Frank hopes to achieve for himself. And indeed, the organising narratives of sportswriting seem to accord with his own experience in a way that those of literature do not: The 'raw material I had up to then – ruminations, fragments of memory, impulses I might've tried to struggle into a short story suddenly seemed like life I already understood clearly and could write about: fighting the battle with age; discovering how to think of the future in realistic terms' (41). Moreover, Frank sees sportswriting less as a 'real profession' than as a disciplined receptiveness, 'an agreeable frame of mind, a *way* of going about things rather than things you exactly do or know' (305, emphasis in original). Sportswriting thus closely corresponds with the good life in Haddam, which Frank professes has far less to do with money than it does the possession of 'a certain awareness' (46).

What saves Frank's philosophy of engagement from banality or smugness is his openness to mystery, a quality that he continues to value throughout the sequence. Mystery inheres even in 'plumb-literal' (100) places like Haddam and is worth seeking out and examining precisely because, in contrast to more celebrated locales, it is unexpected, unannounced, unharnessed. But such mysterious-ness, once again, does not lie solely within the purview of an elite cadre of wandering observers who are in possession of a highly advanced faculty for wonder, and who are able to locate mean-ing behind or beyond the dully familiar. Empathically, ordinary mystery is not locatable on some transcendent plane, but inheres in the material, sensible world. It is detectable in the 'bricky warp' (5) of America's more anonymous cities, in the new-car-smell of a hired Ford Crown Victoria, or when fingering the glossy pages of a sales catalogue. Admittedly, these examples bespeak the pleasures of consumer choice; moreover, Frank registers how the circum-scribed transformations promised by such options – 'freedom-within-sensible-limits' or 'Eternal renewal on a manageable scale' (144) – tend to lead to complacency. Yet, within Frank's insistent attentiveness towards the everyday – a mode of engagement he calls 'literalness' – there remains scope for a critical outlook that has not become wholly accommodated to the world as found. Even his one-time obsession with sales catalogues yielded a 'speculative interest in what's not known' (200). True, mostly Frank's lines of speculation bend towards imagining how his own life might have taken an alternative course had he made different choices. Thus he is perhaps less engaged in reimagining the world than in reimag-ining himself. Still, Frank's approach anticipates more significant transformations. He is after all mobilised by a belief that across the most literal of American locations 'something hopeful and unexpected can take place' (5). What is required to make the most out of these opportunities is an openness to the contingency of encounter. Indeed, such a stance may help prevent one from getting caught in the suburbs' 'worst lie', the 'fragrant silly dream' of 'Life-forever' (312). Thus literalness is a mode of habitation that is not defined by stasis, by permanence, but one that is open to change.

As events unfold in *The Sportswriter*, however, Frank's commitment to literalness is tested almost to destruction. His relationships with others place it under particular strain. For instance, Frank judges his girlfriend, the vivacious trainee nurse Vicki Arcenault, to be his ideal partner because her 'nature is to put her faith in objects more than essence' (58). But he is mistaken in his reading of her: Vicki terminates the affair, in brutal fashion with a punch to the face, after Frank starts behaving in ways that seem counter to her idea of him. Meanwhile Frank's ex-wife Ann Dykstra – whom he refers to merely as 'X' throughout the opening novel – contends that Frank's concentrating on 'being an ordinary citizen' (11) has left him ill-prepared for life's hard knocks. He concedes that her view is at least historically accurate: after the death of their young son Ralph, Frank recounts how he drifted into a state of 'dreaminess', a debilitating sense of dissociation that directly contributed to the breakdown of their marriage. Literalness thus becomes for Frank a vital modus operandi: a way to combat his tendency towards dreaminess, and a means by which he can reattend to and reconnect with the world.

Yet his relationships remain thin. Frank professes he prefers 'to participate briefly in the lives of others at a low level' (205). Kathy Knapp takes this declaration as indicative of Frank's moral minimalism. This term derives from the work of ethnographer M. P. Baumgartner, whose study of an affluent New York suburb in the 1980s describes a community whose peaceable way of life arises from the transience of its members and their indifference to each other – qualities customarily associated with disorder and antagonism.[70] Due to its being so averse to conflict, Baumgartner says it is sensible to 'speak of the suburb as a culture of avoidance'.[71] Knapp takes as further evidence of Frank's moral minimalism firstly his unwillingness to provide comfort and counsel to an old acquaintance, Walter Luckett, who commits suicide a short while later, and secondly his abrupt relocation at the end of the novel to Florida, where he has no ties whatsoever. I agree that these actions demonstrate moral failure, but Frank is at least conscious of and responsive to his own shortcomings. In the novel's reflective coda, narrated sometime after the story's principal events that took place over the Easter weekend of 1983, Frank concludes that Walter's death 'has had the effect on me that death means to have', that is, 'reminding me of my responsibility to a somewhat larger world'. He further muses: 'Though it came at a time when I didn't much want to think about that, and I still don't find it easy to accommodate and am not completely sure what I can do differently.' (358–9) Frank's oblique reference to mourning – something he has previously admitted he does not know how to do – suggests that he has been working at the very limits of his emotional capabilities. He finally accepts that one's past may be of some significance – previously he has insisted 'we are all released to the rest of our lives' (17) – which may indicate a small step in coming to terms with the loss of his son. However, even while his departure for Florida is motivated by a sense of duty to Walter – it begins as an attempt to locate the dead man's lovechild – Frank's account of his pleasurable drifting at 'bottom of the country' seems to describe a relapse into dreaminess. He may have moved out into the larger world, but he has little sense of responsibility towards it.

Yet the following novel *Independence Day*, set five years later, sees Frank firmly reinstated in Haddam; his sojourn in Florida is sheepishly recalled as a period of 'psychic detachment', 'a fugue'.[72] This revision points to a pattern that occurs across the sequence: a model for living, for engaging with others and the wider world, is tested to breaking point in one instalment, and is then undermined following changes in circumstances in the next. Thus the Bascombe novels do not simply chart the development of its protagonist or, at least, I am less interested in how the sequence registers character progression in a conventionally realist manner. Rather, I am concerned with how a shifting suburban spatiality repeatedly demands new modes of interaction, and the manner in which the successive novels appraise these engagement strategies. As the second novel in the sequence amply shows, conceiving of oneself as being as adaptable and processual as space is changeable ultimately has unfortunate moral and political consequences.

Coming to Grips with Contingency: *Independence Day*

Unlike the Harry Angstrom of the second Rabbit novel, Frank Bascombe redux is quite at ease in his local environment. Indeed, whereas he once fancied himself as a 'spectral presence', now he feels '*towny*' (94, emphasis in original), and he frequently employs a first-person-plural voice when discussing Haddam's prospects at the close of the Reagan era. At the novel's opening, for instance, Frank approvingly surveys civic endeavour enabled by 'our proud new tax dollars', as well as local preparations for Independence Day. His enhanced sense of attachment can be explained in large part by a career change: the peripatetic labour of the sportswriter has been traded in for the more grounded pursuits of realty. But his new-found commitment to place has not left Frank wholly inward-looking: he perceives his environs as both unstable and influenced by external forces. Indeed, he diagnoses a subtle shift in mood, a growing uneasiness across the local population in the face of falling property prices, and 'a new sense of a wild world beyond our perimeter' (5). In fact, random acts of violence irrupt throughout the novel. Frank's colleague and erstwhile lover Claire Devine is raped and murdered; the crime remains unsolved. Frank is also a bystander to a murder at a motel he has checked into on the way to see his son Paul who now lives with his mother in Connecticut. Further, Frank's plan for a road trip with his son is envisaged as necessary 'quality time' following Paul's brush with the law for theft and assault; evidently, violence begins at home. But if the novel makes the connection between forces of neo-liberalism and this 'wild world', Frank trusts that the property market will look after everyone's interests. Indeed, if previously literalness enabled sensitivity to change, now Frank's 'existence period' seems to be all about accommodating oneself – and others – to the vagaries of the market place. As he breezily declares, being a realtor 'makes you come to grips with contingency and even sell it as a source of strength' (439). In his line of business, 'change is good', 'instability' always 'promising'; his job, moreover, 'is to make all that seem normal' (406–7).

It is somewhat ironic then that Frank has invested in Wallace Hill, the black section of Haddam, precisely because of the area's perceived stability: 'Reliable, relatively prosperous middle-aged and older Negro families have lived here for decades in small, close-set homes they keep in much better than average condition and whose values [. . .] have gone steadily up [. . .] It's America how it used to be, only blacker' (24). Nostalgia thus appears to have trumped business sense. Perhaps worse, despite having no ties whatsoever with the community – and contradicting his appreciation of the neighbourhood's solidity – Frank presumes that his purchasing of two rental properties will fulfil a longed-for 'sense of belonging and permanence the citizens of these streets might totally lack in Haddam'. Frank's beneficence, however, has an obvious bottom line: his actions, he feels, 'would bestow on me the satisfaction of reinvesting in my community, providing affordable housing options, maintaining a neighborhood integrity I admired, while covering my financial backside and establishing greater sense of connectedness' (26). In the latter aim he is disappointed: the ideal tenants who rent one of his houses leave within two years and the others are alternately belligerent and evasive. Moreover, in a subsequent altercation with his less-favoured tenants, Frank is identified as an interloper by a neighbour who fails to acknowledge him from a previous encounter, as does the police officer who is duly called. Frank's fantasy of himself as a benevolent, civic-minded landlord is thus embarrassingly way off the mark. The disjunction between his self-image and the neighbourhood's attitude towards him is perhaps an inevitable – and certainly a just – outcome of Frank's bad faith and the incoherence of his understanding of place, which appeals simultaneously to permanence and contingency, and to self-interest and community spirit.

The idealisation of other places, a belief in their capacity to accommodate one's self image, is a theme that runs across the novel. Occupying more of Frank's attention than his rentals are his wearisome clients, Joe and Phyllis Markham. Frank's patience with this demanding but unworldly couple – who have started refusing even to view properties that on paper meet their requirements – is admirable. He provides wise counsel: in the face of the Markhams' grudging realisation that their dream of relocating their lives from Vermont to the Haddam area is unaffordable, Frank suggests that 'you are best off coming as close as you can and trying to bring life to a place, not just depending on the place to supply it to you' (76). Indeed, Frank's diligence seems motivated by a genuine desire to help the Markhams. For instance, he worries that, with the couple approaching a 'realty meltdown', they may 'just dribble off elsewhere, feeling the need for an unattainable fresh start, and end up buying the first shitty split-level they see with another agent' (47). Given the therapist-like attention that he lavishes on his clients, Phyllis's verbal slip, where she refers to Frank as a 'relator', is unsurprising; reciprocally, Frank describes her feelings of affection towards him as transference. Their mutual understanding of their business relationship as therapeutic serves as further confirmation that the purchasing of property is understood first and foremost as a technique of self-management. In this manner the second Bascombe novel is closely attuned to the formation of neo-liberal subjectivity.

On the other hand, Frank wishes his clients would curb their self-importance and learn to appreciate the potential of the suburban landscape for surprise and wonder. In short, they need to get over themselves. For instance, where Joe refuses to grant the ageing bedroom community of Penns Neck the honour of being a place, Frank suggests – after witnessing an exhibitionist neighbour besporting herself 'Isadora Duncan style' across the length of the picture window of a nearby property – that it 'has mystery and the unexpected as its hidden assets' (66–7). Thus the quality that preoccupied Frank throughout much of the first novel is revived. Previously, mystery encouraged attentiveness and commitment to place. In the Penns Neck scene, however, its deployment is characterised not by reverence but by flippancy. Moreover, the appreciation of mystery is for personal consumption: Frank's joke is private; the self-absorbed Markhams fail even to notice the incident. Evidently, an appreciation of mystery cannot be shared and, noticeably, Frank's pun suggests his conception of place is predicated on economic advantage. Ultimately, Frank's advice mostly boils down to trying to get the Markhams to be realistic, to moderate their ambitions in keeping with their line of credit. Indeed, getting value trumps all. Frank declares: 'You might think I'd wonder about whether he or she gets their dream house, or if they get the house they originally wanted. Getting your money's worth, though, getting value, is frankly more important – particularly in the current economy. When the correction comes, value will be what things stand on' (73–4). That the Markhams eventually agree to rent Frank's vacant Wallace Hill house – an evidently mutually beneficial arrangement – is thus a fitting resolution. Frank's response is supremely cynical: he declares that 'to me it's ennobling to help others face their hard choices, [to] pilot them toward a reconciliation with life'; in the same breath, however, he contends that he is helping the Markhams 'believe renting is what they should do (being wise and cautious), by promoting the fantasy that each is acting in his own best interest by attempting to make the other happy' (415).

Clearly, Frank's change of occupation has inured him to the commodification of homes. He professes to having no feeling for places, and is unmoved by the sight of his old Hoving Road house, now repurposed as a Christian conference centre. (Perhaps the fact that he benefitted enormously from a tax loophole when disposing of the property goes some of the way to explaining his detachment.) He asks: 'is there any cause to think a place – any place – within its plaster and joists, its trees and plantings, in its putative essence *ever* shelters some spirit ghost of us as proof of its significance and ours?' (442). His answer is an emphatic no; it is only something other people do, like the hapless Joe Markham, who does not even know how to rent a house because he 'can only think in terms of permanence' (418). But even to Frank it is apparent that the defining qualities of his 'Existence Period' – a sense that 'the possibility of imminent change in status underl[ies] everything' (284), being 'anchored only to contingency' (439) – have corrosive effects. He wonders, for instance, whether being able to see himself 'as occupying a fixed point rather than being in a process', which he sees as 'the quiddity of the Existence Period' (285), might improve his relationship with his son Paul. He acknowledges that his ability to see anything being different from how it is, while being a trait which might make for being a good realtor (or for that matter, he suggests, a novelist), 'also seems to produce a somewhat less than reliable and morally feasible human being' (226). And Sally Caldwell, Frank's girlfriend, complains that he is 'noncommittal' (271) and, more damningly, that the Existence Period is 'a simulated way to live your life' (434). Thus the Frank of *Independence Day* demonstrates that some of the qualities which I have so far been arguing need to be better appreciated with respect to spatiality – contingency, process – are far from being in and of themselves positive values. The second Bascombe novel shows that simple identification with suburban change is inimical to either an ethical or critical engagement with space and place. The adoption of mutability as an organising principle after all leads to Frank holding to contradictory standards. For instance, while he is dismissive of traditional, essentialist understandings of place, Frank easily succumbs to uncritical, self-serving nostalgia. Frank's reliability is limited then to his being a barometer, a measure of changeability in turbulent times.

Being Aspirant within Limits: *The Lay of the Land*

The limitations and contradictions of the Existence Period ultimately precipitate its collapse and replacement by a new mode of engagement. Introduced at the end of the second Bascombe novel, 'the Permanent Period' dominates the sequence's third instalment, *The Lay of the Land*, whose proceedings take place over the Thanksgiving holiday in the first year of the new millennium. This new epoch is defined by tranquillity and personal integration; according to Frank, the period marks an 'end to perpetual becoming' and provides 'a licence to think about the past only indistinctly'.[73] The respective titles of the second and third books in the sequence are suggestive of this paradigm shift, with self-determination giving way to acquiescence, and with the certainties of topography substituting the temporal and the transient. The new order is also registered by the protagonist's changed circumstances. Now remarried, Frank has departed Haddam to reside in the modest resort 'townlette' of Sea-Clift on the Jersey shore. He continues to practise realty, though in a much more relaxed fashion than previously, running his own company with the aid of a younger associate, the Tibetan-American and Buddhist Mike Mahoney. However, now in his mid-fifties, Frank is also more keenly aware of his own mortality, not least because of a recent diagnosis of prostate cancer.

But perhaps the most significant development to have taken place between 1988 and 2000 concerns Haddam, which Frank frequently revisits. Stirred by the 1990s property boom the town entered a 'new, strange and discordant phase' (121), during which 'expectations left all breathable atmosphere behind' and the most 'cutthroat [. . .] realty shenanigans' became standard practice. Frank's qualms, however, have less do to with the questionable methods of his industry than the consequences, which left property in Haddam unaffordable to all but the wealthiest incomers. Indeed, Frank understands that this influx, and the town's new desirability, has helped release Haddam from subordination to nearby metropolises; it is finally 'a place to itself'. But upon achieving place-hood, Haddam has succumbed to 'era-lessness'. On the one hand, its present lacks substance and weight; on the other, there is no longer any 'faith in the future', no trust in the redemptive theme running through ordinary civic dramas, such as buying a home (121–2). Further, the town's past is repackaged in ersatz fashion and always to the end of promoting local business. The desultory Civil War re-enactments taking place across Haddam, for instance, are part of an 'effort to rev up sidewalk appeal'. So is the Pilgrim Village Interpretative Center established in the town square. Clad in 'authentically inadequate' clothing, the village's miscast participants give canned declarations about the hardships of pilgrim life in order to remind present-day citizens of Haddam how much they have to be thankful for (69–70). Less eccentric but more depressing is the designation of Wallace Hill as a historic African American neighbourhood, which has the result of pushing up property prices and emptying it of its black residents.

Evidently, something about Haddam is not working as it should. Frank declares that by 1993 he was registering that the 'malign force' at play was nothing other than the economy itself, which has led to property being held 'hostage and away from the very people who wanted and often badly needed it and, in any case, had a right to expect to own it', a state of affairs he now finds 'demoralizing as hell' (123). But Frank also recognises that he is 'implicated' (64) in Haddam's transformation into a fortress of wealth. He readily admits, for instance, that he had given his support to every nimbyish ordinance that 'kept prices fat' (43), and he profited enormously from selling his rentals just as Wallace Hill was being 'gentrified to smithereens' (212). Moral self-disgust prompts his departure for the coast, which promises the opportunity to conduct business 'on a more human scale'. The stability and insularity of Sea-Clift appeals precisely because it precludes the possibility of unchecked economic expansion. Frank declares: 'To me, commerce with no likelihood of significant growth or sky-rocketing appreciation seems like a precious bounty, and the opposite of my years in Haddam, when *gasping increase* was [. . .] a sacred article of faith' (595, emphasis in original). Frank's preference for manageable growth, of being 'aspirant within limits' (595), defines his current business ethics: he requires that his interactions with his clients yield 'productive' or 'acceptable longing' (532) for both parties. Indeed, Frank imagines the 'perfect real estate experience' to be one in which 'everyone does their bit, but no house changes hands'. (Manifestly, these occasional 'positive outside-the-envelope transactions' (401) are the luxury of one who really does not need to make any more money – comfortable circumstances that Frank draws attention to several times across the sequence.) But while he obviously enjoys the easy-going environs of a relatively unfashionable resort town, Frank is wrong to think that it can insulate him from the thrusting excesses of the property market. In any case, far from cutting his ties with his former patch, Frank has retained his Haddam realty licence and frequently takes on referrals. Moreover, the business model in Sea-Clift – 'fill-in and retrench' – is 'not so different from Haddam', and Frank speaks positively of the signs of gentrification in Sea-Clift's Filipino quarter. And, tellingly, he later repeats the sense of his being 'implicated' after making a six-figure sum when selling the ocean-front property next to his own to the forbidding Feensters, whose lack of 'useful longing' helps explain their toxicity as neighbours (308). Thus there would appear to be no escaping the morally compromising aspects of the realty industry; moreover, Frank continues to act as an agent of the kind of change that, in less peaceful conditions, induced moral palpitations.

Thus Frank's 'permanent period' serves as a shelter that insulates him from the worst ravages of late twentieth-century capitalism and as a screen which obscures his own participation in it. As in the previous novels, however, personal circumstances disrupt his carefully engineered modus operandi. Frank is unnerved by the sudden appearance of Sally's long-lost-and-presumed-dead former husband Wally, and is thrown into crisis when his wife of several years decides to return with this gauche and unprepossessing man to his Scottish island home, all because she 'wasn't feeling enough', and wanted 'to experience something [she] never got to experience before' (567–8). The turnabout clarifies for Frank how his attachment to permanence is a device premised on solipsism; he realises how misplaced is his assumption that those close to him share in his unencumbered contentment and have similarly generalised their past 'to a pleasant pinkish blur' (371).

Frank's own past forcibly re-establishes itself in an equally painful manner in a subsequent scene. While reading an article in *Home Buyer's Guide* that mentions the death of a local realtor's son, Frank experiences a moment of epiphany. He realises not only that he has not yet properly mourned his son's death, but also that the various modes of engagement he has devised for himself over the years have been ploys to avoid having to come to terms with his loss. Knapp suggests that this revelation demonstrates how traumatic experience has the capacity to weave together individual and collective suffering, how individual lives are bound together with others.[74] I concur, but also find it revealing that Frank's epiphany results from his reading what is first and foremost a business listings magazine. Frank declares such publications are always enlightening: he reads their 'crowded pages to acquire (by osmosis) some sense of how we're all basically doing, what we need to be wary of, look forward to or look back on with pride or relief'. What he describes as 'spiritual sign-pointers' are 'revealed' in:

old fire stations, rectories or Chrysler agencies that are for sale [. . .] or the number of old homes versus new ones on the sale block, or the addresses and plat maps of new constructions, the ethnicity (gauged by names) of who's selling what, who's doing the cooking and who's going out of business. And finally, of course, what costs what versus what used to cost what. (508)

Frank reiterates his scepticism of the epiphanic, which he insists is a fabrication of the liberal arts, even while he holds the operations of 'plain and simple commerce' to be revelatory. This is not as contradictory as it seems: whereas the former promotes self-importance, an unhelpful sense that 'we are all separate agents, each underlain by an infinite remoteness' (511), the latter demonstrates the inescapable enmeshment of ordinary lives.

The scene, however, seems to equivocate on whether business provides a suitable heuristic for diagnosing social conditions. Frank comes across the copy of *Home Buyer's Guide* while having a drink in an old haunt of his while waiting for his car to be fixed. The bar now has a lesbian staff and clientele; Frank takes pleasure in the capacity of this indubitably commercial establishment to foster 'amiable and tolerant' interaction (505). It certainly compares favourably with the all-male Haddam drinking hole depicted earlier in the novel from which he is thrown out after getting into a fight with a racist regular. But the basis of Frank's participation in the lesbian bar is necessarily transactional. Indeed, it is emphatically so: he is after all buying drinks for himself while waiting for another paid service to be completed, and he even attempts to solicit interest from his server about buying property. As if remarking on the circumstances of Frank's presence, and his studied appreciation of the conditions of local commerce, the barwoman asks: 'when did everything get to be about bidnus?' (505–6). Frank's response is to intone in agreeable fashion the Friedmanesque mantra 'the business of business is business' (506). His rejoinder is both a logical non sequitur and a keen reminder of the difficulty Frank has of divorcing himself and benign commercial exchange from more rapacious varieties of capitalist endeavour.

In fact, Frank's sense of his own life course is inescapably rooted in the commercial world. When Paul derides his father by snarling 'you're all about *development*', Frank understands that his son is not talking about real estate. 'I *do* believe in development' (175, emphases in original) is Frank's emphatic comeback. But his avowal is not only hypocritical – for it flatly contradicts the principal tenets of the Permanent Period – it also unavoidably invokes his own professional interest in the property market. This association is repeatedly confirmed throughout the novel and most decisively of all when, while appreciating a view across Barnegat Bay to the mainland which includes newer homes from 'the go-go nineties', Frank decides that 'there's nothing wrong with development if the right people do the developing' (626). The comment follows his partner Mike Mahoney's decision not to go through with a property deal that will concrete over 'comely' central New Jersey cornfields and woodland with a vast 'flat-as-a-griddle housing tract' (56). But Frank's affirming remarks about extant development suggest he was less concerned about the accrual of eye-watering profits from the rape of the land than with the question of who is profiting. Alongside his somewhat snide observations about his Tibetan-American business partner's ongoing performance of authenticity, Frank is obviously disquieted by the prospect of Asian affluence. For instance, by indulging in wilfully antic behaviour, Frank scuppers Mike's agreed-in-principle sale of a dilapidated Sea-Clift home to a wealthy Chinese-American. Further, Frank speculates that the strained amiability of his Japanese banker neighbour is merely cover for more sinister ambitions: 'Then *bingo!* The buggers own the beach, the ocean, your house, your memories, and your kids are on a boat to Kyoto for immersion language training' (544). Even if semi-sardonic, Frank's projection speaks from a broader complex of anxieties. Tellingly, Frank appears to be comforted by the fact that Filipino newcomers to the area have been taking up service roles. Despite their 'small prospects' (183), they are 'enjoying life'; 'everyone likes them' (182), Frank remarks. His belief in development thus has both economic and racist foundations.

Further, the very progression of the novel sequence itself is inextricably linked with the development of property. Frank speaks of his disenchantment with and withdrawal from the investment council 'Dollars for Doers', which has been 'charged to "transition" Sea-Clift into the "the next phase", from under-used asset to vitality pocket and full-service lifestyle provider using grassroots support'. He adds: 'This even though we all like it fine here. Permanence has once again been perceived as death' (595). But Frank's recent calling time on his own Permanent Period compromises his censure of local boosters. Even more tellingly, Frank refers to the successor to the Permanent Period as 'the next level', echoing the ambitions of Dollars for Doers. Paul's accusation that his father is 'all about development' is then truer than Frank would care to admit. Indeed, the very basis by which the novel sequence transitions from one instalment to the next, and thus also its comprehension of the enmeshment of personal and spatial transformation, is shown here to be indebted to a neo-liberal vision of the world.

The novel's ending would appear, however, to offer a more hopeful vision of spatial and personal change. Being onboard a flight to Rochester, Minnesota for further cancer treatment understandably lends Frank's thoughts a terminal theme. But continued human contact – both through conversation with fellow passengers also bound for a stint at the Mayo Clinic and inferred from the panorama of 'thickening' settlement viewed through his window during his flight's descent – provides encouragement (724). Frank is sufficiently moved to pledge himself to an ethics defined by humility and service or, in his own words, to 'keeping things simple while still making a contribution' (726). And, with 'Here is necessity', he reconfirms the commitment he made to his locality in the first novel. Both principles are condensed in his ardent declaration – which is recapitulated in novel's closing lines – of the need to 'establish the world on a more human scale' (724). Tim Foster reads the book's coda as extenuatory because, 'despite the concerns he harbours from the vantage point of the year 2000', Frank remains 'convinced that an imaginative engagement with space can generate a spatiality – a nexus of society's spatial practices – that is more than a reflection of acquisitiveness'. Foster contends that the two most important lessons learned from Frank's seventeen years of attending to New Jersey's changing landscape are that 'the true measurement of any particular geography has to incorporate human needs, weaknesses and desires', and that '"our doing" might yet result in a different world'.[75] In short, places can be made more habitable through individual and collective action. Further, the articulation 'our doing' potentially redeems Frank of his racism, for it is derived from the Buddhist-inflected wisdom of his business partner. One can thus be committed to locality and remain open to difference.

Helping Others Get Their Narrative Straight:
Let Me Be Frank with You

The fourth Bascombe book, however – with its vantage point of the year 2012 – makes it difficult to sustain such optimism. Now retired, the 68-year-old Frank may be comfortably re-ensconced in Haddam, but Hurricane Sandy has brought death, injury and destruction to the Jersey shore. Frank's old home has been torn from its foundations and tossed on its side like a die; many of his former neighbours' residences have been literally blown away. What scope is there for 'imaginative engagement with space' when there is no longer any here here? The spectacle of ruin is indeed initially paralysing: Frank cannot begin to 'envision the grains of possibility in what's left' of these 'once-sparkling' beach towns.[76] But he is heartened by, of all things, the sight of a washed-up condom, which he takes as 'a sign that humans are drifting back to this spot already – now that it's vacant – and utilizing the beach as they have and should'. Encouraged, he surmises that, 'possibly sooner that anyone's predicting, complex life will resume here' (49). But Frank's appeal to the productive use of the land – a favourite theme of his across the sequence – is somewhat undercut by the fact that '*Flip* companies' – that is, speculators – have moved in quickly to exploit local disconsolation (12); despite the recent catastrophe, the shore is still holding its value. Once again, then, Frank's vision of a benign 'multi-use society' sidelines the corrosive effects of profiteering and wider capital flows.[77] In any case, Frank recognises that his ambulatory musings are enabled by the fact he cleared out at the right moment. In the years following Frank's renewal of his vows to place made while walking in the surf near his Sea-Clift home at the close of *The Lay of the Land*, 'the shore got rediscovered and everything went nuts' (14). This by-now familiar story of his successful navigation of the property market does however enable Frank to revise his understanding of Sea-Clift: belatedly he comprehends that it was 'a bracing atmosphere of American faux egalitarianism' (30) that originally drew him there.

The reason for Frank's current visit to the despoiled coast though extends beyond the economic: he is there to somehow alleviate the 'domiciliary suffering' of Arnie Urquhart, to whom Frank sold his 'tall, glass-and-redwood, architect-design beach palace' (9). Frank feels that 'you bear *some* responsibility to another human you sell a house to'; moreover, the task is, Frank contends, 'a priestly, vocational responsibility', a rare instance when 'the professional and human operate on a single set of rails' (21). The opening story's title – 'I'm here' – thus reworks the previous novel's concluding commitment to place – '*Here* is necessity' – with an undertaking to being present for others. This imperative is the mode of engagement that defines 'the Next Level'. Now 'a member of the clean-desk demographic', Frank sees himself 'freed to do unalloyed good in the world, should [he] choose to' (7). However, his choices – from greeting veterans returning from Iraq and Afghanistan to reading V. S. Naipaul to the blind – are hardly wholly positive or even particularly generous contributions. Perhaps these two examples are supposed to show that being present for others ought to extend beyond officially sanctioned forums and into everyday life. But they also indicate the underlying politics of the Next Level's principal duty. Frank after all has little patience with complaints about the havoc the US has been wreaking across the globe. In his analysis the world's most intractable conflicts have been caused by false divisions: Pakistanis and Indians, he declares 'are the same people, like Israelis and Arabs' (17). As he approaches old age, Frank thus appears to have succumbed to an especially egregious form of US-centric humanism. Further, the eponymous declaration 'I'm here' is gleaned from a newspaper article his wife was reading over breakfast about the hanging of thirty-eight members of the Sioux tribe involved in the Dakota Uprising of 1862. When on the scaffold, the condemned started shouting out 'I'm here' in their own language, as if to give each other strength. Sally is both moved by the account and embarrassed to appropriate the slogan for her own ends; Frank, by contrast, feels no such qualms. His commitment to being present for others, it seems, is predicated on a disregard for both racial difference and histories of state-sanctioned violence.

The limitations of Frank's reigning ethic of engagement are amply demonstrated in the following story 'Everything could be worse'. This second of the book's four stories tells of Frank's encounter with a middle-aged African American woman who turns up unannounced at his Wilson Street home. This woman, Ms Pines, discloses that she grew up in Frank's house during the 1960s. Frank is happy to oblige what he calls 'previous-resident returns', a phenomenon with which he is personally familiar and that he understands to be an inevitable consequence of a twenty-first-century tendency 'to see and buy houses like Jeep Cherokees' (73). Besides, it is little bother helping others to 'get their narrative straight', which, he contends, 'is what we all long for' (74). The visitation provides Ford an opportunity to examine white attitudes regarding the historicity of the suburbs and, more specifically, the matter of who has authority over which historical narratives. Ms Pines's appearance prompts Frank to dwell on residential succession in Haddam. He initially presumes, incorrectly as it turns out, that she is a representative of the town's 'black trace' (65) still holding on in the neighbourhood where he once owned rental properties. Wallace Hill is now dominated by 'a new wave of white young-marrieds who work two jobs, are never home, wouldn't think of having children, and pride themselves on living in a "heritage" neighbourhood instead of dreary townhouse where everything works but isn't "historic"' (66). Frank's account of the prizing of period architecture by white gentrifiers, coupled with their disconnect from local social history is hardly news. Noticeably, though, Frank and Sally's attitudes to housing are not all that different: in their Wilson Street house they have 'kept the "older-home" fussiness of small rooms', for Sally abhors 'the spiritless open-concept bleakness of the re-purposed' (79). And when Frank welcomes Ms Pines to explore the house with a complacent 'you won't find much changed', her pointed reply, 'we'll have to see' (82), both underlines and contests his assumption that the ownership of historic property equates with a custody of history. Ms Pines seems the perfect herald to disabuse Frank of his belief that he knows the past. Not only is she a history teacher, she also informs him that her father grew up on Clio Street – the very same street on which Frank once owned property. And Clio, Ms Pines informs him, was the muse of history (88). Frank recognises that suburbs are rarely credited with a sense of history, but Ms Pines's visit forces home that the history of American suburbs is one defined by property and race, a history that Frank – whose investments in a historically black neighbourhood contributed to its gentrification – is incontrovertibly a part.

Frank is not unmoved by Ms Pines's story: indeed, he is somewhat perturbed by the fact that, despite his background in selling houses in Haddam, he has been left ignorant of his own home's status as a local historic milestone, that is, its having been an early mixed-race household in all-white neighbourhood. He reacts by positioning himself as the arbiter – and even the author – of Ms Pines's narrative. She suffers Frank's repeated interruptions that involve his trying to demonstrate how much they have in common or the extent to which her account of familial anguish corresponds with white experience; Frank's suggestion that what he is hearing 'sounds like a story in *The New Yorker*' leaves his visitor staring 'with incomprehension' (98). And when Ms Pines is only part-way through her narrative, Frank begins to imagine writing the story himself, or telling it to his amazed wife. Similarly, the news that Ms Pines's scientist father converted the basement into a private laboratory strikes Frank as 'a good story for an as-told-to project – like the Underground Railroad stopping at your house', as well as 'a secondary-value consideration for resale' (100). In short, what Frank wants is to get this black woman's narrative straight, but for his own benefit, not hers.

As with all the Bascombe books, a short period of time – usually, a matter of weeks – has elapsed between the narrative's action and the act of narration. Frank's retrospection is tinged with embarrassment. The numerous inanities that Frank babbles before Ms Pines owe much to the discomfort he feels when having conversations with African Americans, which he admits tend to devolve into 'phony, race-neutral natter about making the world a better place just by being alive'. If only he could just 'let silence do its sovereign work and see if something of more material import opened up' (86). As his ludicrous comments about Paul Robeson suggest, he is not very good at keeping his mouth shut, but there is a moment of revelation when Frank tries to picture the Pines family occupying the space of his home while 'trying to portray a cohesive mixed-race family unit'. Whether or not this is an appropriate scenario, it enables Frank to register that 'it would do any of us good to contemplate the house we live in being peopled by imperfect predecessors. It would encourage empathy and offer [. . .] perspective' (103). After hearing that Ms Pines's story ends in tragedy Frank indeed responds empathically. He wonders whether what she is feeling by returning for the first time in over forty years to her childhood home and the site of the violent deaths of her entire family is not grief but an emotion that needs some new word. On the other hand, Frank refers to the 'spectacle-grim-oddness' of their encounter. He does rather treat Ms Pines like a spectacle: throughout her visit he scrutinises her clothes, her skin tone and her 'Kewpie-doll face', and he repeatedly imagines the sight of them conversing together from the perspective of his neighbours. But what seems to elude Frank – as well as the reader – is what Ms Pines makes of her visit. She declares that it was revealing to come back, but does not reveal what she has experienced or understood. They part with what Frank hopes is a feeling of mutual understanding, of significant human contact. Even this sense of amicability is under-cut by the sight of a realty sign announcing a price reduction being put up in a neighbouring yard, which for Frank indicates that a much more hard-nosed set of relationships continue to determine his neighbourhood's composition and character. Friendly feelings between strangers, it would appear, are quite unable to temper the more brutalising forces of the property market.

The title of the volume's second story, 'Everything could be worse', is drawn from conversation at the end of the preceding story. This transmission and repurposing of a fragment of dialogue is an operation that repeats across the rest of *Let Me Be Frank with You*: Frank's suggestion to Ms Pines that his not making much of an impression on things is 'the new normal' – almost the last thing he says to her – provides the title for the succeeding story, and so on. The overlapping manner of the book's four stories is thus homologous to the progression of the sequence overall. The effect of this repeated patterning is to confirm not only that the four books indeed comprise a sequence but also a sense that the sequence's various modes of engagement are not discrete or framed by neatly cordoned time periods. Frank's strategies for dealing with space and with others overflow the sequence's formal boundaries in a manner that recalls the French term for the form, *roman-fleuve*. The pattern established by the sequence promises continuation; the books' individual endings are thus always provisional. Such pro-visionality may certainly be interpreted optimistically, for it reinforces a sense of the ongoing production of spatial forms and social relationships. The continual replacement and recycling of strategies for engaging with changing spatiality may also counter a limiting understanding of history as linear and progressive. Yet the sequence concludes with Frank feeling thwarted and exhausted. At a time when greater scrutiny of our own arrangements is needed. Frank admits that he asks less of where he lives than he used to (110). His feelings of futility appear convenient, for they coincide with the clarification of his own complicity in his suburb's racial formation. As a putative suburban Everyman, then, Frank is an unreliable and redundant figure. Yet, as demonstrated by both Updike's and Ford's endeavours, the novel sequence remains a sophisticated vehicle for interrogating suburban historicity and change.

CHAPTER 2

Suburban Gothic and Banal Unhomeliness

For those with at least some exposure to post-war American culture, 'suburban Gothic' is likely to be a familiar cultural mode. It is prevalent across various forms, both popular and 'serious'. Its tropes are readily identifiable, and its motivations seem intelligible. Indeed, the decaying tract homes, insidious duplicating technologies and sequestered monstrosities arguably all serve to evoke a horror of suburban surveillance and conformity, or to articulate anxieties about the violence and perversity of family life hidden behind closed doors. Thus it would seem reasonable to generalise that late twentieth-century works of fiction and feature films, such as *The Stepford Wives* (1972; 1975; 2004), *Blue Velvet* (1986) and *The Virgin Suicides* (1993; 1999) make use of the Gothic principally as a means to call into question a white middle-class dream of security and prosperity predicated on home-ownership and the nuclear family.

The familiarity of suburban Gothic certainly owes a great deal to its situation within a broader generic tradition. Like so many Gothic narratives, suburban Gothic is centred on buildings and built environments which seem to provide suitable stages to play out concerns to do with status and power, as well as tensions arising from various conflicts, both psychological and social. Further, in characterising bright new suburban landscapes in altogether familiar Gothic terms – as ruined, haunted, labyrinthine – suburban Gothic would appear to be drawing on a long-running vein of American literature. Suburban Gothic's apparent scepticism directed towards the narratives of progress voiced by promoters of the United States' suburbanisation echoes earlier Gothic stories written in a decidedly anti-rationalist mood. Charles Brockden Brown's *Wieland* (1898), with its portrayal of a doomed utopian community, and several of Edgar Allan Poe's tales imbued with 'the spirit of the perverse' cast doubt over the Enlightenment thinking undergirding the recently constituted United States. Meanwhile, many Southern writers, from Poe to William Faulkner and Flannery O'Connor, have contributed to the development of a regionally inflected Gothic which explores 'the tensions between a culturally sanctioned progressive optimism and an actual dark legacy'.[1] The darkest shadow, of course, is that cast by slavery. Thus, from the late eighteenth century to the present, a persistent element of American Gothic has been the distrust of the transformative potential of the projects of modernity, in particular, the mutually constitutive discourses of nation building and progress.

Perhaps, though, suburban Gothic is less a distinctly American than a middle-class formation which finds expression across national cultures. Aspiration and fall, David Punter contends, are the abstract qualities that define Gothic fiction; their typically dramatic rendering in Gothic narrative is reflective of a class of people nervy about their own status. This should hardly be surprising, since aspiration and fall are the very mechanisms through which 'the middle class is forged, yet they are the elements which continually seek to undermine its stability'.[2] The place where tensions about status most frequently coalesce in Gothic writing is precisely where one is supposed to feel most secure: the home. The uncanniness that pervades middle-class domestic space in Gothic narrative from about the middle of the nineteenth century onwards can be characterised, according to Anthony Vidler, 'as the quintessential bourgeois fear', the 'fundamental insecurity [. . .] of a newly established class, not quite at home in its own home'.[3] Thus American suburban Gothic could be understood as an articulation of the unease of a still-unsettled upwardly mobile diaspora. Such a view perhaps makes most sense in relation to narratives of the early post-war decades, which are typically focalised through suburban 'pioneers'. More recent material, perhaps marking a generational shift, rather confirms Angela Carter's famous observation of the mid-1970s that 'we live in Gothic times': what was once a marginal genre has come to occupy a central, and increasingly commodified, place within culture. As Fred Botting has it, 'monstrous figures are now less often terrifying objects of animosity'; instead, they are more likely to provide 'sites of identification, sympathy, desire and self-recognition'.[4] The monsters and mansions of recent suburban Gothics that have found success on screen – particularly comedies such as *The Addams Family* (1964–6; 1991), *The 'Burbs* (1989), and *Edward Scissorhands* (1990) – are more often than not associated with a creativity and individualism that is threatened by the bland tyranny of suburban life. But if the wholesale admiration of Gothic figures in late twentieth-century suburban Gothic is new, the implicit critique of the suburbs in these comedies remains largely the same. In any case, it is quite unusual to see the Gothic being mobilised to explore severe socio-economic precarity and injustice; other modes seem more appropriate.[5] All this rather confirms Punter's contention that the Gothic is, essentially, a genre that speaks to bourgeois concerns.

I suspect, however, that the familiarity and legibility of recent suburban Gothic is mostly a consequence of its emergence from a twentieth-century tradition of suburban critique. Suburban Gothic can certainly be understood to be working in close accordance with the outpouring of polemic which dominated discussion about suburban life in the post-war decades. Initially the most influential voices in this chorus of denunciation were to be found in bestselling, more-or-less scholarly historical or sociological studies. Typically, such material bemoaned the loss of rewarding communal lives left behind in the inner cities, or otherwise the spirit of independence that supposedly had previously marked American life. As well as excoriating the inauthenticity and uniformity of the hastily thrown-up suburban habitats and the tendency of their infantilised residents towards mutual surveillance and conformity, many of these studies attended to the particular effects of suburban life on men and women: some consider the plight of the alienated, emasculated corporate drone, while others focus on the psychologically debilitating effects of the limiting domestic roles conferred on women.[6] These concerns also found repeated representation in contemporary literary fiction, most of which was written by white, middle-class men, such as John Cheever, Sloan Wilson and Richard Yates. Indeed, the violent deaths that punctuate the conclusions of Cheever's 'O Youth and Beauty!' (1953) and Yates's *Revolutionary Road* (1961), as well as the temporal confusions that shape Cheever's most famous short story 'The Swimmer' (1964), would seem to correspond to the narrative conceits of later, more explicitly Gothic tales with suburban settings. The preoccupations of suburban Gothic have also long found echo in cognate popular modes, including noir and science fiction.[7]

So far, so familiar. Yet might not assertions of suburban Gothic's familiarity serve only to banalise the mode? For if the suburban Gothic is to be understood as merely rehearsing the critiques of the early post-war period, its Gothic qualities and capacities approach redundancy. Quite simply, the Gothic is not being utilised to say anything that is not already well known about the suburbs. This is rather the problem with an otherwise energetic and extensive study of the topic, Bernice Murphy's *The Suburban Gothic in American Popular Culture* (2009), which concludes that the suburban Gothic 'deserves to be considered one of the most significant and revealing undercurrents in American popular culture'.[8] But what Murphy 'reveals' is that the suburban Gothic has all along been posing precisely the same 'despairing questions asked by the authors of *The Split-Level Trap* back in 1960 – "What has been happening to these people? What is missing, what is so terribly wrong in this pretty green community?"'[9] Such questions are purely rhetorical. Moreover, the very persistence of these 'anxieties' produces nothing more than a comforting confirmation of particular kinds of knowledge regarding suburban conformity and inauthenticity. The suburban Gothic, in Murphy's account, is then an altogether safe, reassuring mode, its uniformity mirroring, indeed helping to produce, the perceived conformism of the suburbs it supposedly attacks. There is little scope for the Gothic's vaunted tendency to confound, to exploit uncertainty. To be sure, there is no recognition in Murphy's analysis of how indetermination is so often constitutive or, as Allan Lloyd Smith has it, a 'narrative necessity, providing the essential possibilities of mystery and suspense'.[10] Instead of expecting from Gothic narrative revelation and confirmation, as Murphy does, perhaps then it might be more productive to focus on its capacity to destabilise commonplace understandings about space and place.

However, to argue that uncertainty is the Gothic's principal purlieu is to lead oneself out onto unstable ground. Scholars of the suburban Gothic – as well as critics of the suburbs who resort to Gothic tropes – have sometimes become ensnared by their own self-implicating truth claims. In such instances, the very distinction between critic and the object of their enquiry (or contempt) is threatened with collapse. For example, Victoria Maddon, following Murphy, focuses on the anxieties that suburban Gothic apparently both harnesses and perpetuates. She suggests that the suburbs, being the product of an age of uncertainty, constitute a persistently liminal zone that produces 'a most disquieting sense of epistemological disturbance'.[11] However, like Murphy, Maddon merely reiterates a set of commonplaces about the suburbs – that they promote conformity, for example, or that their idyllic and uniform surfaces conceal all manner of dark impulses. Further, Maddon's evident desire to codify both the suburbs and the Gothic leads to a paradoxical but revealing identification with suburban culture. She asserts: 'Liminal figures are fundamentally gothic: they disturb because they do not fit in neatly. They are outliers within a social system that values straightforward definition above all else.'[12] Such a neat and straightforward definition of the essential qualities of the liminal would seem, on Maddon's own terms, more likely to reassure and sustain rather than disturb and disrupt the 'social system' of the suburbs.

More productively, Kim Ian Michasiw discusses the ways the suburbs have been installed as Gothic 'stations', which are offered to consumers as 'places [. . .] to be scared of'.[13] These reassuring fears often displace other anxieties. The couching of suburbs as Gothic environments by numerous elite critics, Michasiw argues, obscures the increasing difficulty they have in differentiating themselves from the mass, which occurs in part because, in order to distinguish one from the other, 'the critic must embrace and take as real the very set of signs that have raised the security fences' of gated communities.[14] In general, then, it may be wise to be wary of any critic who speaks breezily about the articulation of cultural anxieties, and to always ask what other concerns relating to the object under scrutiny might be being displaced by such claims. Having problematised a 'banal' mode of interpretation – that which 'reveals' the already familiar, or which resolves anxieties into certainties – this chapter, through readings of three quite different novels, attempts to delineate a more fruitful way of appraising the suburban Gothic. My approach focuses on the texts' various narrative conceits to draw out how the suburban Gothic might trouble secure forms of knowledge, problematise habituated modes of storytelling and thereby provide a more critical and self-reflexive appreciation of the historicity of the American suburbs. My approach requires caution: if too certain about what the texts enable, my own readings will succumb to banality. I turn first, however, to Freud's concept of the uncanny, not only because it remains the dominant paradigm for comprehending unhomeliness, but also because Freud's own explanations are troubled by a surfeit of certainty. I suggest how, if handled carefully, the uncanny can be deployed to reimagine suburban histories in productive, and perhaps unsettling, ways.

Domesticating the Uncanny

Surprisingly absent from Murphy's study is any mention of the uncanny, which, in the wake of the publication of Sigmund Freud's seminal essay 'Das Unheimlich' in 1919, has constituted a principal conceptual frame through which to understand the capacity of domestic buildings and spaces to be disturbing. In his celebrated etymological excavations of the German word *heimlich* ('homely'), Freud notes how the word shares certain meanings with its opposite, *unheimlich*. The comforting qualities connoted by *Heimlichkeit* ('homeliness') – intimacy, familiarity, cosiness, security – compete with opposing, less reassuring associations: withdrawal, concealment, secrecy, mystery. For Freud this linguistic ambivalence usefully models the mechanism of psychical repression. That which seems uncanny, he explains, 'is something which is secretly familiar (*heimlich-heimisch*), which has undergone repression and then returned from it'.[15] But Freud's observations about the word *heimlich* are suggestive of the way homeliness is predicated on the repudiation, the keeping at bay, of elements that disturb. Homes – especially those nostalgic incarnations, still very much present in Western imaginaries, that stand isolated within natural surroundings: the farmstead, the forest cottage, the house on the hill – are typically organised around the divisions between inside and outside and, secondarily, order and disorder. That which is unsettling is only ever the thickness of a wall, or an unexpected knock at the door, away. Thus the uncanny draws attention to the brittleness – or, perhaps better, the solubility – of the binaries that define the home, and to the home's vulnerability. But domestic uncanniness is less frequently associated with a penetration from without than with a possibly more unnerving kind of disturbance from beneath or within. In these scenarios the home is rendered uncanny by a barely perceptible but nonetheless disturbing shift, a sliding away from the familiar. Such estrangement might also be caused by an obscuration, either sudden or gradual, of elements of the home's ordinary landscape, or of an inability to distinguish between dream state and conscious reality. The domestic uncanny, therefore, involves a subtle dislocation, a loss of bearings leading to an inability to navigate an environment that is normally fully known. In his study of the architectural uncanny, Anthony Vidler notes that it is the English equivalent of *das unheimlich* that provides useful etymological clues to such disorientation: the word uncanny is derived from 'beyond ken', in other words, that which lies outside one's scope of understanding.[16]

Freud, however, was dismissive – notoriously so – of explanations of the uncanny that appealed to intellectual uncertainty. Such rationalisations were incomplete, he declared, to the extent that they failed to account for the processes of repression. These limitations were most obvious in relation to works of literature that trade in uncanny sensation, such E. T. A. Hoffman's short Gothic tale 'Der Sandmann' (1816), which Freud analyses in some detail. Without recourse to the revival of formerly repressed psychic material – say, anxieties about castration – such stories indeed make little sense. The uncanny feelings stirred by narratives such as Hoffman's therefore have to do with their capacity, through symbolic substitution – for instance, the loss of eyes for the threat of castration – to remind readers of early psychical conflicts that were repressed in the process of the ego's development and adaption to society. An obvious objection to Freud's insistence on the explanatory power of repression is that it presumes that, in order to experience a particular story as uncanny, different readers must each be in possession of a similarly stocked unconscious. But if the uncanniness of Hoffman's 'Der Sandmann' is caused by its rekindling of repressed anxieties relating to castration, female readers will necessarily be left unaffected. Freud does, though, offer a more global, socio-historical explanation whereby uncanniness has to do with 'primitive' fears and beliefs, for example, in magic, or relating to death and the return of the dead. Modernity has marginalised such tendencies, and most individuals who consider themselves rational and civilised have surmounted them. Yet they are 'still so strong within us and always ready to come to the surface at the slightest provocation'.[17] Moments which seem to confirm the truth of these age-old beliefs are thus experienced as uncanny. But while it involves a form of repression, Freud acknowledges that this variation of the uncanny is quite distinct from that which is derived from infantile complexes. Of course, it is the latter that interests the psychoanalyst far more, even if it draws him into the relatively unfamiliar territory of fantastic stories. For it is in imaginative writing rather than actual experience, Freud realises, that the more complexly conditioned instances of uncanniness are most frequently to be found.

One of the most significant lines of criticism, which is articulated across much of the considerable body of literature written in response to Freud's essay, focuses on his repudiation of intellectual uncertainty as an explanation for the uncanny, and his determination to assimilate the phenomenon to a scientific methodology. This ambition to codify the uncanny as the product of a discrete psychic mechanism ignores – or, rather, disavows – what is most interesting about such feelings, which often seem potent precisely because of their apparent irreducibility to any familiar classificatory system, or indeed their blurring of the very distinctions of familiar and strange. Noticeably, there is something about the uncanny that eludes Freud. Towards the end of the essay he seems increasingly uncertain about his approach and finally concedes that his investigations have produced only 'preliminary results'. He declares that further inquiry is necessary into aesthetic matters, which suggests the troubling possibility that he has not after all got the measure of stories like Hoffman's.

Many have seized upon Freud's uncertainty as evidence of his flawed approach.[18] His insecurity has in part to do with his theory's reliance on imaginative stories, which Freud attempts to render transparent with his own conceptual apparatus. Of course, literary materials often prove less pliant than anticipated. Some have taken Freud to task for what they perceive to be his highly selective reading of 'Der Sandmann', and find it telling that he has far more to say about the story's male characters than he does the female ones.[19] In one of the most influential responses to Freud's essay, Hélène Cixous notes that the story's most important female figure, the doll Olympia, is relegated in importance: Freud declares she is 'nothing else than a materialization' of the protagonist Nathaniel's attitude towards his father in infancy. Moreover, the explanation is worthy only of a footnote, which, Cixous suggests, constitutes a 'typographical metaphor of repression'.[20] Olympia's sidelining enables Freud to discuss an all-male psychodrama at length. Might then his determined focus on the loss of eyes in the story, and its apparent uncanniness, have something to do with a sense of the limitations of his own reading, which blinds him to other conflicting and possibly more troubling interpretations, such as Nathaniel's desire for death, or his homosexuality? Thus Freud's own tools have the potential to work against his aims. Indeed, the essay threatens to render the very project of psychoanalysis – putatively scientific, but revealed to be reliant on the explanatory power of fantastic stories – somewhat uncanny.

The treacherous quality of the uncanny – its potential to destabilise all kinds of critical apparatus – is precisely what has drawn so many to it. Those attending to architectural manifestations of the uncanny have found this aspect especially revealing and productive. For example, in his discussion of unhomely homes, Vidler outlines the bases for the spatial uncanny in the romantic imagination, which he contends was less dependent on the 'temporal dislocations of suppression and return or the invisible slippages between a sense of the homely and the unhomely' than on 'tropes of spatial instability signifying an abyssal drive toward nothingness'.[21] Inspired in particular by the carceral labyrinths of Giovanni Battista Piranesi, Thomas De Quincey and others found abyssal repetition to be a fitting metaphor for the romantic mind. However, such radical withdrawal rendered romantic interiority uncanny, in part by virtue 'of the "doubling" inherent in the incessant movement without movement' and partly because it 'reinforced the ambiguity between real world and dream'.[22] In her study of the domestic uncanny in the work of contemporary female French novelists, Daisy Connon draws on Cixous's and Julia Kristeva's feminist criticisms of Freud. Both theorists contend that the disturbances of the uncanny are potentially generative, for they motivate the abandonment of falsely coherent identities and routinised ways of thinking. The uncanny, therefore, may provide a crucial source of creativity. Declares Connon, the uncanny is not only 'a breakdown, a symptom or a form of *dis-ease*', but also 'an inherent, creative possibility within each everyday moment, retrievable within all the comfortable and familiar structures that surround the subject'.[23] In addition, the uncanny provides inspiration for more ethical modes of behaviour. As Connon suggests, rather than automatically provoking a repressive othering of the strange, uncanny experiences 'should command the subject to perceive vulnerability in the self, to acknowledge her own foreignness. Such a model of alterity must be embraced as an ethics of approaching the unthematizable difference of the foreigner in the national community.'[24]

By contrast, the strange and the uncanny in accounts of the suburban Gothic are typically reduced to altogether predictable themes: 'anxieties' relating to uniformity, conformity, alienation and so on. There is an irony here of course: in suburban Gothic it is so frequently sameness that is presented as strange or monstrous. Once again, recent scholarship has rationalised these unsettling elements as having the same root cause: a set of specific 'cultural anxieties', which provide such disturbances with a familiar narrative frame. Explanations of the suburban Gothic that attempt to domesticate it, to situate it within familiar interpretative frameworks – as Freud did the uncanny – are manifestations of what I wish to call the banal unhomely.[25] By reiterating banal unhomeliness, critics confirm their – and our – safe remove from these sites, which become fixed objects of secure knowledge, just as the post-war suburbs were for their haughtily distant detractors. Further, as Catherine Jurca reminds us, the tropes of unhomeliness and dispossession have long served to mystify the exclusions that sustain white suburban middle-class privilege.[26] There is a risk, then, that attributing the significance of suburban Gothic to a set of (conventional) anxieties merely reinforces the ideological project that emphasises white middle-class suffering. At the same time, I do not mean to deny that anxiety can ever have significant explanatory power; that degree of certainty would be both untenable and hypocritical. On the other hand, many suburban Gothic narratives are themselves inescapably banal; as in the criticism I have discussed, the putative anxieties these stories deal in are in fact familiar comforts, diversions which avoid implicating readers in more uncomfortable race- and class-based politics. What I am attempting here, then – as Connon and others have sought to do with the uncanny in relation to the domestic – is to identify ways in which Gothic narrative might facilitate a more sophisticated and less compromised understanding of domestic sites and suburban histories, and the often-contradictory investments that continue to be made in them.

In the remainder of this chapter I examine a trio of suburban Gothic novels published in the final three decades of the twentieth century. The first is Anne Rivers Siddons's *The House Next Door* (1978). The novel, the author's second, was a bestseller, and received strong praise from leading American horror writer Stephen King. In the final chapter of his 1981 study of the horror genre, *Danse Macabre*, King declares 'as a gothic, [Rivers Siddons's] book succeeds admirably', and he especially appreciates its 'steady down-turning funnel toward disaster'.[27] For me, however, *The House Next Door* is interesting for the way it repeatedly models, to the point of making strange, the typical trajectory of banal unhomeliness: its narration of suburban uncanniness and horror continually relaxes into expressions of domestic contentedness. (Tellingly, this is an aspect of the novel that rather irks King.) In doing so, Rivers Siddons's novel is suggestive of how these supposedly disturbing stories often have ultimately reassuring consequences.

Next I turn to Gloria Naylor's *Linden Hills*, first published in 1985. As with her acclaimed debut, *The Women of Brewster Place* (1982), the title of Naylor's follow-up novel refers to the book's setting. In fact the settings of the two books are part of the same fictional universe, and share a border. They could not contrast with one another more, however: one is a poor, cramped black urban neighbourhood, the other – Linden Hills – a fabulously wealthy black suburban subdivision. The appeal of the latter is superficial and ultimately corrupting; Naylor's novel is usually read as a morality tale – and a highly pessimistic one at that – about the plight of the black bourgeoisie. Indeed, as one early reviewer had it, *Linden Hills* represented the dark side of *The Cosby Show* (1984–92), the upbeat TV sitcom about a successful upper-middle-class black family, which went on air the year before the novel's publication.[28] Noticeably, *Linden Hills*'s account of its suburban setting is laden with something that *The House Next Door* rather lacks: an appreciation of local history, as well as an understanding of locality's situation within a broader, national story. (The neglect in Rivers Siddons' novel perhaps marks a presumption that white neighbourhoods, and white experience more broadly, may be construed as universal.) But like *The House Next Door*, *Linden Hills* is preoccupied by the effects of its Gothic mode, especially when it interacts with other kinds of narrative. An outcome of these generic collisions is the production of an impure, polyvocal and democratic history that seems to facilitate rather than stymy resistance.

Finally I discuss Jeffrey Eugenides's debut novel *The Virgin Suicides*, published in 1993. I examine how the book's uncannily familiar Gothic tropes can disrupt the overly familiar way in which stories about the suburbs tend to be told and, in doing so, say something unsettling about the most familiar of American spaces. Precisely what *The Virgin Suicides* disturbs has to do with the suburbs' location within American history. If suburban Gothic has tended to critique the manner in which suburbs supposedly have become disconnected from history – to the point of establishing a comforting truism – Eugenides's novel reconstitutes the post-war suburbs as a historical space, as a site of conflict undergoing change. Eugenides's Gothic motifs – doublings, infestations, ruination – coalesce around the irruption of repressed ethnic memories into the cultural blankness of the suburbs. If this sketch of an amnesiac society suffering a return of the repressed still sounds all too familiar, the novel's various Gothic narrative effects problematise the telling of a certain kind of normative suburban history that could be described as the remembrance of forgetting. The foremost of these effects is the first-person-plural narrative voice which, operating as a peculiarly indeterminate retrospective chorus, serves to question the reliability and coherence of recent histories of the suburbs. Eugenides's Gothic foregrounds a current tendency to misread and misremember the suburbs, a tendency which produces a simpler, safer version of them that confirms one's apparent separation and distance from such troubling places.

Satisfying Symmetries: Denaturalising Banal Unhomeliness in Anne Rivers Siddons's *The House Next Door*

The presumption that the post-war suburbs are free from history certainly makes the Gothic mode seem inappropriate. Murphy notes some of the earliest suburban Gothics show an awareness of this problem. For example, one of Richard Matheson's victims of suburban haunting complains: 'It doesn't make any sense. Why should a place like this be haunted? It's only a couple of years old.'[29] A common cause of suburban haunting is that these newly built residential developments, while possessing at most purely decorative references to the past, have been built over lands once populated by other peoples. Typical of this strand of suburban Gothic is the 1982 film *Poltergeist* and its sequels. Here the residential subdivision's development over a much older burial ground – possibly Native American, though the film's sequels suggest otherwise – is the stimulus for paranormal activity. The desire for a share of the American good life quite detached from disturbing histories of displacement and dispossession is shown for what it is: an utterly self-centred materialism. For sure, such a critique was probably most keenly felt during the Reagan years, a period so often derided in precisely these terms. Gothic horrors such as *Poltergeist* thus moralise that suburban America's ignorance of or disregard for the past will always result in that past coming back to haunt it.

Is there anything more to suburban Gothic's preoccupation with the presence of the past than a simple reworking of the biggest cliché in the book of American hauntings, the house built over a(n Indian) burial ground? There is of course something salutary and potentially instructive about stories that deal with histories of racial erasure. Moreover, the violence and horror of supernatural disturbance seems a fitting response to the monstrous arrogance of a wilfully amnesiac society. But so transparent have these stories become, so obvious and familiar are their mechanisms, that their allegorical power is quite exhausted. They have become inert cultural objects – effectively, dead metaphors – with little capacity to disturb. Meanwhile, their historical referents remain mystified: we are rarely invited to care much about the identities of those whose graves have been desecrated.[30] Thus these stories present a highly codified 'disturbance' that provides little or no impetus to critique the bases of suburban privilege.

So over-familiar are certain tropes of haunting, that it should come as no surprise that they are sometimes installed in self-conscious ways in suburban Gothic narrative. A character in Rivers Siddons's *The House Next Door*, for instance, reiterates the scepticism of Matheson's suburbanite, but goes a step further when she wonders: 'If it was an old house, I'd almost think it was haunted, but who ever heard of a haunted contemporary less than a year old? Maybe there was an Indian graveyard on the property once, and the natives are restless.'[31] The allusion to the disturbed spirits of long-buried Native Americans confirms an interpretation that many readers will have been anticipating by this point in the novel. The eponymous house, a modern design marvel seemingly fashioned from little more than glass and light, is after all built on a wooded and stream-crossed vacant plot that is viewed by the residents of neighbouring properties as having been primordial in character. Further, the house itself seems sustained by, and indeed, a part of, the plot's verdant habitat. In the architect's plans, 'the woods pressed untouched around [the house] like companions. The creek unfolded its mass and seemed to nourish its roots' (23). And the house 'grew out of the pencilled earth like an elemental spirit that had lain, locked and yearning for the light, through endless deeps of time, waiting to be released' (22). This imagery seems prescient: the house's erection coincides with the appearance around the plot of the eviscerated remains of wildlife and neighbourhood pets. Worse is to come. The successive occupants of the house each suffer a serious of misfortunes that are sufficient to impel them to sell up and leave. Highly focused individuals become distracted and disorganised. A freak fall leads to a miscarriage. Those with fragile mental or physical health experience traumatic collapse, while several visiting neighbours are turned temporarily into automata, driven entirely by lust or murderous intent.

The repeated suggestions that some malevolent spirit which occupies the site has been disturbed by the house's construction and is bent on repelling all who trespass on its territory are, however, red herrings. It transpires that the house's 'curse' is located not in its plot, but in its plans. The novel's denouement reveals that the talented young architect who designed the house has had a small number of other projects realised; all of his clients come to a bad end. Even his eventual murder and the razing of the house by neighbours fails to exorcise the curse completely, for the original plans are discovered by another party who, unaware of their unfortunate history, wish to see them realised. The novel's final lines, voiced by this eager young middle-class couple, echo earlier observations: '"It looks like it's growing right out of the ground, doesn't it?" "It looks like it's alive"' (251). The implication is obvious: the malevolent force somehow immanent in the plans has not been finally expelled.

The fact that the source of disturbance is, as it were, written into an architectural design, might suggest that there is something profoundly flawed and unlivable about the organisation of suburban space. But Rivers Siddons does not appear to imply this. After all, the house is utterly modern and unlike anything local residents have ever seen; it could hardly be said to be representative of the suburb in question or American suburbia generally.[32] The novel is rather more preoccupied by the readiness of its upper-middle-class suburban characters to attribute special powers to designs, particularly – as demonstrated by the quotations in the previous paragraph – their ability to come to life. More significant, though, is the way these designs seem to promise fulfilment to those who look upon them. The young woman who clutches the plans in the novel's epilogue raptures: 'It's just exactly what I've always wanted, right down to the ground. I didn't know exactly what I wanted until I saw it, and then that was just it' (251). Such inattention to context echoes the complacency of the novel's other wealthy characters, who are shown again and again to be wholly satisfied, to feel fully realised by their properties and their comfortable lifestyles. Indeed, Rivers Siddons's novel warrants scrutiny precisely because it is less preoccupied with suburban conformity than it is with suburban comfort. This self-satisfaction, moreover, is shown to impede historical narrative.

The house's story is told by Colquitt Kennedy, whose own home neighbours the malignant development. Colquitt begins her account by underlining how she and her husband Walter have sacrificed their professional and social reputations by going public about the events that have taken place next door. Few in their set appreciate the attentions of the outside world, and absolutely no-one is prepared to countenance supernatural explanations. For Colquitt, the situation requires desperate measures; things have escalated to the point where somebody is surely soon to get killed. Yet, despite the urgency of her story, she cannot help being distracted by her own comforts and achievements. The novel's opening pages repeatedly allude to the reassuring aspects of her life, which, she declares, has 'a satisfying symmetry' (12); her best friend Clare Swanson, meanwhile, is said to be 'square, sturdy and somehow comfortingly basic-looking (11), and she and her husband Roger comprise 'a satisfying unit' (12) in the Kennedys' world.

These could all be merely requisite gestures for the narrative, establishing the calm before the storm. However, a sense that self-satisfaction is rather the novel's principal focus is underlined by the sheer number of references to comfort, which, the novel confirms, has much to do with keeping the outside world at bay. When bad news threatens, Colquitt endorses the simple suburban pleasure of 'good drinks' with the saying 'living well is the best revenge'. That she lazily surmises the phrase to be some 'old Spanish proverb or something' (13) suggests further a misunderstanding of the bases for, if not the function of, her creature comforts.[33] And then, much later in the novel, after the disturbances of the house next door have reached their most terrifying, Colquitt's account settles once again upon the peace and satisfaction afforded by her environment and habits. She declares: 'There was joy and contentment and a rich enoughness to the things we said, and ate, and read and watched, and did. I do not remember it as a bad time at all. I am very grateful – glad – for those days of proving' (240). Their withdrawal after such an ordeal is of course understandable. What is peculiar, however, is the weight this 'rich enoughness' is given in Colquitt's account, her gratitude for it and her belief that such repose may be perfecting. Such contentment defuses Colquitt's story and works against her stated aim of warding people away from the house next door with its apparently fantastic capacity to charm. It would appear then that, like their successive neighbours, the Kennedys have fallen under the spell of their own lifestyle.

The House Next Door does make explicit reference to the apprehension of strangeness, and the tendency for the strange and the familiar to coalesce. Indeed, the one time the term 'uncanny' is used in the novel comes early on, in order to register Colquitt's feelings about 'all the areas of accord and pleasure', the perfect self-sufficiency that she and her husband, free from the encumbrance of children, 'have built with each other' (24). To a certain extent, this predicts the unnerving and indeed destructive manner in which the house next door seems to afford its inhabitants and onlookers a sense of complete fulfilment. But just as noticeable is the manner in which the out-of-place is quickly resolved into domestic familiarity. One of the house-next-door's occupants, who is recovering from a nervous breakdown following the death of her son, is said to look 'haunted', which, Colquitt notes, 'was not a word for this twilit suburban backyard' (87). Another member of her party detects 'the slight skew of normalcy too' (89). And yet, repeatedly, these perceptions of uncanniness are only fleeting, and are smothered by familiar comforts. For instance, moments before, Colquitt finds the sounds of birdsong and classical music emanating from the house next door immediately reassuring: 'The unease and alienness of the past few minutes washed out of my mind' (84). If such soothing music offers only temporary respite, a pattern is established. After returning home from a party to welcome her new neighbours, around whom 'little winds of fear and strangeness seemed to whip' (89), Colquitt finds the neighbouring edifice's 'grace and beauty' winning. She is moved to declare 'whatever happened over there, it doesn't change how the house looks' (91). Later in the narrative, after returning from a brief vacation, Colquitt concludes that 'the house and its terrible short history seemed to have lost its hold on me' (165). Repeatedly, suburban comfort seems to intrude, interrupting accounts of uncanniness and neutralising the tensions they produce.

The novel's stuttering narration, which enacts a continual retreat from strangeness and horror into familiar comforts, would seem then to provide a critique of suburban complacency and withdrawal. After all, the residents' inability to deal with the threat, and their refusal to admit how much power the house next door has over them, serves only to prolong the ordeal. Moreover, the story ends with the destruction of the house and the dissolution of the community, which is shown ultimately to be unsustainable. But what is more interesting to me about *The House Next Door* is how it echoes, at the level of its narration, the trajectories of the banal unhomely. Rivers Siddons's novel is neither principally about nor propelled by anxiety, yet it models the banal unhomely through its repetitive transfiguration of disquieting strangeness into reassuring comforts. On the other hand, the very repetitiveness of this manoeuvre – an aspect of the novel which Stephen King found so exasperating – is potentially defamiliarising. Thus, rather than seeing Rivers Siddons's novel as critiquing a complacent middle class unable or unwilling to recognise its own privileges, I see it as denaturalising or even sending up banal unhomeliness, which tends to mystify such privilege through its focus on dispossession.

For a Gothic novel set in the American South, however, *The House Next Door* is oddly muted about race and the 'dark legacy' of the region's past. As most commentators agree, central to the Southern Gothic – undoubtedly the best-established and most recognisable of all regional Gothic modes – are engagements with the still unresolved trauma and repressed historical guilt sourced in slavery. Southern Gothic's articulation of the unspeakable, moreover, acts as a rebuke to the region's – and nation's – progressivist mantras.[34] In Rivers Siddons's novel, references to race and racism are so few and far between that their cropping up has a jarring effect, such as the suggestion that the house's evidently ambitious architect would have happily taken on the KKK as clients if it were the only way of getting his plans off the page (30), or the brief appearance of the Parsons' elderly black servant, who seems just one more antique object in a delightfully eclectic 'showplace' of a home (177). Indeed, the novel is noticeably diffident about its setting. The narrator-protagonist just manages to concede that she lives in Georgia, though the 'very New South city' (11) – presumably

Atlanta – in (or near which) she resides goes unnamed. Colquitt's understanding of the collision of Old and New South, which she sketches at the opening of her retrospective account, relates entirely to class tensions among whites. She distinguishes between old and new money, represented by, respectively, an unshowy but sophisticated established white upper-middle-class milieu and pretentious or merely trashy arrivistes. The Kennedys, naturally, identify with the former set. Declares Colquitt: 'we are *of* them precisely because we understand the way they choose to live. It is our way too; [in it] we find grace and substance' (12, emphases in original). The distinction between 'them' and 'our', and that emphatic '*of*', hints at aspiration, an as-yet-incomplete identification. This duality is echoed by Colquitt Kennedy's full name: she shares her unusual first name with places in southern Georgia, which in turn were named after a local antebellum personage.[35] Her surname, more obviously, bespeaks a different heritage and set of political impulses, and indeed, Colquitt reports, rather self-consciously, 'we watch the news, we are active in our own brand of rather liberal politics' (12).

But the other, disavowed kind of people begins to encroach on this Old South enclave, threatening to disturb its graceful rhythms and symmetries. The unappealing Jennings family lives 'catty-cornered across from the Guthries' (13). The awkward geometry is instructive: their lawn is usually strewn with 'Day-Glo-coloured plastic tricycles and wading pools and swing sets'; their too-loud and too-numerous children terrorise neighbourhood pets and are liable to make foraging forays into other people's kitchens. The Jenningses have inherited the family home, once the seat of a 'substantial family'; the current occupants thus represent a social fall. More are to come: the first of the ill-fated residents of the house next door are Buddy and Pie Harralson, newly married provincials who are the beneficiaries of the latter's father, a wealthy and reportedly corrupt state legislator from the south of the state. Pie's garrulous naivety and indiscrete jewellery draws polite scorn from her new neighbours, but the disturbances of the house ensure that the Harralsons do not stay around for long. Ultimately, however, the neighbourhood is overrun by the sort of folk whose existence Colquitt has to admit she has never before much acknowledged:

'hungry-faced' gawkers whose class background is as evident from their dress ('the women wore polyester pants or shifts and some had flat plastic curlers in their hair' (233)) as it is from their trash ('Beer and soft-drink cans and Big Mac boxes littered the mown lawn and drifted into ours' (237)). This tide of subhuman sensation seekers is drawn in by the Kennedys' telling the story of the house next door to a popular magazine in order to dissuade anyone else from buying it, moving in and succumbing to the same fate as its previous owners. The consequences of Colquitt and Walter's actions are thus almost as bad as continued inaction would have been.

And yet despite the invasion and ultimate destruction of the neighbourhood, one of the novel's final images bespeaks complete self-satisfaction. Obliged to shop for groceries at a 'damp, dingy' lower-end supermarket (so as not to run into their now-hostile neighbours), Colquitt catches sight of herself and her husband reflected

> in the mirror over the meat counter, two tall, slender, graceful people in well-cut slacks and heavy sweaters. I thought we looked like attractive strangers, people you see on the streets and in restaurants or passing cars whom you do not know but know instinctively are *of* you, one of your own. I thought too that Walter and I looked far more alike that I had ever realized. (221)

It would seem then that the Kennedys' attempts to cling to a genteel identity have led to a loss of individual identity. In fact this is the only time the novel resorts to conventional Gothic imagery to articulate suburban conformity. But Colquitt's apprehension of herself and her husband as 'attractive strangers' is by no means an instance of horror or troubling dislocation. Indeed, this second use of the emphatic 'of' demonstrates the couple's final accomplishment of southern grace: whereas before they aspired to belong to a rarified social set, now the Kennedys see others as belonging to and bolstering theirs. The scene is also reminiscent of Freud's anecdote in 'Das Unheimlich' in which the psychoanalyst recounts mistaking for a stranger his own reflection in the mirror of a train compartment. Freud recalls that he 'thoroughly disliked his appearance' and surmises that his negative response contained 'a vestigial trace of that older reaction which feels the double to be something uncanny'.[36] By contrast, Colquitt's confrontation with her own double is wholly reassuring, articulating her ultimate complete fulfilment. The scenario could of course be taken as an implicit critique of the emptiness at the core of the Kennedys' arrivisme: at the very point which they feel they have finally joined the club they have become pariahs. Thus their social ambition has distinctly antisocial effects. Yet the novel can also be understood to be operating in a manner counter to the banal unhomely, whose focus on dispossession and uncanniness distracts from the material benefits of suburban life. Although it appears quite unable or unwilling to countenance questions of race, through its continual attention to suburban comfort Rivers Siddons's text foregrounds the forms of self-deception that provide the bases for the banal unhomely.

Generic Fusions: Narrating Histories of Black Suburbanisation in Gloria Naylor's *Linden Hills*

Gloria Naylor's 1985 suburban Gothic *Linden Hills* has in common with *The House Next Door* a decidedly upscale residential setting. In many other respects, though, Naylor's novel occupies very different territory: the eponymous Linden Hills is an entirely African American settlement situated in the North. And unlike Rivers Siddons's southern white suburb, Naylor's wears its history on its sleeve. Indeed, the novel opens with a twenty-page preamble that charts Linden Hills' development. This account begins with the purchase in 1820 of 'the worthless northern face of a rich plateau' abutting a cemetery by one Luther Nedeed, a decidedly peculiar-looking black man hailing from Tupelo, Mississippi. It then provides details of the land's subsequent improvement by Nedeed's successive clone-like descendants, and concludes with the fashioning of an 'ebony jewel', the country's wealthiest and most desirable African American neighbourhood.[37] This history is presented as apocryphal and contested; indeed, the novel's opening lines announce that the precise location and borders of Linden Hills have been disputed by multiple parties for years. What is clear, though, is that Naylor is sketching a history of forgetting. The first to settle

Linden Hills after Nedeed are 'parasites and outcasts' ejected from the South following the Civil War; they require the short memories of the dead that bordered their homes 'for their left-of-center carryings-on' (5–6); their children would later welcome Linden Hills' development, 'wanting nothing better than a way to forget and make the world forget their past' (10). Moreover, the Nedeed of the Depression era envisages transforming Linden Hills into a wholly conventional romantic suburb of 'smooth curved roads, [. . .] long sloping lawns and manicured meridians' that flaunts its ersatz periodicity with 'imitation Swiss chalets, British Tudors and Georgian town houses flanked by arbors choked with morning glories, wisteria and honeysuckle' (10). The new suburb's solidity and grandeur would be 'enough to bury permanently any outside reflections about other beginnings' (11); further, Nedeed imagines that Linden Hills will provide the entire basis for all future generations' historical memory. The motivation for all this, it seems, is to showcase a flourishing black middle class – less a talented tenth than a glittering one per cent – in order to engender racial uplift over the long term. Nedeed even imagines 'true black power' (11) to be manifested not by rebels and nationalists like Nat Turner or Marcus Garvey, but by wealthy black suburbanites.

The novel is obviously deeply pessimistic about such a project and, by extension, the advance of an increasingly visible black middle class in the wake of the passing of Civil Rights legislation.[38] Linden Hills is shown to be contradictory to is core. It is predicated on a racial separatism that is nationalist in character but which duplicates the racial exclusivity of white suburbia. In the 1930s, Nedeed establishes the Tupelo Realty Corporation – a kind of black equivalent to the Federal Housing Authority – which offers low-interest mortgages, but also inscribes racially restrictive covenants into its leases. More damningly, Nedeed's endeavours are understood to be ultimately little more than a conjuring trick. The subdivision's complacent residents have not only willingly traded in historical memory for status and luxury, they have also chosen to forget 'that a magician's supreme art is not in transformation but in making things disappear' (12). The occupation of Linden Hills is enabled by hundreds of individual Faustian pacts with Luther Nedeed – Lucifer indeed – which inevitably lead to, on the one hand, the disappearance of residents as they become 'completely devoured by their own drives' and, on the other, the evaporation of the original dream of black empowerment. While the Nedeeds had manufactured a history that 'spoke loudly of what blacks could do' (16), ultimately, 'Linden Hills wasn't black, it was successful'; the shining surface of their success 'only reflected the bright nothing that was inside of them' (17). In this manner Naylor's novel chimes with some of the more sceptical reactions to the enormously successful television situation comedy *The Cosby Show* (1984–92), which was criticised for avoiding references to black history and experience – and of white racism in particular – and for emphasising instead the importance of individual endeavour as the basis for social advancement.[39]

Naylor's novel quickly inhabits a Gothic register. For instance, much is made of the devilish and macabre qualities of the Nedeeds, including their baleful, toad-like appearance, their uncanny ability to duplicate themselves perfectly over the course of five generations, and their perpetual occupation of the roles of undertaker and mortician. In addition, the novel gives account of the secret torments of the Nedeed wives. The latest incarnation of Mrs Luther Nedeed spends most of the novel imprisoned with her dead infant in the basement of her home. This brutal punishment has been inflicted upon her by a husband who suspects his wife of infidelity, an act that threatens, in his eyes, to corrupt the carefully managed Nedeed legacy. Crowning this most traditional of Gothic tropes – that is, subterranean female entrapment – is the irruption of the woman's despair: her blood-chilling cries can be heard on the wind across Linden Hills. Thus the novel's most determinedly Gothic attributes appear to articulate, on the one hand, the maintenance across a century and half of various structures of privilege and, on the other, the forlorn plight of those consigned to history's dark chambers.

So far, so gloomy. But Naylor's novel simultaneously operates in another mode, allegory, which potentially skews its Gothic trajectory. To be sure, allegory and Gothic have certain historical and generic affinities. They are both construed as being antithetical to literary realism, with the former generally understood to be an antecedent of the realist novel, the latter a reaction against it. Further, many Gothic narratives, notably Ann Radcliffe's and those of her imitators, are laden with allegorical import. In contrast to the relative transparency of allegorical devices, however, the fearful figures of Gothic texts so often retain a residual allure that complicates or confounds the reception of their moral consignments. Further, Gothic materials undermine the very bases by which we can make sense of allegory. As Fred Botting contends, 'knowledge and understanding do not constitute the primary aim of gothic texts: what counts is the production of affects and emotions, often extreme and negative'.[40] Reciprocally, allegory is less likely to rely on the mainstays of Gothic narrative – mystery and suspense – since these elements are liable to obscure, or distract attention from, its tenor. What is remarkable about Naylor's novel, though, is the manner in which the modes of Gothic and allegory are set on a collision course. Their interface takes spatial form by being played out on suburban streets. The novel provides resolution by synthesising an alternative, potentially more productive mode of historical narrative.

The book's principal allegorical vehicle comprises the travails of close friends Lester and Willie, two young black men whose life ambitions lean toward poetry rather than property. The novel follows the pair's working their way down through Linden Hills' increasingly exclusive crescent drives, servicing well-appointed homes on their way in order to make a bit of money in the days leading up to Christmas. The men's encounters with various residents, each morally compromised in their own way, is narrated in episodic fashion, culminating with their confrontation with Nedeed at his house situated at the suburb's lowermost reach. The novel's various actors and the geography of its setting thereby echo one of the most famous of all allegorical works; patently, *Linden Hills* is a pastiche of Dante's *Inferno*. There are too many parallels to mention, but among the most salient are Willie and Lester's substituting for Dante's more august poet protagonists. Naylor's imaginary suburb is stratified in quite the same manner as Dante's pit of the damned. With its sequence of descending crescents, each more wealthy, prestigious and corrupt than the one above, Linden Hills is clearly meant to be apprehended as a manifestation of Hell on Earth.[41] Indeed, it is even crested by a portal – the gates of Willie and Lester's school, no less – whose motto about abandoning ignorance echoes the famous lugubrious imperative emblazoned on the gates of Hell. Linden Hills' other polarity meanwhile is occupied by the satanic figure of Luther Nedeed, whose ancestral home at the foot of the hillside constitutes a veritable sink of corruption. Willie and Lester's progress and their witnessing of the various torments of the debased of course correspond to Dante and his companion's systematic exploration of the nine rings of hell. At various stages Naylor's protagonists are sorely tempted by the status and lifestyle afforded by a Linden Hills address; their arrival at and escape from Nedeed's residence and its frigid environs at the novel's denouement mirrors the final confrontation with and evasion of Satan at the ice-bound centre of Hell by Dante's adventurers.

If Dante and Virgil's expedition constitutes an allegory of the journey of the soul towards God, which necessarily involves the recognition and rejection of sin, Willie and Lester's involves a recognition and rejection of depthless avidity for other, more humane values and pursuits: community, poetry, history. There are, however, considerable risks, in this day and age, in the use of such an antique literary mode. By drawing so heavily on Dante, Naylor's use of allegory is certainly self-conscious. Yet it is still hard not to bridle at what reads as the novel's crude moralising. (Many of its early reviewers seemed to respond in the same way.)[42] While historians and sociologists have produced a number of trenchant and nuanced accounts of black suburbanisation, Linden Hills stands as one of the very few literary accounts of African American suburbia.[43] Its lack of subtlety – indeed, its apparent complete refusal to countenance that there might be any value at all to black suburbanisation – is then all the more disappointing.

The novel does though attempt something rather more complexly critical through its coupling together of Gothic and allegorical modes. These two registers seem to spring from different sources, each sited at opposite poles of the novel's fictional world. Descending from the brow of Linden Hills, Willie and Lester are repeatedly confronted by the disturbing howls that seem to emanate from further down the slope. Willie becomes troubled by nightmares; indeed, he seems to share some bond with the woman who, unbeknown to him, is languishing in a locked basement at the bottom of the hill. Her cries appear to draw him to her; they seem destined to meet. In fact, it transpires that they have their given name in common, almost: the last Mrs Luther Nedeed is called Willa. Willie and Willa are similarly preoccupied by the recovery of texts that enable very different readings of present formations than that which has been authorised by Luther Nedeed. Willie is a poet who never writes down his creations. He is proud of the 665 poems has stored away in his head; presumably the next one that he composes will need to get the measure of the Devil. Willie is inspired to do just that in part by snatches of poetry – from old friends Walt Whitman, T. S. Eliot and Wallace Stevens – that he hears or recollects on his descent through Linden Hills and which seem to provide the beginnings of a critique of the hypocrisy and complacency that defines life on the hill. Willa meanwhile discovers the writings of the previous Nedeed wives hidden in old bibles and cookery books stored in the basement. They give account of these women's isolation and disempowerment, and the desperate strategies they employed to mitigate their suffering or to hasten their own demise. Like the fragments of poetry for Willie, these textual traces of previous madwomen in the basement provide Willa the wherewithal to reconstruct a sense of herself and the resolve to change her situation. Like *Jane Eyre's* Bertha, Willa meets a fiery end, though she does at least manage to take her husband down with her. (Willa's self-sacrifice also frees her near-namesake and his friend from Nedeed's clutches.) Thus the novel's Gothic elements are almost as derivative as its allegorical frame (Willa's incarceration at times also echoes the stories of Poe – 'The Pit and the Pendulum' and 'The Fall of the House of Usher' in particular – and perhaps too Charlotte Perkins Gilman's 'The Yellow Wallpaper'.) There is something paradoxical about all of this. The willing relinquishment of historical memory by the residents of Linden Hills leads to their loss of identity, indeed, to their literal vanishing; the reclamation of history, Naylor seems to show, can only be done through a recycling of familiar texts, which lends the novel an indistinct, hybridised character.

A suburban history that is intertextual and polyvocal seems entirely preferable to the converse, however. Once again, *Linden Hills* opens with a historicising narrative that gestures towards a number of disputes and confusions but which ultimately clarifies how the development of Linden Hills owed everything to Nedeed initiative and endeavour. The historiography of Linden Hills – and by implication the rise of a suburban black middle class – is manifestly a key concern of the novel. The last person Willie and Lester meet before arriving at Nedeed's house is the elderly Dr Daniel Braithwaite, Linden Hills' official historian. The fact that Braithwaite has been installed by Nedeed in the property just above him – the second-most prestigious address in the entire neighbourhood – indicates the importance of his role but also, of course, his utter degradation: the lowest ring of Hell in Dante's *Inferno* was after all reserved for traitors. Braithwaite's house affords him a panoptic view of every residence in Linden Hills, a facility he employs to help him write an exhaustive history of the suburb. Lester makes the reasonable objection that, due to the historian's reliance on the Nedeed family records, Braithwaite's account is bound to be partial. Not so, responds the academic emeritus: reputable historians look at the big picture, drawing on innumerable, diverse sources 'to come up with the whole story, the real story if you will' (263). But his putatively impartial history is politically inert. Braithwaite contends that he has compiled 'a record of a people who are lost' (261), but insists that nothing will come from his work, and that no historian should ever pass judgement on his object of study. It is this determined passivity that discloses Braithwaite's close alignment with the Nedeed project. After all, Braithwaite speaks of the impossibility of 'being able to stop the course of human history, a collective history or an individual one'; Nedeed, who had watched Linden Hills unfold, 'understood that' (257). Moreover, the resources that the historian has accessed and accumulated are frequently referred to in monetised terms: the information sourced from the Needed archive is said to be 'priceless' (262); Lester marvels that Braithwaite's voluminous library, in which considerable shelf space is devoted to black history, must be 'worth a fortune' (254). As well as being apolitical, then, Braithwaite's endeavours are entirely privatised. Unsurprisingly, the historian's ambitions are limited to his receiving suitable professional recognition for his magnum opus. Braithwaite's occupation of the very base of Linden Hills and his proximity to Nedeed thus seem absolutely justified.

In counterpoint to Braithwaite's presumption that his history has captured the truth of Linden Hills in the manner of a 'written photograph' are inserted sections from Eliot's poem 'Gerontian'. The lines of verse rather obviously satirise the aridity and the self-deception of Linden Hills' aged historian: 'Here I am, an old man in a dry month / Being read to by a boy, waiting for rain'; 'Think now / History has many cunning passages, contrived corridors / And issues, deceives with whispering ambitions / Guides us by vanities' (263–4). The text implies these lines are recollected by Willie, who in any case has already denounced the impassiveness of Brathwaite much more pithily: 'I can't buy that [. . .] that's not being human' (256). But perhaps what is most insidious about Braithwaite is his totalising mania: he intends that the twelfth and final volume of his series will conclude with an account of Lester and Willie's descent through Linden Hills, which Braithwaite has been observing all along. This decidedly metafictive moment of horror – less about being written out of a narrative than being written into one – mobilises a potent critique of authoritative suburban histories. Braithwaite's desire for finality is surely to be understood as stultifying and controlling, affording his subjects neither autonomy nor dignity. Indeed his insistence on closure, on producing the finished picture – a 'written photograph' – echoes those armchair critics of the post-war suburbs whose work, though less exhaustive, presumed these spaces had realised their final form, and who were of course informed greatly by photography. Thus, while it is evidently pessimistic about black suburbia, Naylor's novel nevertheless offers a critique of the dominance of certain suburban stories – including, perhaps, its own one-dimensional depiction of a wealthy black neighbourhood. The standard lapsarian narrative, here appropriated to undergird a counterfactual history of black suburbanisation, is exposed as serving elite interests. The novel's various Gothic and allegorical elements that jostle for attention do not merely provide vehicles for cautionary messages; the hubbub of quotations, with their criss-crossing trajectories, underscore the unoriginality of that singular, final 'record of a people who are lost', as well as its failure to account for certain past injustices and its refusal to provide useful critical tools for those living in the present. Thus it is by way of its intersecting narrative voices that *Linden Hills* may be seen as working against the banal unhomely. Naylor's novel suggests, then, that suburban Gothic requires augmentation if it is to provide a useful counternarrative to banal unhomeliness. In the following section I discuss a novel that uses a somewhat different technique – the hyperbolic proliferation of Gothic elements – to achieve a similar end.

Out of Time: Suburban Gothic and White Ethnicity in Jeffrey Eugenides's *The Virgin Suicides*

It is tempting, given the discussion in the previous section, to draw a distinction between the suburban Gothics of white and African American writers, with the former avoiding serious engagement with history and the latter completely preoccupied by the politics of suburban historiography. It would, though, be inappropriate to generalise about suburban stories written by African American writers on the basis of *Linden Hills* for the simple reason that it stands as one of few ever written. It is more reasonable, however, to argue for *The House Next Door*'s representativeness of a broader awkwardness about history in suburban Gothics written by white authors. This ambivalence takes different forms. Indeed, it would seem that a desire to live in a place without a past has rather given way to representations of suburban landscapes which have not been allowed to age. In several films produced in the 1980s and 90s, suburban environments are explicitly cast in the image of 1950s televisual representations. As such, the suburbs are more easily characterised as both artificial (because they resemble an idealised media image) and oppressive (because they are defined by conservative 'family values' and the presumption of white privilege). Robert Beuka is critical of the insistent 'relegation to the past' of these environments, which, he argues, shows how suburbia has become entirely 'overdetermined' in millennial America. In films such as *The Truman Show* and *Pleasantville* (both released in 1998), Beuka complains that the suburb is 'depicted less as a lived place than as a signifier of certain co-optive, even totalitarian impulses that lurk beneath the fabric of centrist, middle-class American culture'.[44]

This layering of 1950s and contemporary suburbia takes a more distinctly Gothic turn in David Lynch's *Blue Velvet* (1986). The uncanny quality of its New England town setting derives in large part from the blurring of visual references to 1950s and 1980s American suburbia. Lynch has suggested that this disorientating sense of doubling and of time compression – what Laura Mulvey refers to as its 'amorphous temporality' – expresses his fascination with the parallels between the Eisenhower and Reagan eras, in particular, their shared championing of a suburban vision of the good life.[45] Whether they feature haunting or time compression, what films such as *Poltergeist* or *Blue Velvet* have in common is their insistence that suburban lives are not properly engaged with American history. Suburbanites embody either a refusal to acknowledge the past, or a desire to live wholly within it. Neither outlook leaves much scope for the appreciation of suburban histories, troubling or otherwise. Yet might not such histories be an area suburban Gothic could conceivably and productively inhabit? Or, to put it another way, might it not be *more* disturbing to consider suburban pasts as being closely imbricated with American history than wholly detached from it?

Jeffrey Eugenides's *The Virgin Suicides* shares with *Blue Velvet* and the other aforementioned films a strong sense of time being out of joint. In part it is the insistently elegiac tone of Eugenides's novel which makes it seem as though it stands outside time. *The Virgin Suicides* is narrated by a group of middle-aged men who periodically come together to try to recall and explicate the most dramatic yet unfathomable event of their adolescent lives. The calamity in question is the multiple suicides of the five daughters of the Lisbon family, their neighbours in Grosse Pointe, Michigan, the elite Detroit suburb in which the men grew up during the 1970s. The very palpable nostalgia that pervades the novel relates the men's failure to come to terms with the deaths; manifestly, they are still in mourning. As Debra Shostak observes, the suicides have 'stopped time for the narrators, who seem to live in a timeless zone of contemplation of the Lisbon deaths'.[46] But it is not only the novel's narrators who appear to dwell in a 'timeless zone'; their parents also seek suspension from history. The preference of the novel's first-generation suburban settlers for sheltered, anaesthetised lives is considered by the narrators to be a traumatised response to the experience of war and loss. Yet the narrators also find reasons to believe that such pasts have not, and cannot, be fully shaken off by a move into the suburbs; indeed, as I will show, it seems suburban-isation refocuses attention onto these pasts.[47] This seems to retell an entirely familiar story: those who escape from history into the suburbs are destined to suffer a return of that repressed past. But, in addition, *The Virgin Suicides* effects a number of uncanny sym-metries between the traumas of suburban pioneers, the previous experiences of their parents, and the subsequent ones of their off-spring. Despite its apparent atemporality which is in keeping with so much suburban Gothic narrative, Eugenides's novel actually insists on resituating suburbia in history. Such historicisation is by no means straightforward: *The Virgin Suicides* articulates not only the ambiguous presence of history in the post-war suburbs, but also their ambivalent presence in the history of post-war America. Both of these moves are enabled through a number of identifiably Gothic motifs and textual strategies.

For instance, that most ubiquitous of Gothic devices, doubling, proliferates throughout the novel. The narrators repeatedly com-ment on how the Lisbon daughters appear indistinguishable from one another, and on how they consider themselves to be the girls' doubles.[48] Largely this is a consequence of the men's refusal or inability to see their female counterparts as individuals; as Shostak argues, it better serves the narrators' own mythic and somewhat self-aggrandising narrative to view the girls as a group of sacrificial virgins rather than experientially distinct teenagers. (Just occasion-ally they manage to catch glimpses of the girls' individual sub-jectivity; Shostak argues these moments enable a counter-reading to the novel's dominant, misogynist narration.)[49] But there are other doublings of which the narrators seem very much less aware. Ordinary perceptions of maturation are continually scrambled in the men's account, with many figures appearing simultaneously aged and youthful. The novel opens with an image of the youngest Lisbon sister Cecelia in the bath, blood from her slit wrists clouding the water, her 'small body giving off the odor of a mature woman' (3). Later, the exact reverse of this image is presented, when an old Greek neighbour, Mrs Karafilis, is similarly spied in the bath: in her nakedness she appears 'shockingly' like a girl (174). At the very end of the novel the narrators reveal themselves to be middle aged and balding (249); this moment is jolting too because the narrative has hitherto been almost entirely focalised through their teenage selves. Then there is Joe the Retard, at once wizened and infantile, who appears as an early foreshadowing of the narrators' entrapment within their own adolescence (28). These doublings, which pass without comment from the narrators, seem to correspond not only to their own trauma, but also the existence of other, competing traumas associated with their home environment: those of their parents – grandparents even – who are still troubled by their own pasts, and who have moved to the suburbs in order to escape them. The novel's continual making strange and confused the inevitability and orderliness of the processes of growing up and aging is expressive of the contradictions of post-war suburbia: first, that there is still so much history in a place which is supposed to have broken free from the clutches of the past; and, second, that this moment of supposed historical evacuation has itself become historical, with all the problems that recollection and narration entail.

Also like Lynch's film, an insectile motif runs through *The Virgin Suicides*. In *Blue Velvet*, the placidity of the opening suburban scenes is sharply undercut by repulsive close-ups of seething insects, which seem to be boiling up from underground. Such imagery rather confirms the commonplace that the calm exterior conformity of the suburbs is just a facade which hides nests of depravity. In *The Virgin Suicides*, the insects' significance is more complex: like the instances of doubling discussed above, they invite various interpretations. The narrators, once again, tend towards mythic readings, but the inclusion of other material and commentary seems always to encourage from the reader more historically grounded explanations. The first such account is of the swarm of fish flies which rises annually from the algal bloom on the nearby polluted lake to deposit a layer of corpses on virtually every man-made surface. The girls' deaths occur in synchrony with this apparently most natural of life cycles, and thus their demise appears inevitable. Indeed, the day before her first suicide attempt, the youngest Lisbon sister Cecelia is reported to have drawn her initials through a scrim of their remains, suggesting a willing identification with ephemeral nature (4).

Later, an infestation of Dutch elm beetles prompts the organised removal of the neighbourhood's entire natural and protective

canopy. The surviving Lisbon girls are the only people in the neighbourhood who fight to save their tree; responding to a picture of the
girls' struggle, the narrators declare 'they seem to be worshipping it
like a group of Druids' (183–4). The girls' lives – and deaths – seem
to the narrators to be merely part of some great elemental, timeless
force. This tendency of the boys obscures both the girls' individual
subjectivity as well as the historical specificity of their suburban
habitat. Yet the insects also relate decidedly human concerns, in
particular, the physical and social landscape of post-industrial
Detroit. The fish flies, for instance, are actually associated less with
the lake's water or fish than the pollution-induced mat of algae,
which gets even worse the year after an industrial spill. The elm
trees are said to be the only topographical feature that distinguishes
their suburb from the city of Detroit (34, 44), which in the logic of
post-war white flight was inextricably associated with the violence
and poverty of its black population. The disquiet about infestation
certainly echoes the anxiety, anger and disgust expressed by white
suburbanites threatened by black encroachment.[50] On the other
hand, the insects seem also to relate the longer journeys of certain
arriviste suburbanites: one of the Lisbon girls insists that 'if boats
didn't bring the fungus from Europe in the first place [. . .] none of
this would have ever happened' (181).[51]

In addition to the fish flies and the beetles, the neighbourhood
resonates with the thrum of crickets. Despite all attempts to eliminate them with chemicals, the crickets perpetually sing 'from every
direction, always from a height just above our heads, or just below,
and always with suggestion that the insect world felt more than
we did' (58). Once again, the narrators consider the insects as part
of an eternal natural order: the crickets evoke for the narrators
an ancient sentience, which their parents are said to be more in
tune with. Yet this mythic construal marks a realisation that their
parents have histories which predate the environment which, as
adolescents, is all they have ever known. Thus, all of the insects
seem to herald – or perhaps mock – the suburb's failure to divorce
itself physically and socially from the city which produced it, and
from which most of its older inhabitants have come.

To be sure, these infestations, which help depict the suburb as
plagued, diseased and dying, contradict its inhabitants' apparent

belief that they live in an immortal and pristine world. Indeed, up until Cecelia's death, the first of the suicides, the narrators claim that no-one has died in their suburb (35). Perhaps this incredible feat is attributable to the strong sense that nobody is really truly alive; the residents are, in a very modern sense, undead. Different explanations are offered for this living death. Some seem to have to do, once again, with traumatised responses: to the experience of war (35), and also to the black city – 'occasionally we heard gunshots coming from the ghetto, but our fathers insisted it was only cars backfiring' (36). This unpreparedness for dealing with death prompts blackly comic scenes when the city's gravediggers go on strike. Mortuaries fill up and corpses have to be shipped out of state in refrigerated containers (36). Mr. Lisbon also struggles to find a suitable cemetery in which to bury Cecelia. Alternatives remind him of threatening ethnic difference: one is near the Palestinian section and resounds to the call of the muezzin. And where that ethnic difference has been erased, other equally unpleasant associations are invoked. Another cemetery is by the remains of what was Poletown. That neighbourhood has been razed by GM to build a new factory which never got off the ground; the massive expanse of waste ground abutting the cemetery reminds Mr Lisbon of Hiroshima. Cecelia is finally laid to rest in the flattest, blandest and most distant cemetery in town, which is located between two freeways. Even the headstones are laid flat; the only things that punctuate the horizon are cheap plastic American flags. But even this wholly deracinated environment – the next best thing to crossroads, perhaps – is no place to put the past in its place. Again this is articulated by Gothic imagery: excessive watering by family members acting as caretakers has caused flooding, and 'a trail of deep footprints from grave to grave made it appear the dead were walking at night' (36–8).

The various markers of ethnicity that buffet Mr Lisbon during his fraught search for a place to bury his daughter herald an increasing preoccupation of Eugenides's suburban Gothic. They also suggest a distinctly Freudian conception of the uncanny, that is, one that is predicated on the return of the repressed. I contend that *The Virgin Suicides* foregrounds the brittleness of newly established suburban identities that are based on a shared whiteness but which are constantly threatened by reminders of repressed 'ethnic' attachments. This rationalisation, however, is not a banalising, dehistorising move. The fragility of suburban whiteness derives from home ownership being confirmation both of the European national identities of new immigrants *and* of their having become fully assimilated middle-class Americans. In other words, the home becomes a site of the collision of two equally powerful but potentially incompatible identities. My hypothesis that suburbanisation encouraged competing, contradictory identifications runs counter to classical theories of assimilation, which presume that suburbanisation inevitably leads to, and equates with, full adjustment and incorporation. The remoteness of (typically) second-generation immigrants from urban-located ethnic communities and their similarity to other suburbanites in terms of age and class are supposed to all but neutralise significant ethnic attachments.[52] In his study of race relations in post-war Detroit, Thomas Sugrue insists that this shift happened relatively early: 'Beginning in the 1920s – and certainly by the 1940s – class and race became more important than ethnicity as a guide to the city's residential geography. Residents of Detroit's white neighbourhoods abandoned their ethnic affiliations and found a new identity in whiteness.'[53] Meanwhile, some African American writers have provocatively argued that the assumption of whiteness occurred almost the instant European immigrants set foot in America. James Baldwin famously argued that there were no white people in Norway; immigrants from European countries only achieved whiteness through acts of racial prejudice and violence and the assumption of material privileges predicated on such racism.[54] Malcolm X is reported to have said that this typically happens with lightning speed, the first word of English any immigrant learns upon arrival in the States being 'nigger'.[55]

Recent historiography of immigration and assimilation – responding to the 'white ethnic revival' of late twentieth-century America of which Eugenides's fiction is undeniably a part – suggests the picture is more complicated than these accounts would suggest.[56] David Roediger has argued in *Working toward Whiteness* (2004) that the adoption of a white identity by European immigrants often did not happen upon disembarkation, and was frequently piecemeal: new immigrant notions of racial identity were sometimes informed by their own understandings of whiteness and non-whiteness from living in Europe; often, their whiteness was questioned by immigration officials and employers, which sometimes led to a closer identification, and sometimes political alliances, with blacks. For my purposes, though, the dynamics of 'racial' identification and homeownership are the most significant. Echoing Oliver Zunz's study of immigrants in Detroit, Roediger argues that in the early and mid-twentieth century the desire felt by new immigrants for homeownership was readily understood as a powerful 'racial longing':

> The passion for home owning intersected with broadly defined questions of 'racial' identity. It spoke to group values reflecting how immigrants thought about both sides of the Atlantic. When President Herbert Hoover characterized the desire for a home as a 'racial longing,' he implied that the Anglo-Saxon 'race' was his point of reference. However, when the Lithuanian newspaper *Lietuva* editorialized on home ownership as a way to 'honor' one's nationality, it referred to another set of complex, powerful, transnational 'racial longings'.[57]

Of course, there were many other, more prosaic motivations, mainly to do with security and independence, which help explain why rates of homeownership amongst immigrants often exceeded those of wealthier and better established native-born white Americans.[58] If homeownership confirmed particular national or 'racial' attachments, it is tempting to argue that such powerful identifications had to be diluted and even abandoned in order that immigrants could assimilate to a white identity required by restrictive covenants being established across swathes of urban and suburban America from the 1920s onwards. However, in these self-segregating communities, many new immigrant homeowners could indeed have it both ways. Roediger suggests that 'restrictive covenants held out the seductive possibility that neighborhoods could be imagined both as white and as the property of a European "racial" group'.[59] To a great extent this perception was enabled by the support given by local 'ethnic' institutions – Catholic churches, and even synagogues – to 'neighborhood improvement associations', whose function was to ward off incursions from non-whites.[60]

But in many instances, immigrants and their descendants were indeed encouraged to disinvest in their ethnic communities and identities. Even after racially restrictive covenants were deemed unconstitutional following the Supreme Court's *Shelley v. Kraemer* decision (1948), residential discrimination persisted in more informal, covert ways. In certain cases, some European immigrants and their descendants were actively discouraged from settling in white neighbourhoods. One of the most notorious instances was the scheme implemented by the residents, realtors and bankers of Grosse Pointe, the 'Grosse Pointe Point System', which came to national prominence in 1960. As one its practitioners openly admitted in court that year, the system was intended to make it more difficult for those of south or east European descent to acquire a mortgage in order to purchase property in the neighbourhood. Whereas no restrictions were placed on would-be residents of north-west European descent, those with Italian, Greek or Polish heritage wishing to move into the area had to achieve certain point scores to win admission. (Jews were required to achieve the highest scores; blacks and Asians were barred altogether.) Applicants were judged on a number of factors, including their 'degree of swarthiness', their employment, the manner in which they dressed and even the upkeep of their former home. Private detectives were employed to determine the latter.[61] Thus in the specific case of Grosse Pointe, for certain immigrants who were determined to suburbanise, assimilation – even if posed – paid dividends.[62]

In *The Virgin Suicides*, however, despite the machinations of neighbourhood associations and other local actors, ethnic identities have emphatically not been abandoned. In this most upper-middle-class suburban neighbourhood, Europeanness abounds, and not only in its cosmopolitan assortment of surnames: many households are referred to as German, Italian, Polish and Greek. Hyphenated identities are avoided; these residents seem more European than American. Quite possibly this insistence on Europeanness is a consequence of the narrators' historical situation. Several of them are declared to be the grandchildren of immigrants; perhaps they are motivated by the politics of white ethnic revival so ascendant in the latter part of the twentieth century, and are attempting to recover and reassert what their parents were all too keen to abandon in the white dreamscape of post-war suburbia. Notably, though, markers of Europeanness are not evenly distributed throughout the novel. Rather, as the suburb becomes increasingly identified with European ethnicities, its essential Americanness becomes more and more insecure. An initial differentiation between Europeanness and Americanness is made towards the beginning of the novel: the 'immigrant kid' Dominic Palazzolo, who is on a short stay with relatives, confirms how the narrators 'expected a European to look': 'frail, diseased and temperamental' (19–20) – the very image of an Ellis Island immigrant. Their emphatic identification of Dominic with Europeanness, of course, confirms the narrators' own Americanness, whatever their own ancestry. After he leaves, though, it seems no longer so easy to make such distinctions. Indeed, Dominic's departure is considered to be a possible reason for Cecelia's first suicide attempt – it seems she is besotted with him – which sets in motion the rest of the novel's incidents. Cecelia kills herself using a method which mirrors the failed attempt of the lovelorn Dominic: throwing herself out of the upstairs window of her home. Dominic falls into 'calculated shrubbery' (20); Cecelia is impaled on fence spikes. The subsequent organised removal of the 'murdering fence' by the Lisbons' neighbours, and in particular, their indifference to the carnage so caused to their properties, leads the narrators to sense 'how ancient they were', and to realise 'that the version of the world they had rendered for us was not the world they really believed in' (55). Quite on cue, this insight is followed by the nonchalant emergence of Europeans behaving for all as if they had never left the Old World: 'the old German couple appeared in their grape arbor to drink dessert wine. As usual they wore their alpine hats, Mr Hessen's with a tiny green feather, while their schnauzer sniffed at the end of his leash' (56). Thus once the figure of the itinerant immigrant is dispelled, Europeanness comes increasingly to seem settled in the suburb.

The bald presence of these almost comically unassimilated Germans perhaps bespeaks the micro-management of racial and ethnic accession in Grosse Pointe. Once again, there were no restrictions placed on prospective house buyers of north-west European ancestry, even those whose preferences – whether for drinks, dress or dogs – deviated from the American. It was quite a different matter for those of south and east European descent, and accordingly, in the novel the households of Italians, Poles and Greeks are rendered quite differently, with each acquiring decidedly Gothic characteristics. First there are the Baldinos. The suspicion that they are mafiosi transforms them, in the locality's imagination, into modern Gothic villains, and underneath their garden with its laurel trees imported from Italy is rumoured to be an underground hideaway and a network of tunnels that connects even with the Lisbons' home (10–14).Then there are the Stamorowskis. As the Lisbons' house is overcome by 'creeping desolation' as the family's withdrawal from, and abandonment by, the community becomes complete, the narrators comment: 'We always thought the bats had come with the Stamorowskis from Poland; they made sense swooping over that sombre house with its velvet curtains and Old World decay, but not over the practical double chimneys of the Lisbon house' (89). Finally, there is Old Mrs Karafilis, who is kept in the basement of her otherwise assimilated Greek family's home – a subterranean chamber she has made over to look like Asia Minor, in which 'she is waiting to die'. As the narrators declare, she is 'shaped and saddened by a history we knew nothing about' – her experience is of the fearful brutality of war (in her case the expulsion of the Greeks from Turkey in 1923). Indeed, when she was a girl she hid for weeks in a cave to save her own life. This is why it seems she becomes interested in the plight of the Lisbon girls and is able to 'enter into telepathy with them': 'On the day she heard about the girls' new incarceration, she jerked her head up, nodded, didn't smile. But had already known, it seemed' (171–4).

Why are these particular households fashioned as Gothic? The answer seems ultimately to lie with the Lisbons, who are in fact about the only family whose ethnic heritage is undisclosed. Aspects of their Europeanness survive as the faintest adumbrations: their surname is an obscure reminder of such a past, as is their mother's Catholicism, whose outlook seems otherwise entirely Puritan – even her own priest remarks that her preference for austere modern choral music 'is what you might expect to find in a protestant household' (136). Indeed, the interior of the Lisbons' home is devoid of any references to their Old World heritage; instead it is replete with 'stark colonial furniture', and even a painting of Pilgrims plucking a turkey (25). These conscious symbols of an originating American people are reminiscent of what Alison Landsberg describes as the 'prosthetic memories' installed by the protagonists of various early twentieth-century immigrant narratives who sought to imagine themselves as Americans, and through which they were able to disassociate themselves from their European pasts.[63] Likely, the Lisbons' ancestors left European shores some time before the arrival of the 'new' immigrants – indeed, during the homecoming ball, the Lisbon girls are likened to 'pioneer women', their unflattering dresses having 'the stoic, presumptuous qualities of European fashions enduring the wilderness' (118). Whatever the Lisbons' precise origins, their forgetting has a singular purpose. The Lisbons' prosthetic genealogy, which extends back to the Pilgrims, serves to obliterate some other lived, non-American history. The overtly Gothic motifs – the tunnels, the bats, the telepathy – serve then to reconnect forcibly the ethnically unmarked home of the Lisbons with locations marked by the Old World. These motifs, along with the Gothic collapse of the Lisbon home, suggest that the abandonment of European ties in exchange for a deracinated suburban home cannot but produce trauma. In this suburban Gothic narrative, there is an irreducible element of the home which is not American. It is the uncanniness of these perceptions – the simultaneous appropriateness and inappropriateness of Old World associations in New World domestic space – that helps to unhouse the suburban home.

Arguably, Old Mrs Karafilis's comprehension of New World suffering, enabled by her Old World experience, relates a further uncanny aspect of the novel. Its central Gothic conceit – young women trapped in a ruined building – is of course a dominant trope of classic European Gothic fiction. At the same time, *The Virgin Suicides* borrows from earlier American Gothic tales – notably Faulkner's 'A Rose for Emily' (1919) with which it shares a first-person-plural narrator. 'A Rose' is told by the male townsfolk of a provincial Mississippi town who have over several decades become fascinated by an ageing spinster, Emily Grierson. Grierson has sequestered herself in her own townhouse, which like the Lisbons' upmarket suburban home, has fallen from its high estate into dilapidation. But whereas her domestic quarters are finally penetrated by the male narrators and her murderous secret and sexual perversity revealed, there is of course no such disclosure in *The Virgin Suicides*, despite the boys' physical access into the Lisbon home. References to the baleful appearance of the Lisbon house and the 'miasmic vapors' (145) emanating from its environs also evoke Poe's 'The Fall of the House of Usher' (1839). Actually, Eugenides's Gothic has more in common with Poe's: both texts suggest their narrators are far from reliable, and both refrain from explaining the full mystery of their incarcerated women. Moreover, this most canonical of American Gothic stories features a setting which seems more Old World than New. These stories, then, indicate how a residual Europeanness seems to colour any attempt to articulate a purely American Gothic.

The Virgin Suicides does not, though, find a single dysfunctional family to be guilty of cultural amnesia. One of the final scenes recounted is of a debutante party. Crassly, this celebration of a Grosse Pointe girl's 'coming out' into womanhood is held immediately after the three-quarters successful combined suicide attempt of the remaining Lisbon daughters. But then, most reportedly attend precisely to put the Lisbons out of their minds and to restore their faith in a specifically American narrative of success: 'Raising champagne glasses, people said our industry was coming back, our nation, our way of life' (236). The narrators' recollection, then, stands as an act of remembrance by a group of individuals of an event held by a community in order to forget about a family who refused to remember. This layering of memory and denial, a persistent feature of the novel, also implicates the male narrators. Their recollections offer no cathartic release, they dispel no ghosts; moreover, they demonstrate that the narrators' response to trauma is simply to create their own collective prosthetic memory. Retrospectively, the narrators fashion their faltering attempts to engage with the girls into a 'communal conversation' (66); their rereading of Cecelia's diary enables them to 'hold collective memories of times we hadn't experienced' (42). Their choric narrative echoes Cecelia's diary in that it 'depicts [. . .] an unformed ego' (42) – to the point where 'the first person singular ceases almost entirely' (44) – a consequence, it seems, of her (and similarly their) endless watching of others.

Relentlessly, the novel shows such forms of public memory to be flawed, partial. In their quest for objectivity and inclusivity, the narrators resort to documents and the remembrances of others. Perhaps predictably, what results is an account full of holes and contradictions. Cecelia's diary, for instance, does not confirm the supposition, based on her behaviour, that she was in love with Dominic Palazzolo (32); in establishing a motivation for her suicide it is utterly inconclusive. The narrators attempt to arrange chronologically a series of photographs to better account for the tragedy; their narrative, however, continually requires them to jump between their numbered exhibits. In any case some photos are missing, and others undermine shared memories – one in particular seems to suggest the 'creeping desolation' of the Lisbon house was all in their minds (89). Many of the neighbours' accounts are contradictory or coloured by self-regard. One testimony relating to Cecelia the moment before her death is drolly dismissed as the 'hallucination of a bifocals wearer' (47). The two people deemed the most reliable of witnesses fail utterly to provide: the girls' counsellor is the one of the few individuals who could not be tracked down (she may have anyway been working under false credentials), and Trip Fontaine, prom king to Lux Lisbon's queen, is considered reliable precisely because he never tells. (In any case, he always moved in a haze of marihuana.) Yet, even the most doubtful of accounts from the boys themselves are folded into the narrative: Paul Baldino's tall tale of travelling the neighbourhood's tunnels and coming up into the Lisbons' home to glimpse Cecelia lying in bathwater clouded with her own blood provides the striking 'remembered' image at the novel's opening.

In addition, the narrators' account features a number of historical incongruities. For instance, far from triggering a cyclical superabundance, the fish flies of the northern lakes were in actual fact decimated by pollution. The reference to Poletown is anachronistic; its demolition was not to take place until 1981. Thus, once again, the narrators' account is partial not only in ways they readily acknowledge, but also in ways to which they are less prepared to admit. These disavowals parallel the manner in which they refrain from referring to Detroit or Grosse Pointe by name for the entirety of the narrative. This avoidance serves to render their memories mythic, timeless. At the same time, these anomalies and omissions undercut their narrative, demonstrating it to be limited and self-serving. The novel's 'choric' narration, then, shows why we should not trust the collective stories we tell of the suburban past. Further, it implies there is no reliable or coherent subject to narrate suburban memories, and no discrete, stable site from which to tell them.

Only by paying attention to the Gothic's formal devices, its textuality, is it possible to gain a perspective on what Cathy Davidson has described as the mode's 'challenge to history, its rewriting and unwriting of history'.[64] The suburbs have for so long been understood as places people go to in order to forget, or to avoid conflict. Instructively, *The Virgin Suicides* shows how such forgetting is far from inevitable, but equally, how the remembering of that forgetting is inevitably conflicted. Eugenides's suburban Gothic insists that the place we presume to know so well can never be fully known; this is a consequence not of its being outside history, but of its becoming history. But perhaps this formulation sounds a little too pat and self-satisfied. So I will conclude instead by referring to the way *The Virgin Suicides* encourages one to get one's story straight about it, to pin the novel down, and to reread it repeatedly to achieve this end. One is thus reminded of one's similarity to the narrators, who go over and over the same evidence in order to be able to settle on, as they say, a 'story we could live with' (241). It is this instance of doubling that is by far the most disconcerting of all.

CHAPTER 3

Some Shared Story: Suburban Memoir

Now I am looking hard and I cannot locate our lives amidst all the
sameness below, and that is what terrifies me. That is what terrifies and
instructs. A child absorbs such a vision and begins to sense, at some level,
the imperative of making a bigger meaning of things. I wonder whether
all these people living just like me might be *my* people – all of us, perhaps,
with some shared story. I wonder whether the pattern below might be a
mass of connections joining me to some whole.

David Beers, *Blue Sky Dream: A Memoir of America's
Fall from Grace*[1]

If the novel constituted the principal vehicle for telling suburban
stories in the post-World War II period, in the decades around
the millennium it has given ground to another platform: memoir.
Such a development should come as little surprise. As members of
the suburban baby boom have entered late middle age, they have
become increasingly willing and able to tell their own life stories.
Those who were cradled by the newly built habitats of the 1940s,
50s and 60s are liable to feel an especial affinity with these places.
After all, they came into the world at the same time, a period
often couched as a moment of optimism; by the same token, the
maturation of the suburbs provides memoirists with an analogue
to their own ageing. This personal affinity is typically tempered,
however, by an awareness that a suburban upbringing is hardly a
unique experience. In the opening quotation, David Beers describes
how a realisation of the ubiquity of his way of life first occurred in

childhood, while flying above his suburban neighbourhood in a light aeroplane with his father. The perspective is terrifying because it is so depersonalising; the details of a life diffuse into abstraction. But it is also instructive: identifying one's situation within a much larger pattern promotes an understanding of how one's life – and those of countless others – has been shaped by impersonal forces. The memoirist's retrospection may constitute a similar sort of optic, and perhaps that is what Beers is really describing here; as another memoirist claims, to have begun life in a middle-class suburb 'entitles a person to a generic memory'.[2]

These observations invite two sets of questions that will be addressed in this chapter. The first relates to memoir's articulation of the suburb's temporal dimensions. What are the consequences of the memoirist's retrospection meeting that forward-looking 'moment of optimism' of the post-war suburbs? How might this interaction reshape understandings of suburban history? Can the suburban memoir, for instance, describe a trajectory other than one of decline and disillusionment? And do memoirists presume the suburbs only ever looked forward, or are these places shown to be installed with memories too? Peter Balakian's memoir *Black Dog of Fate* (1997) for instance, demonstrates how the past can indeed inhabit suburban environments in different ways. Traumatic histories need not infiltrate suburban streets and houses in the most predicable ways: as haunting, as the return of the repressed. By contrast, suburbs can provide refuges, protective habitats in which vital reparative work can take place. *Blue Sky Dream* (1996), Beers's richly observed account of the Californian aerospace suburbs in which he grew up, complicates the familiar lapsarian narrative of post-war suburbia by carefully attending to multiple, often conflicting trajectories, an approach that is further inflected by his own obvious yearning for a life when the future seemed a far simpler prospect. Finally, D. J. Waldie's intriguingly fragmented study of Lakewood, California, *Holy Land: A Suburban Memoir* (1996), shows that the suburban city in which he has lived for most of his life is indeed haunted by various brutal histories, including the Holocaust. The grid on which Lakewood is built opens out onto the world; it is the 'antithesis of a ghetto'.[3] Such a bold claim about the suburb's connectedness, however, also facilitates an appreciation of

Lakewood's discomforting proximity to histories of genocide and exclusion.

The second set of questions relates to the imperative to tell a shared story of the suburbs. How does its narration negotiate the generalisations and abstractions so characteristic of suburban representation? How do suburban memoirs meet the seemingly contradictory requirements for both critical distance and attention to detail? The passage from Beers's memoir suggests that the lofty God's-eye view of his childhood habitat threatens the traditional autobiographical 'I', which shrinks from such disembodied truth telling. In his suburban memoir Waldie is especially preoccupied with the legacy of aerial perspectives of the suburbs. Yet Waldie demonstrates not only how the abstractions of planners and photographers have influenced people's lives, but also that such patterning provides a vital imaginative resource, enabling one to see how suburbs, and the lives made in them, are networked within broader geographies and histories. This cartographic perspective facilitates other narrative modes that seem better able to make sense of a social or environmental subject than the conventional autobiographical 'I'. Indeed, suburban memoirs typically employ more pluralist modes of writing, from autoethnography to prosopography, in order to situate individual stories within wider historical trajectories and social formations. To do otherwise would fail to get an adequate measure of the suburban past.

From the Baby Boom to the Memoir Boom

The emergence of the suburban memoir rides on the back of a much broader surge in the popularity of memoir that gathered momentum in the early 1990s. The much-used term 'memoir boom' is no hyperbole: in the last twenty-five years the form has come to dominate bestseller lists in the US. At the beginning of her study of the memoir boom as an industrial phenomenon in the US, Julie Rak notes two illuminating statistics: the number of biography titles sold between 1940 and 2004 increased more than tenfold; between the years 2004 and 2008, sales of personal memoirs exploded by 400 per cent.[4] In addition to the sheer volume of memoirs published and purchased, the period has seen a startling proliferation of sub-genres, from the 'misery memoir' to the usually more upbeat dad memoir, dog memoir and 'shtick-lit' of recent years.[5] The memoir boom is arguably also a democratising development: increasing numbers of non-celebrity memoirists have found significant readerships, and a variety of online outfits have sprung up dedicated to the production of memoirs and family histories of any member of the public willing to pay for the service.[6]

For G. Thomas Couser, this trend is hardly surprising; indeed, he argues that the significance of memoir, 'by far the most inclusive and democratic of genres', relates to its having roots not in literary writing but in the ways in which ordinary people represent their everyday lives.[7] However, for the many others who bemoan what they perceive as the self-regard and lack of literary merit of much recent memoir, the form's democratic credentials are hardly worth celebrating. And if memoir has been repeatedly critiqued as a manifestation of a kind of cultural atavism, even more febrile have been discussions in the media following revelations that a number of memoirs were found to include substantially exaggerated or fabricated elements. On the other hand, memoirs have become a significant cultural space in which to contest accounts about individuals and events presented both in the media and in other memoirs. These developments have prompted Ben Yagoda to declare 'there has never been a time like it'. Memoir, he concludes, 'has become the central form of the culture: not only in the way stories are told, by the way arguments are put forth, products and properties marketed, ideas floated, acts justified, reputations constructed and salvaged'.[8]

Spikes in the popularity of memoir have, though, been registered at several different moments throughout the last two and a half centuries. For instance, V. S. Pritchett noted in 1958 a 'tremendous expansion in autobiographical writing', which he attributed without much enthusiasm to the influence of 'psychological theory'.[9] In his history of memoir, Yagoda observes that the current 'anti-memoir screed' reproduces very closely the same criticisms – that memoirists are mostly self-important, and memoirs largely insignificant – as those made in the late eighteenth century.[10] It is also the case that the post-war years saw the publication of a handful of memoirs focusing on domestic life in the new suburbs.[11] The recent memoir boom is then not an entirely novel phenomenon, and neither are suburban memoirs. But one thing that cannot escape attention is the obvious echo between the two terms, the baby boom and the memoir boom. For sure, one frequently offered explanation for the recent 'craze' for memoir is that it is an expression of the narcissism of the baby boomers; first-person personal narrative, this line of reasoning presumes, was always going to be a popular mode of expression for the so-called 'me generation'.[12]

Perhaps more revealing, though, is the way in which critiques of the memoir boom and of the post-war suburbs are similarly shaped by disdain for mass consumerism. Julie Rak shows that the memoir boom has frequently been understood in terms of overproduction and a concomitant reduction in the quality of writing: the memoir has become merely an industrial product with little capacity to cultivate its readers.[13] Quite the same kind of thing was meted out to the suburbs in the decades after World War II. As Malvina Reynolds's popular folk song had it, suburbia's mass-produced landscape, its proliferating flimsy 'little boxes', could only ever propagate an equally uniform and degraded population: both suburban houses and their inhabitants, Reynolds sings, are 'all made out of ticky-tacky'.[14] If Reynolds insists on suburban conformity, the lack of individuality among suburbanites, other critics skewered the suburbs for both their self-centred individualism and their baleful uniformity. For Lewis Mumford, the overproduction of suburban housing and consumer goods thwarted ambitions for social detachment. Flight to the suburbs, once predicated on a desire 'to be your own unique self; to build your unique house, mid a unique landscape', has metastasised into a mass movement whose inevitable consequence was the expansion of 'a low-grade uniform environment from which escape was impossible'.[15]

Rak notes the similar repeated emphasis placed on the voracious hunger of memoir readers, and on the stoking of an undiscriminating, base appetite by corporate publishers. As well as being overproduced, the memoir is over-marketed; indeed, the genre is all but a marketing ploy, a mere expression of market forces. The unthinking mass readership, easily manipulated by the media industry, is of course a theme that echoes across the twentieth century. But the especial focus on the development of a mass appetite and, therefore, a non-rational, corporal mass, suggests not only disdain for but also anxieties about the encroachment of the lower class into the territories of bourgeois culture. As Catherine Jurca has persuasively argued, the contempt for suburbs and suburbanites common to the twentieth-century American novel was largely prompted by a need to reassert social status in the wake of mass suburbanisation. As homeownership was rapidly democratised, new rhetorical strategies were required to maintain status; suburban living and homeownership, once benchmarks of middle-class privilege, had to be called into question in order to keep membership of the middle classes beyond the reach of this upwardly mobile mass.[16] A similar dynamic is at play with criticisms of the memoir. Assertions of the form's lack of literary credentials are a reaction to its democratisation; invocations of memoir's overproduction and of its mass consumption are predicated on a vision of literary culture whose membership is more highly regulated and narrowly based in terms of class composition.

Bodies in Motion: The Multiple Trajectories of Suburban Memoir

Given the parallel hostility to the suburbs and to memoir, it is unsurprising that authors of suburban memoirs are either rather defensive about their projects, or otherwise keen to assert how their writing responds to such preconceptions. For instance, in his self-published memoir *Growing up Levittown: in a Time of Conformity, Controversy and Cultural Crisis* (2011), Steve Bergsman attempts to rebut hostile accounts of the suburbs in general, and of his hometown, Levittown, New York, in particular. He devotes whole chapters to such material – Reynolds and Mumford provoke his ire especially – and counters with his insider's perspective, providing details of his family's history, the flourishing cultural life of the suburb and the maturation of its environment. If Bergsman's book proves only one thing, it is Yagoda's observation that memoir has become a key site for the construction and contestation of reputations. A peculiarity of the suburban memoir, however, is that its location is often presumed to have more of a reputation than its author. Thus suburban memoirs can be understood to straddle the frequently referenced divide between celebrity and non-celebrity narrative.[17] They typically tell a story that is bigger than an individual life; in various ways they attempt to narrate a collective story, and to resituate their settings within wider historical and cultural frames.

Bringing the Pain of the Past into the Landscape of the Present: Peter Balakian's *Black Dog of Fate*

Peter Balakian's critically acclaimed, award-winning *Black Dog of Fate: A Memoir: An American Son Uncovers His Armenian Past* (1997) is unquestionably of a different order to Bergsman's memoir. Balakian's own profile is not insignificant either: he is a professor of literature, a translator and a published poet. Typical of suburban memoir, though, Balakian's book presents his own life as one element within a much larger frame. In an article about *Black Dog of Fate*, Balakian relates the scepticism expressed by friends upon their hearing that he was writing a memoir: surely, they responded, his life was not important enough to yield one – or, at least, not yet. Balakian effectively agrees: 'I would explain that I actually was interested in subjects bigger than my life; a memoir, I insisted, didn't have to be a story just about the self and its little journey through its little world.'[18] The subject of Balakian's 'memoir across generations' is the traumatic, supressed history of the Armenian Genocide. *Black Dog of Fate* relates Balakian's need to reach beyond his own 'little world' – across continents and generations – precisely because no obvious trace of these past events was to be found in the contented New Jersey suburbs of his childhood. In its repeated distinction between an 'Armenian past' and the 'suburban present', however, Balakian's memoir would appear to be reinstalling a familiar critique of the suburbs as deracinated sites floating free from history, whose modern comforts encourage their residents to shrug off any feelings of responsibility to the past.

Balakian contends that while he was growing up only his maternal grandmother, Nafina Aroosian, provided him a sense of connection with the shadows of history. 'When I was with my grandmother' he recalls, 'I had access to some other world, some evocative place of dark and light, some kind of energy that ran like an invisible force from this old country called Armenia to my world in New Jersey. It was something ancient, something connected to earth and words and blood and sky.'[19] Her endless inscrutable folk stories suggest to the young Peter that his suburban world is not all that there is or, in her own words, 'that there is mystery [. . .] that appearances are deceiving' (11). Only long after his grandmother's death does Balakian begin to understand the significance of her 'strange shadow' (31), when he learns that she witnessed countless acts of dispossession and slaughter during the Genocide and had, along with her two infant children, survived one of the murderous death marches through the Syrian desert orchestrated by the Turks in 1915. Her stories, he comes to feel, are a kind of gift, meant to hibernate within him – or better, he thinks, to marinate or cure, 'since we are a people so steeped in food' (18) – until he is ready and able to harness them. His mother, by contrast, despite her steadfast commitment to her extended family and to Armenian cuisine, repeatedly asserts her family's Americanness and repudiates other Armenians for being 'too ethnic' (45). Second and third generations appear to unite in disavowing the ethnic attachments of the first. As a boy Balakian identifies with his surroundings against his family. The interminable Sunday dinners with relatives seem only to keep him from the easy pleasures of his suburban environment. And on hearing of his parents' plans to move from their almost entirely Jewish street in Teaneck to a brand-new upscale development in the neighbouring suburb of Tenafly, the young Peter resists by declaring to his mother that he is a Jew (49).

Balakian tells of how, in his teenage years, he sinks into a life of 'suburban indulgence' (109), a state of complacency that threatens to leave him entirely insensitive to his grandmother's cryptic yet urgent messages. (He is saved by the tough-love of his father, who sends him away to a private school, an intervention that Balakian comes to appreciate only later in life.) But *Black Dog of Fate* does not show how Balakian manages to uncover hidden histories in spite of his suburban upbringing; rather, in a number of different ways, the suburbs seem to facilitate access to the past. First, Balakian is keen to show that suburbia harbours 'a kind of memory' distinct to itself. True enough, it does not involve the kinds of memory embodied by his grandmother, which seemed 'connected to something larger than my life' (30); rather, it is associated with 'a personal web of sensations', 'the body in motion [. . .] that sense of limitless potential' (28).[20] To be clear, Balakian is not here referring merely to memories of his suburban youth from the vantage point of middle age; rather, he understands suburban memory to characterise what it was like 'to be thirteen and dreaming' (28), a stir of sensual recollections 'spilling into myth and nostalgia' (29). Interestingly, the soundtrack of Balakian's suburban adolescence – a melange of rock 'n' roll, blues and folk – which he says 'defined his sense of time because it embodied events in memory' (29), is understood to be not unlike those other, more mysterious memories associated with his grandmother that seem to reach far beyond the suburban present. In the voice of Bob Dylan, for instance, Balakian hears 'an estuary of tradition' and 'poetic opacity' (29). But if suburban memory is mostly bound up with the sensual world and with possible futures, it nonetheless has the capacity for sophistication; if it is largely self-centred, it is also self-reflexive. In his paean to the Four Tops' 1966 hit 'The Same Old Song', which 'celebrated memory and the act of memory indelibly imprinted in the experience of a song in the grooves of the disc' (29), Balakian suggests the popular music of his youth corresponded closely with, and maybe even encouraged, a particular kind of suburban dreaming, in which the past was continually being replayed in the present. Thus suburban culture, it may be surmised, provided some of the tools, and maybe even a training ground, for engaging in quite sophisticated kinds of memory work.

Second, Balakian demonstrates how his grandmother, despite her gnomic stories, dream-telling and old-world foodways, readily appreciated suburban modernity. Unlike the Greek grandmothers of Jeffrey Eugenides's first two novels discussed in Chapter 2, Nafina Aroosian is not presented as an entirely incongruous figure, or as a source of embarrassment to be hidden away in the basement of the family home. Balakian remembers his grandmother as confident and mobile, and recalls his regular walks with her in their local neighbourhood, or across the Hudson in New York City. Once, quite disorientated, they wander the streets of Upper Manhattan together, her stories continually spooling. Her strange tales may seem other-worldly to the young Peter, but the situation of their telling in the here and now is crucial and in a certain way also appropriate. These stories, Balakian comes to feel, are encoded testimony. The vehicle of this testimony, the beguiling imagery of myth and dreams, is anathema to the modern world. Its subject, however, is anything but: as Balakian remarks, the Armenians under Ottoman rule in 1915 had the misfortune to experience one of the defining events of modernity. Their walks on the more familiar side of the Hudson are said always to end with them looking down from an overpass in silent admiration at the construction of the Garden State Parkway (11). Balakian later incorporates these memories of their standing together on the bridge over the unfinished highway into the published poem 'The History of Armenia' (192–4). Evidently, in both the memoir and the poem, Balakian conceives of his grandmother as a living bridge between the suburban present and the fateful events of 1915. Her encoded testimony is unfinished business; Balakian understands his task precisely to be 'to bring the pain of the past into the landscape of the present' (195).

Third, Balakian comes to understand that for his parents, the suburbs promised safety and respite from the horrors of the past. Balakian does not, however, cast their eager assimilation as denial. Rather, the prosperous New Jersey suburbs provide a place of repose, an environment in which these memories, still with so much potential to cause pain, could be safely contained, carefully transmuted and ultimately made available to the next generation. Balakian contends that his parents ensured – 'often in unconscious and instinctual ways' – that he and his siblings were 'Americans first. Free. Unhampered, unhaunted, unscarred by the unspeakable cruelties of Armenian history' (297). He considers this to be the greatest gift they could have bestowed on their children. Yet the past has not been banished; it shadows these comfortable houses and re-emerges periodically in unconscious ways. At the same time, his parents and other relatives are able and willing to tell Peter what 'he needs to know' once he has reached the security of adulthood. Indeed, towards the end of his memoir, Balakian refers to what he has come to see as the 'strange sweetness of our life in suburbia' (295); its strangeness, echoing the mystery of his grandmother's stories, relates his sense of its containing something quite beyond the realms of the obvious. Balakian does note that his parents' suburban assimilation was made much easier by their whiteness and their affluence, and by the fact that they were Protestant (both his grandparents' families having been converted from Armenian Orthodox Christianity by American missionaries in the nineteenth century); he also acknowledges that they were cognisant of but acquiescent about racial exclusion in their own neighbourhood. Nevertheless, Balakian finally understands his family's suburban homes 'not as symbols of American material comfort or upward mobility, but as emblems of peace and refuge from a world of horror and death' (300). Thus, the location of Balakian's suburban memoir is neither incidental nor merely problematic; rather, it is understood to be essential to the maintenance and narration of memory.

'Living the Inevitable Future': Remembering 'Aerospace Suburban Gentility' in David Beers's *Blue Sky Dream*

In *Black Dog of Fate*, Balakian understands the significance of the suburbs to be their reparative function, their capacity to contain and manage the effects of an anterior trauma. Of course, one should not presume that suburbs always provide such a benign environment. Some black and gay memoirists, by contrast, have good reason to recall their suburban hometowns as isolating and threat-filled.[21] The most common course taken by suburban memoirs, however, is in a sense the reverse of the one described by Balakian. Suburban memoirs less frequently tell redemptive stories than they do lapsarian ones. For sure, an Edenic paradigm has been a common feature of life writing since childhood began to receive extensive attention by authors in the eighteenth century.[22] But instead of focusing on the personal loss of a childhood idyll, many suburban memoirs emphasise a broader disillusionment, usually that of their authors' parents, whose investment in the dream of the post-war suburbs is shown to be, if not wholly misjudged, then at least impaired by circumstance. The very title of David Beers's *Blue Sky Dream: A Memoir of America's Fall from Grace* (1996), for example, registers the falling away of this dream; indeed, the memoir takes as its principal subject the trajectory of the post-war suburban generation or, more specifically, the course of the many thousands of suburban families affiliated to the state-contracted aerospace industries that boomed during the Cold War. Beers's chosen title suggests a downward course; his memoir, however, recounts something much more complex.

The 'blue sky' vision of this new suburban society entailed a complete trust in technology and technocracy as bases for progress, as well as a strong sense of their vanguard position in American society and their own continual forward momentum. A central icon of this blue-sky optimism was the Polaris missile, developed by Lockheed, the corporation which employed Beers's father for over thirty years. Polaris, Beers notes, was almost always depicted as bursting out of the ocean as though commencing a perpetual, vertical ascent, thereby leaving little room to imagine the nuclear warhead-carrying missile's ultimate destination and purpose. Presumably, such imagery also helped reduce any qualms that members of the 'aerospace suburban gentility' (34) may have had about how their lives of privilege owed everything to the manufacture of weapons of mass destruction and other military systems. The clean, open spaces of the modern suburban home held a similar promise. Beers comments that his parents' brand-new tract home in a brand-new subdivision on the fringes of San Jose, California helped orientate them toward the future by providing them 'an up-to-date emptiness', 'a certain perfection of potentiality' (39). Beers sees that the presumption of suburbia's inspiring lack of history, its emptiness, ought to be interpreted as a twentieth-century reworking of manifest destiny. Certainly, the century-old orchards and the slower way of life based around agriculture in what was once known as the Valley of Heart's Delight were quickly displaced without much compunction by the arriving aerospace families. Beers suggests their faith in a distinctly 'blue sky' trajectory explains this lack of sentiment: 'We did not, after all, come to the Valley of Heart's Delight to join the circular rhythm of nature': 'Our imagination was linear, proceeding forward and upward, and our lines did not curve back on themselves as did the seasons. We saw promise in the clean possibilities that arose once every blossom had been erased, never to return (53). Thus *Blue Sky Dream* shows that often it was their complete faith in technological progress that enabled aerospace suburbanites to ignore conflict and to presume they were 'living the inevitable future' (14).

Nevertheless, like other suburban memoirists, Beers attempts to narrate a suburban history. If *Blue Sky Dream* shows only one thing, it is that the 'inevitable future' did not turn out quite as expected. But Beers's account, which is especially attuned to how the fortunes of the aerospace suburbs have been dictated by broader political and economic forces, does not simply dispel the blue-sky myth of continual progress merely by showing that what goes up must come down. The interest of Beers's memoir has precisely to do with the way it renders the history of the post-war suburbs as a series of contradictory trajectories and transitions which cannot be mapped out clearly, as if on a graph. True, Beers states that his father's career at Lockheed 'perfectly traced the arc of the Cold War aerospace industry' (14) and, initially at least, his account of his father's life as an organisation man follows a familiar-enough script. As a young man Hal Beers was a jet fighter pilot for the American Navy. Flying at 40,000 feet, 'an altitude at which visibility appeared unlimited' (12), he embodied 'America's favourite story, the story of a son who zooms past his father's sternly conventional expectations, the son who roams far and returns transformed' (8–9). But even while it continued to celebrate this familiar masculine archetype, America was soon to need a different kind of man, one who forewent mobility and vision for a sedentary working life situated in vast, windowless structures, a man who was content to work on abstract elements of projects whose details he was prohibited from sharing with either co-workers or family members, and whose larger purpose and ultimate consequence he might never know anything of himself.[23]

Life as an organisation man working within the military-industrial complex evidently takes a toll on Beers's father. He is shown to have frequently taken out his frustration on members of his family and on the very structure of his suburban home. Pointedly, the damage caused by his punches and kicks to doors and walls becomes increasingly hard to disguise, and so the house is increasingly less able to embody the pure potential of industrial technology, on which its very existence is predicated. But if the divergent trajectories of blue-sky optimism and the plight of the organisation man seems a straightforward, predictable development, Beers further complicates matters by relating the effects of, for instance, the paradigm shift caused by the personal computer revolution. From the 1970s a rival technological and corporate culture took hold of the valley, which was of course quickly renamed in its honour. Its ascendancy was driven in part by its employment of a 'lean and mean' business model that was anathema to the aerospace corporations, and partly because it articulated a more attractive myth of technology: 'unlike missiles or satellites or lunar modules, the personal computer could be touched, could be put to use by nearly *anyone*' (149, emphasis in original). The Beers family's hostility toward the relative affluence and self-satisfaction of these Silicon Valley arrivistes, and to the way they 'seemed to glorify impermanence' (150), ironically reflects very closely the contempt expressed by the likes of Joan Didion in response to the arrival of aerospace families in decades previous.[24] And yet the aerospace industries did not go the way of the orchards; on the contrary, they saw a resurgence during the military build-up of the Reagan era. The career of Beers's father is revitalised as a result, and home life becomes noticeably happier. But both Beers and his father are expressly ambivalent about this upturn, as it is without question the result of another discomforting trajectory, the 'massive transfer' of federal subsidy 'from one group less fortunate to another very fortunate indeed' (169).

Thus Beers's memoir charts not only the historical complexity of the aerospace suburbs but also some of the moral complexities arising from living in them. In the wake of Reagan's 'generosity', Beers's father comes less to regret that his career was mostly unrewarding than to 'fear that he had travelled too far along a path morally doomed' (192). This is a not a debilitating kind of moral self-disgust; evidently, the shallow optimism embodied by those bright images of Polaris, and the clean, empty suburban houses has fallen away, to be replaced by a critical consciousness, an increased understanding of the political and economic shifts which have sustained his class's affluence. That Hal Beers's career 'perfectly traced the arc of the Cold War aerospace industry' (14) is then a measure of his good fortune: he was always in the right place at the right time, whether as a beneficiary of the 'billowing economy' and 'updraft of national will' (12) that sustained his careers as a test pilot and then as an aeronautical engineer, or as the recipient of a generous early retirement package before brutal cuts were made to the aerospace workforce shortly after the Cold War's close. Beers's father also recognises that his long stint at Lockheed owed much to his being male and white. Ultimately, even his frustration with his role as an organisation man is recognised as another facet of his privilege: his malign behaviour in the home has the fortunate effect of warding his children off from joining an industry with bleak prospects. (Beers contrasts the career trajectories of those who had the simple misfortune to join the industry at a later point in time, often following a parent's lead, or those who faced discrimination on the basis of their race or gender.) On the one hand, then, Beers's account strenuously avoids the 'sentimental dispossession' of early narratives of the organisation man, such as Sloan Wilson's 1955 novel *The Man in the Grey Flannel Suit*, which denies the privilege of middle-class suburbanites by emphasising how much they suffer. On the other, *Blue Sky Dream* describes the same mechanism employed in these earlier stories, whereby suffering acts as a stimulus to social mobility.

However, Beers cannot help but return: his parents, after all, still live in the same (albeit modified and updated) suburban house. Their neighbourhood is a landscape that embodies both stasis and change. If the suburban veneer 'remains implacably pastel' (269), a more substantive transformation has taken place: 'To be white and middle class in this neighbourhood today means something very different than when I was growing up' claims Beers. What was once an optimistic 'frontier parish' is now an 'enclave of worried, tenuous affluence' (225–6). Beers notes how some things from the post-war years, however, remain unchanged. His mother, for instance, has 'kept her mystical imagination' deriving from her Catholic faith, which he understands to be 'her own way of defeating the banal, of living at once inside the moment and outside of it' (238). Beers expresses respect for his parents' capacity to critically comprehend their own suburban habitat and life courses. Indeed, ultimately he evinces a belief that the trajectories of the blue-sky suburbs, as conflicted and compromised as they are, have nonetheless providing his parents with a clearer sense of purpose that he himself feels. By contrast, having left for a West Coast city – a life choice he considers less courageous than his parents' pioneering move to a sketchy suburbia – Beers feels he possesses, 'merely, a nervous sense of the shifting movements of air' upon which he 'float[s]' (266). Thus Beers's memoir is lapsarian to the extent that it narrates a coming to knowledge. Yet it is also perceptibly nostalgic for the original, now dissipated, blue sky dream, that commitment to a shared vision of a singular trajectory.

Like most suburban memoirs, *Black Dog of Fate* and *Blue Sky Dream* attempt to tell shared stories, to mediate between individual and collective experiences of particular places across time. Of course, all memoir does this to a certain degree. Every life involves, and is shaped by, networks of relations with other people and places; any narrative of an individual life will likely make little sense if it fails to account for some of these interactions. Suburban memoir, however, is defined by place and time, in terms of both setting and narrative trajectory. *Black Dog of Fate*, principally concerned with the lasting effects of a historical trauma, is expressly presented as a 'memoir across generations'. (Though in fact all suburban memoirs are liable to be trans-generational, even if they describe only the experiences of the author and his or her parents.) In order to tell its shared story, *Blue Sky Dream* employs, in a self-conscious fashion, a different mode: autoethnography. In the memoir's prologue Beers purports to analyse an arrangement of early family photographs hanging in the hallway of his suburban home. With its 'naive, even primitive' style of expression, the collection of 'pictographs' constitutes 'a family totem typical of our tribe' (1). Beers goes on to use the latter term, which is frequently prefixed by the first-person-plural possessive pronoun, throughout the book to describe the inhabitants of the aerospace suburbs. Beers's use of lexis associated with classical anthropology – 'primitive', 'tribe', 'totem' – is jarring: this is a people who have put their trust in science. Beers evidently considers the conceit an appropriate defamiliarising strategy. After all, white, middle-class cultures are so rarely the subjects of anthro-pological scrutiny: Beers's performance as ethnographer helps to elucidate the contradictions and denials that characterised this class, particularly those which relate to its own privilege and histor-ical contingency. For instance, while his tribe 'believed themselves without myth', their habits of self-presentation were laden with a 'dense mythology' (1) that Beers presumes to explicate; further, even though they felt themselves to be living the inevitable future, Beers seeks to demonstrate that his blue-sky tribe was an anomaly, 'a strange and aberrant moment that is now receding into history' (14). The autoethnographic mode is appropriate also because it draws attention to the affective consequences of generational succession. Beers once belonged to the blue-sky tribe; indeed, as a child he represented its continuation. Now, though, he feels distanced from it, its 'receding into history' is felt as loss. If autoethnography posits the self as necessarily part of, or as emerging out of a collectivity, Beers communicates how the passing of this social milieu is liable to leave a subject suspended or, as he puts it, 'float[ing]'.[25]

The text examined over the concluding section of this chapter, D. J. Waldie's *Holy Land: A Suburban Memoir* (1996), leans towards yet another mode to tell its shared story: prosopography. This term refers to that kind of historical project which takes as its focus the patterns of behaviour, habits and interactions of a distinct group of people defined by geography, period and/or social role. Prosopography is motivated partly by the historian's wariness about drawing conclusions solely from the narrative accounts of important or otherwise eloquent individuals. Indeed, prosopographers are 'not interested in the unique but the average'; they examine the common characteristics of a narrowly defined group by means of a collective study of the lives of its members, the sorts of everyday experience for which there is usually a scarcity of historical evidence.[26] To be clear, Waldie's memoir is not in fact a work of prosopography, and certainly not in the strict sense that most historians would understand the term. It does not, for example, draw on a sufficiently large and therefore representative sample of cases. (However, in his role as an officer for the suburban municipality in which he has lived all his life, dozens of local residents write to him and discuss their lives in a seemingly generic fashion. He also repeatedly references official opinion surveys. Thus Waldie has at his disposal a wealth of biographical material about his city.) Neither are Waldie's subjects selected in the disinterested way that is proper to prosopography, nor does the memoir (unsurprisingly enough) treat biographical material as so much data to be analysed with the tools of the statistician. Nevertheless, Waldie shares – and his memoir is shaped by – the same motivations as prosopography:

the desire to register and evaluate patterns across ordinary lives, and to consider how these patterns relate to broader historical processes. Additionally, Waldie resists letting his own biography speak for the suburb; the memoir is characterised by a continual turning away from the details of his own life – which he describes at different moments in the first, second and third person – to the habits and stories of his fellow residents. But as I explore in the next section, Waldie's work evinces some discomfort with locating meaning within such patterns. After all, abstraction has frequently been mobilised in order to deny the suburbs' habitability. Waldie's suburban memoir is marked by ambivalence toward pattern, which is shown to have considerable potential to both obscure and elucidate ordinary experience.

'Abstract and Ordinary': Life on the Grid in D. J. Waldie's *Holy Land: A Suburban Memoir*

These four aerial photographs (Figures 3.1 to 3.4) were taken in 1950 by William A. Garnett, who had been assigned to document the construction of Lakewood, the suburban tract of 17,500 houses situated on former farmland twenty-three miles south-east of downtown Los Angeles. Along with Levittown, New York and Park Forest, Illinois, Lakewood, California was one of the United States' first planned communities of the post-war era. But if this suburban city now seems fairly unremarkable, Garnett's widely published and exhibited photographs continue to influence the way American suburbs are conceived.[27] In *Holy Land*, Waldie, a lifelong resident and long-time chronicler of Lakewood, says the following of Garnett's work:

> The black-and-white photographs show immense abstractions on ground the color of the full moon. [. . .]
> The photographs celebrate house frames precise as cells in a hive and stucco walls fragile as an unearthed bone.
> Seen from above, the grid is beautiful and terrible. (5)

In a recent essay on Garnett's work, Waldie suggests that the abstractions of aerial photography were a necessary response to

Figure 3.1 'Grading, Lakewood, California', 1950. Photograph by William A. Garnett. Copyright: © William A. Garnett Estate

Figure 3.2 'Foundations and Slabs, Lakewood, California', 1950. Photograph by William A. Garnett. Copyright: © William A. Garnett Estate

Figure 3.3 'Framing, Lakewood, California', 1950. Photograph by William A. Garnett. Copyright: © William A. Garnett Estate

Figure 3.4 'Finished Housing, Lakewood, California', 1950. Photograph by William A. Garnett. Copyright: © William A. Garnett Estate

the 'immensity of the landscape, its relative sameness and its rapid commodification'.[28] Yet, the process of recording the subdivision of the landscape for human habitation entirely worked against producing a humanised portrait of Lakewood. These habitats may have been designed for living, but Garnett's photographs present an eerie necropolis, deathly in its regimentation.

Garnett did not approve of what he had been commercially hired to illustrate, commenting: 'Seventeen thousand houses with five floor plans, and they all looked alike, and there was not a tree in sight when they got through.'[29] Certain aesthetic decisions articulate his derision; indeed, his grand panoramas are actually always selective and partial. Waldie remarks that many of Garnett's Lakewood photographs depended 'for their effect on what they lacked: an internal scale of reference, the organizing line of the horizon, identifiable human figures'. Further, 'it's always late afternoon in those photographs. The sunset is pouring tarry shadows across the barren backyards of not-yet-homes. Their frail stucco walls are blisteringly white in contrast.' In fact, Garnett reproduces what was already by this time a cliché of aerial photography: 'pattern as substitute for narrative'.[30] It is a pattern – geometric forms repeating without apparent limit – which has been repeated endlessly. Typically, these iterations are meant to inspire contempt or dread. In *The City in History* (1961), Lewis Mumford appears to borrow from Garnett's barren and repetitive forms for his withering portrait of the new suburbia, which he barrages as 'a multitude of uniform, unidentifiable houses, lined up inflexibly, at uniform distances, on uniform roads, in a treeless communal waste'.[31] In the same decade Garnett's photographs 'merged with contemporary newsreel footage of atomic bomb test buildings in the equally featureless Nevada desert' and, following the publication of titles such as Peter Blake's *God's Own Junkyard: The Planned Deterioration of America's Landscape* (1964), became symbols of environmental devastation. In the 1980s and 90s the same handful of images informed a new battery ranged against the suburbs – for example, Mike Davis's attack on the paranoid corporatised citadels of suburban Los Angeles in *City of Quartz* (1990) and the New Urbanists' excoriation of sprawl, of which Howard Kunstler's claim that the suburbs are a place 'where evil dwells' is possibly the most startling.[32] Waldie contends that 'the "myth of suburbia" w[as] founded, in part, on the continuing shock of seeing that long-ago Lakewood from the air'. He further muses: 'I sometimes think the suburbs became the thing labeled "suburbia" because of altitude and broken hearts.'[33]

Evidently, one thing that is central to Waldie's project is to counter this persistent and pernicious 'myth of suburbia' with a more sensitive appraisal of the history of Lakewood. He notes for instance that the fixed image of the suburbs as 'an ominously vacant landscape' was already out of date when the photos were first published, by which time Lakewood was 'crowded with 90,000 citizens, a majority of them children under the age of 15'.[34] In *Holy Land*, Waldie also gives account of Lakewood's improbably speedy incorporation, as well as the effects of planning and ordinances on the environment – including, pointedly, the planting of trees out-side of every house. He also alludes to subsequent social changes, for instance, the maturation and departure of the baby-boom gen-eration, and the Hispanicisation of Lakewood. He devotes even more time to situating the suburb's development within wider histories, including the early colonisation of and later waves of migration to Southern California, the evolution of urban planning and management, and even the hydrology of the Los Angeles basin.

But Waldie is not only attuned to these broader histories and transformations; he also insistently narrates events, lives and land-scapes at ground level and at walking pace. *Holy Land*'s particular emphasis on the rhythms and intimacies of the suburban everyday partly reflects Waldie's embodied experience. A lifelong eye condi-tion has meant Waldie has never been able to drive; he has always walked to work from the same tract house in which he grew up. For sure, *Holy Land*'s attentiveness to ordinary experience acts as a riposte to Garnett's malign influence; in its introduction, Waldie quips, 'you can't see the intersection of character and place at 500 feet' (vi). But alongside the rather obvious irony that Waldie is effec-tively claiming to have superior vision to the aerial photographer, the statement's pithiness belies an ambivalence that is typical of Waldie's writing. While Waldie accuses Garnett of having depicted only lifeless patterns, lattices of intersecting streets and empty houses, he nevertheless reiterates the same structures emphasised by the photographer. While Garnett fails to witness character and place, Waldie still sees intersections. Thus *Holy Land* is a narrative that does not simply contest ingrained prejudices about the suburbs but additionally attempts to explicate, and mediate between, the polarities of spatialised experience – the structural and the personal, the historical and the everyday, the static and the shifting – without necessarily seeking some final resolution between them.

Waldie's critique of the manner in which aeriality has shaped the suburban imaginary in the US is highly reminiscent of Michel de Certeau's account, in *The Practice of Everyday Life*, of looking out over Manhattan from the 110th floor of the World Trade Center. Such a viewpoint, asserts de Certeau, allows one to feel removed from the ordinary confusion of the city's streets and their claim on one's body. It is a position which enables the viewer to take possession of the city, 'to be a solar Eye, looking down like a god'.[35] This is the totalising perspective of city planners and administrators, which renders the city both legible and immobile. The planner's scopic drive entails a repudiation of embodiment and mortality, a desire to be removed from and to eliminate the 'intertwining daily behaviors' down below. Indeed, these 'geometrical', 'panoptic [. . .] constructions' are – like Garnett's chiaroscuro patternings – life-denying visions: 'the voyeur-god created by these fictions [. . .] knows only cadavers'.[36] Instead de Certeau wishes to register the 'blind mobilit[ies]' of urban practice: the myriad, dispersed journeys of pedestrians whose shortcuts and detours alter and fragment the authorised meanings and uses of the city, and whose personal nominations of places generate a 'foggy geography' of poetic and mythic associations that flouts the 'rational transparency' of regulatory regimes.[37] These private, everyday practices produce hidden histories that render the city habitable; in doing so they 'invert the schema of the *Panopticon*'.[38] De Certeau's insistent association between pedestrian spatial practices and opacity, mobility and narrative, as opposed to the 'perspective vision and prospective vision' of the planned city, would seem to correspond closely to *Holy Land*. Waldie counters Garnett's totalising depictions of an inert suburb with a series of fragments which communicate diverse personal stories and the author's own ambulatory experiences across Lakewood. Neil Campbell, who has written extensively and eloquently about Waldie's work, concurs, though he draws on a similar distinction made by another theorist: 'George Bataille, although an unlikely ally of Waldie, famously referred to this viewpoint from above as eagle-like and 'Icarian' – related to Icarus – in contrast with 'the "old mole"' working down below 'in the bowels of the earth [. . .] where bodies rot as opposed to [. . .] the purity of lofty space' (153).[39] Campbell goes on to identify Waldie – who, once again, has poor eyesight and walks everywhere – as the 'lowly old mole'; his intimate experience of his surroundings is tactile, 'impure' and 'hybrid'. Campbell argues that it is through a panoply of 'organic, earthy, "breathing" images' that Waldie creates his 'phenomenological, affective landscape vision of suburbia'.[40]

And yet, Waldie does not repudiate entirely the abstractions of Garnett's aerial photography. Indeed, if Waldie's rendering of Lakewood can rightly be said to be impure and hybrid it is because *Holy Land* combines two seemingly contradictory ways of appraising a landscape: one detached, static and wholly visual, the other situated, dynamic and more fully sensual. Waldie's re-inscription of abstraction constitutes a reverse discourse, that is, a repurposing rather than a rejection of the language and imagery that defines and denigrates the landscape of suburbia. Such redirection enables a richer and more nuanced account of Lakewood that further emphasises the suburb's multiple connections with other places, both past and present, with which it shares its highly patterned form. But it is also a tactic which bequeaths Lakewood a certain indeterminacy, which may further help to resist the persistent prejudices of the Icarian perspective. This indetermination is produced by the paradoxical operation of situating abstraction. On the one hand, historicising Lakewood's abstract form connects it to innumerable accounts of social endeavour. Some of these histories are haunting, or perhaps better put, contaminating, since their residue is less spectral than corporeal: Icarus may see only cadavers, but they are rising from the soil. On the other hand, Waldie shows how the abstract patterning of the landscape has shaped his own perspective and informs his understanding of his environment's history. Indeed, some of Waldie's early memories of Lakewood blur with Garnett's photography. About this apparent cross-contamination of imagery Waldie is ambivalent. He seems to accept the troubling possibility that the Icarian perspective has conditioned even his own childhood recollections, perhaps because the converse – that Garnett's vision has been personalised, domesticated – is equally likely. As I will go on to show, Waldie's memoir is a continually self-reflexive – indeed, self-implicating – narrative: the situating of abstraction so often involves a reciprocal situating of self, a positioning that is both mutually constitutive and disruptive. This dynamic is one of the most important characteristics of Waldie's suburban memoir, though it is by no means unique. Jan Campbell and Janet Harbord argue that the most important aspect of the rise of autobiography in academic writing is how it 'forces a dialogue' between the traditionally opposed terms of theory/experience, ontology/epistemology, global/local. It is an interaction that has the potential to disrupt and transform understandings of both elements of these binaries, though Campbell and Harbord acknowledge that 'such exchanges are rarely conducted in the spirit of mutuality'; rather, they are played out within 'the struggle for status, authority, discernment'.[41] In articulating the hostilities between visionaries (Garnett) and denizens (Waldie) of the suburbs, *Holy Land*'s imbricated account of abstraction and experience is situated firmly within such struggles.

Waldie arguably makes a similar case to de Certeau, who describes how the 'rich indetermination' of place names articulates a 'poetic geography' that overlays the geography of literal, permitted meanings.[42] But de Certeau rather privileges private perceptions and local understandings of place, presuming that city dwellers never also harness more expansive perspectives or abstract visions. While both Waldie and de Certeau insist that the 'blind mobilities' of urban and suburban living are predicated on broader structures, a key difference between their outlooks has to do with their treatment of those structures. De Certeau imagines that abstract urban forms rarely function as intended at a local level: everywhere they are 'punched and torn apart'. The 'imposed order' is always only a 'sieve order'; urban practice inevitably invests in the fabric of the city a dynamic polysemy.[43] Rather than imagining ruptures and the creation of habitable interstices in the abstract forms conceived by the planners of Lakewood, Waldie leaves intact the structures he aims to critique. The ambivalence of these structures, for Waldie, is what produces a poetic geography; ambivalence is a sign of their very habitability, and also their interconnectedness with other places and histories.

The influence of Lakewood's abstract form on Waldie's narrative is immediately apparent. *Holy Land* certainly appears as patterned as Garnett's photographs. The text is organised into 316 short numbered sections; just like the suburban landscape of Lakewood, then, *Holy Land* is a tract that has been subdivided. But if the text resembles a site, the reverse is also true. Early on in the memoir Waldie refers to Lakewood's construction site with a term – 'interleavings' (3) – that invokes textuality (as well as a text's materiality). It is, further, an expression suggestive of the imbricatedness of lives, histories and habitats. Noticeably, however, the text's carefully arranged units are of unequal length. The implication would appear to be that while suburbs may be highly ordered, suburban lives are not entirely uniform. On closer reading though, what Waldie's memoir demonstrates is that these lives *are* largely uniform – or, at least, similarly circumscribed – but that this fact alone is unrevealing. In section 172, Waldie declares:

> The critics of suburbs say that you and I live narrow lives.
> I agree. My life is narrow.
> From one perspective or another, all our lives are narrow.
> Only when lives are placed side by side do they seem larger. (94)

Informed principally by Garnett's vast panoramas, critics of suburbs fail to see the bigger picture.

Throughout *Holy Land*, Waldie intersperses personal memories with accounts of other Lakewood residents. Their anonymisation would seem to perpetuate abstraction, a distancing from lived experience. But the stories of Mrs A, Mr H, Mr L and others, together constitute something akin to a prosopography of Lakewood, a study of interactions and shared experiences. Waldie focuses especially on the compulsive behaviour of many of these individuals and the consequences of their behaviour for others – behaviour that is at once repetitious and a 'defection from predictability' (20). Noticeably, Waldie's account is self-implicating: 'There is a neurological disorder', he notes, 'which compels its sufferers to write' (18). Waldie's writing thus not only describes but also embodies the negotiation of compulsion. The story of Mr H, for instance, is an account of failure, of the impossibility of negotiating compulsion in purely legalistic terms. Mr H hoards tons of dead machinery in his yard. The city responds by following procedures: conferences, warnings, deadlines to extensions; all sidesteps to confrontation. After more than ten years, the city's procedures at last exhausted, Mr H is jailed; his bank forecloses his mortgage, and 'his house is taken from him' (24). Evidently, 'The city with its codes cannot make Mr. H a good citizen' (20). Usually, though, compulsion is negotiated more humanely, through 'honest hypocrisy' (20), or with tenderness. Waldie shows that this latter quality, along with a capacity for reflexivity and responsiveness, is vital equipment for any historian of the ordinary. Waldie's seemingly compulsive narrative returns again and again to the same stories, the same people, the same places. But each return is informed by new knowledge, and each interaction stimulates new associations. Waldie's history of Lakewood is finely attuned to the patterning of ordinary lives; repetition is the process which drives the accretion of this history of the everyday.[44]

The principal abstraction which informs *Holy Land*, however, is the grid. From the air the grid appears 'beautiful and terrible'; on the ground it is experienced in equally ambivalent ways. It is 'a compass of possibilities' (4), providing its residents both orientation and infinite opportunity. This is a capacity Waldie elsewhere suggests can breed anxiety: if you can be anywhere, you are really nowhere. But Waldie also concedes that 'the grid limited our choices, exactly as the urban planners said it would'. He insists, however, 'the limits weren't paralysing. The design of the suburb compelled a conviviality that people got used to and made into a substitute for choices, including not choosing at all. There are an indefinite number of beginnings and endings on the grid, but you are always somewhere' (116). Thus, again, abstraction does not preclude situatedness. Further, Waldie is concerned to show how abstractions give shape to lives, and how the form of the grid is only meaningful in so far as it is embedded in established human relationships and results in social encounter. It is perhaps telling, then, that the more abstract and apparently complete renderings of Lakewood's grid are often less than useful as guides. The blueprint map produced by the city's planning department, for instance, is so large as to be awkward to use. It is highly detailed, showing every house lot in the city: 'The rows of lots look like the illustration of a fold of skin in a high school biology book' (125). There is, however, something uncanny in this comparison. On the one hand, reassuringly, the map's seemingly organic forms suggest that, yet again, there is an inevitable coalescence between ordinary human life and abstract renderings of its situation. On the other, the invocation of human skin cells brings to mind the inhumanness of Garnett's aerial photographs, which Waldie says are 'like cells in a hive', and which the Getty Museum, which acquired six of Garnett's photographs in 2004, compared to 'views through a microscope'.[45] Further, the scientific reference also reminds that the very fabric of human being is, in essence, a structure. Thus the abstract can always be humanised; equally, the human can always be rendered abstract. Such indeterminacy seems a necessary consequence of rejecting prescriptive accounts of Waldie's own environment. Yet it also recognises that the persistent influence of the God's-eye-view of outsiders has shaped his own perspective.

The grid's capacity for infinite extension – rendered so fearful in Garnett's photographs – is invoked repeatedly by Waldie to connect Lakewood outwards to other geographies and histories. In so doing, Waldie corresponds with contributors to the 'New Suburban History', who have demanded more sophisticated, imbricated accounts of the development of cities and their suburbs than those offered by classic suburban histories, 'whose inward focus', Kevin Kruse and Thomas Sugrue argue, 'often obscures the larger social, political and economic process that reshaped modern America'.[46] Equally, we might situate Waldie, as Neil Campbell does, within the practice of 'Critical Regionalism'. This is a cultural strategy which, according to the architectural historian Kenneth Frampton, seeks to mediate, deconstruct and critique 'the impact of universal civilization with elements derived indirectly from the peculiarities of a particular place'.[47] According to Campbell, both Frampton and Waldie present 'a radical vision of "critical regional" space as complex, layered, and multiple, a palimpsest comprising past, present and future that opposes any effort to reduce or limit its capacity through narrow definition or "rootedness"'.[48] I have already begun to show how Waldie produces Lakewood as 'complex, layered and multiple' through its structure and dispersed narrative focus; Campbell usefully describes Waldie's suburban memoir as a 'distributed biography'.[49]

For Waldie, the grid is once again never purely an abstract, universal form and thereby placeless: it is always geographically situated; further, it possesses a complex history which has been shaped by relationships of power. For millennia settlements have been built on a grid in recognition of the authority of a distant centre of power; through its very form the new colonial city is articulated as an extension of the metropolis.[50] Lakewood, though, is defined not by one but by two urban centres, which competed for control of the land and, in particular, for the water reserves beneath the land on which the suburb was built. This historic rivalry explains why Lakewood's streets count back to Los Angeles while its house numbers progress from Long Beach. Further, those two cities are situated on different grids: unlike Long Beach, whose grid aligns with the cardinal points, as is typical in the American West, the centre of Los Angeles is oriented on a northwest-southeast axis, a consequence of the city's origins as a Spanish settlement. Waldie delights in showing that Los Angeles was once as wholly abstract as Lakewood had been; its late-eighteenth-century *diseño* depicts 'a city where winds blow only from the north, and where the sun each day might light the sides of a small square house equally' (117). Waldie also traces genealogies of the grid through various authorities. Tellingly, though, his different accounts produce competing origins: one finds a source in the work of the Roman architect Vitruvius; elsewhere, Waldie declares, the 'grid came from God' (21). The history of grid is as complex as it is indeterminate.

Waldie's expansive vision of the grid, which 'opens outwards without limits' (118), also reaches into the interior spaces of the modest houses of Lakewood. He speaks for instance of the interior doors of his family home whose near-square panels resemble the layout of the surrounding streets. The doors, like the suburb, are 'abstract and ordinary' (25). Mass-produced and regularly patterned, these objects are also inescapably material, with the capacity to shape ordinary life. Waldie dwells on the material qualities of his bathroom door: its age and solidity, and the workings of its lock (25).[51] In the same section he attends to the body of his father, who dies of a heart attack trapped behind the same door. Yet, like the door, his father's death never entirely loses its sense of being abstract either – whether measured by the dimensions of the rooms in which Waldie and his father lived together, and in which his father dies, or as suggested by Waldie's journey with his father's body to the hospital, which involves a series of right-angled turns across the grid of Lakewood. The abstract and ordinary are qualities shared not only by spaces and objects but by the bodies and lives shaped by them.

Equally abstract and ordinary is Waldie's Catholic faith, which informs his vision of Lakewood as 'holy land'. If the grid's every intersection invokes in abstract the crucifix, the suburb's modest material circumstances require humility. Indeed, Waldie declares that he believes 'that each of us is crucified', and that 'his own crucifixion is the humiliation of living the life he has made for himself' (3). Carissa Turner Smith contends that central to Waldie's spiritual geography of suburbia is an acceptance of the limitations of place, an understanding that habitation entails a life of habit; reciprocally, 'the habits of faith are a burden that yet provides shelter'.[52] Waldie is emphatic about how his sense of his very being is predicated on his habitat's form and the habitual behaviour it precipitates: with the book's opening line he declares 'he thought he was becoming his habits, or – even more – he thought he was becoming the grid he knew' (1). In imagining himself crucified by the grid, Waldie expresses the sacrifices involved in accepting the limitations of his locality, but equally, how such an intimate relationship with place may enable, even constitute, a connection with the divine.

It is important, though, to recognise Waldie's sense of his own agency; if his becoming his own habits suggests automatism, he also speaks of 'the life he has made for himself'. 'The life [. . .] made' is certainly suggestive of Lakewood's systematised manufacture. But while acknowledging the involvement of process, Waldie insists that his faith is not merely a product of environment; it is a decision. His faith may be constituted by a way of life shaped by habitat, but it is a life chosen. Waldie makes the much the same case about his father's faith, which he compares to the design and mass-production processes involved in the construction of Lakewood's tract houses. He declares for instance that his father's kindness did not flow forth from him, like an innate passion, but was something acquired through much 'spiritual calculation, as a product might come from a conveyer belt'. Waldie promptly adds, however, 'you are mistaken if you consider this a criticism, either of my father or of the houses' (7); that they are both manufactured belies a complexity of process and of deliberation. Moreover, Waldie recounts in detail the collective endeavour of Lakewood's fabrication. He implies, therefore, that his father's faith was facilitated by a greater social framework. Turner Smith is right, I think, to suggest that Waldie conceives of his father as a classic post-war organisation man, whom William H. Whyte decried as having traded an independent mind for a 'belief in "belongingness"'.[53] The curriculum vitae of Waldie's father certainly indicates an institutionalised life as he moved seamlessly from church to military to corporation (96–7). But Waldie's portrait is a more sympathetic, or at the very least, more balanced view than Whyte's, as he insists on his father's relative autonomy. Waldie declares that his father's life expressed that 'it was necessary to choose, but only once', because 'every choice limited God's choices, and cut you off from other graces' (61). If this summary seems mildly sardonic, Waldie's appreciation of his father's legacy certainly cuts across Whyte's characterisation of the organisation man as someone who has 'left home, spiritually as well as physically, to take the vows of organisation life'.[54] Turner Smith suggests that for Waldie, choosing to live in his father's home 'is one of the elements of his father's faith that he has retained'.[55] For both Waldie and his father, then, the home provides the crucial locus for a spiritual life.

In *Holy Land* Waldie declares, baldly, that 'sometimes I think the only real forces here are circumstance and grace' (138). If he considers the contingent and the divine to be discrete forces, in an abstract sense, he regularly *feels* them to be entwined. Indeed, Waldie has expressed that his 'sense of place' 'enmeshes the ghostly and the definite [...] like the Word made flesh'. It is precisely this coming together, this dialogue between all that is spiritual and material, that Waldie 'understand[s] to be prayer'.[56] Indeed, one way of interpreting *Holy Land*, with its many short, numbered sections, is as a book of prayer. After all, Waldie admits how each of the stories he tells seems to him insignificant, until 'at Mass on Sunday, I remember them as prayers' (111). However, he shows how Lakewood as a divine landscape is emphatically not merely a private vision, but one with historical and social dimensions. Waldie declares that it was precisely the grid that enabled what was once worthless land to 'be redeemed'. Thus the land's holiness is not primordial but entirely predicated on the suburb's structure. The final sections of the memoir depict the communal devotions of Good Friday services in Waldie's local church, which always culminate in the veneration of the cross. *Holy Land's* final lines, from one of the hymns sung, the *Pange Lingua*, address the cross itself: 'Sweet the wood / Sweet the nails / Sweet the weight you bear' (179). It is an invocation of materiality that recalls Waldie's devoted attention earlier in the memoir to the materials and manufacture of the frame houses of Lakewood. The suburb's form and fabric is then understood to be sufficient to support an individual's faith, and a faithful community.

Despite the memoir's title and its conclusion in Catholic ceremony, I do not think that Waldie means for the grid's significance to be reducible to a Christian vision. Once again, Waldie suggests that the Word of God provides the grid one possible aetiology among many. On the other hand there are certain things the grid – 'a plan above the earth' (4) – fails even to touch. For instance, the last quarter of the memoir is much concerned with the geology of Southern California, with a particular focus on water management; this venturing underground might well be described as a 'deep history' of the region. But one of the most resonant sequences in the book is the one that attends to the concentration camps of Nazi Germany. If the grid may be said to have its origins in Roman civilisation, or in a Christian deity, its ultimate realisation is to be found in modernity. Says Waldie, whenever 'places to live must be built quickly, cheaply, and profitably, they are built on a grid of right angles' (99). The neat rectangles of the barracks for political prisoners at Auschwitz, and the wooden sheds at the nearby Birkenau camp built for the extermination of Jews, were built on a grid. The parallels with Lakewood are numerous and discomforting. Waldie notes that 'Birkenau means "Birch Wood"' (99), and that the camp was built on what had been farmland. The planners of the camp and his home town alike were preoccupied with population densities. There were similar oversights in the design: for instance, regarding the burial, or disposal, of bodies. No provision for any cemetery was made in Lakewood: to this day the dead are buried out of town (135). Meanwhile, 'when spring thawed the waterlogged ground of Birkenau, frozen corpses rose to the surface' (135).

Birkenau, Lakewood's monstrous double, is only mentioned in two consecutive sections out of 316, but it haunts Waldie's text. Patterns repeat: the orientation of sleeping prisoners to the cardinal points in the Birkenau sheds is matched by members of Waldie's family slumbering in their Lakewood bungalow, and by his dead parents, whose graves face east, directly towards Lakewood. These echoes may appear to risk confirming Garnett's vision of the inert, unliving suburb, which would leave Campbell's reading of Waldie's *Holy Land* as a 'critical region' seeming somewhat optimistic. But Birkenau is not the only memory which haunts the suburb: indeed, Waldie shows that if Lakewood is anything, it is an assemblage of visions of the ordinary and the abstract, the one always haunting the other. As de Certeau argues, such present absences are what make somewhere a place; indeed, 'haunted places are the only ones people can live in'. De Certeau, however, is referring to personal memories about places, those 'enigmatic', 'inward-turning histories, pasts which others are not allowed to read'.[57] Waldie, though, demonstrates that private memories of space are always already shaped by panoptic visions, which in turn can be modified and repurposed by personal imaginaries.

A most telling instance of this interplay comes in one of the relatively few scenes from Waldie's childhood. Waldie remembers making 'cities' with a friend in the dry soil of his backyard. His laying out of 'roads, parking lots and rows of roofless houses with pale dirt walls' (131) inevitably brings to mind the construction of Lakewood; their uncovering of a bone, 'half the smooth jaw of a cat' (131), recycles the same 'beautiful and terrible' imagery of the Garnett photographs. Of course, it could equally be said that it is this childhood memory which informs Waldie's reading of Garnett. So, Waldie's repetitions, as well as being accretive, as I have suggested, are also indeterminate, a quality that disrupts Garnett's deadly repetitions, so dependent on 'the bombadier's appraising exactness'.[58] But even if one accepts that the panoptic may be to an extent domesticated, personalised, it is essential to see that Waldie is concerned not purely with the legacy of Garnett, with this binary of the private and the panoptic. His boyhood games in the soil communicate with numerous other stories, both collective and individual. The games are said to always end in the same way: the cities are slowly flooded with water from a garden hose until the mud walls of their houses melt. This resonates with anxieties about the city's vulnerability to the liquefaction of the soil in the event of an earthquake, or perhaps concerns about the influx of a saline plume from the Pacific Ocean following the overdraught of the Los Angeles basin's aquifers, or for that matter the death in 1951 of a boy who was buried by the wet sand he was playing in on the building site of one of Lakewood's subdivisions. Just as the building of Lakewood involved an 'interleaving of houses and fields' (3), Waldie's suburban memoir is a 'complex, layered and multiple' construction. Such complexity is necessary to adequately account for the ways any suburb's material circumstances and discursive reality interact with private and shared memories and experience, and equally, the suburb's situation within wider regional and national histories.

CHAPTER 4

Houses, Comics, Fish: Graphic Narrative Ecologies of the Suburban Home

In *The Production of Space* (1974), Henri Lefebvre invites his readers to 'consider a house':

> The house has six storeys and an air of stability about it. One might almost see it as the epitome of immovability, with its concrete and its stark, cold and rigid outlines. (Built around 1950: no metal or plate glass yet.) Now, a critical analysis would doubtless destroy the appearance of solidity of this house, stripping it, as it were, of its concrete slabs and its thin non-load-bearing walls, which are really glorified screens, and uncovering a very different picture. In the light of this imaginary analysis, our house would emerge as permeated from every direction by streams of energy which run in and out of it by every imaginable route: water, gas, electricity, telephone lines, radio and television signals, and so on. Its image of immobility would then be replaced by an image of a complex of mobilities, a nexus of in and out conduits.[1]

Lefebvre's 'critical analysis' is instructive, for it helps defamiliarise this most ubiquitous and unassuming of sites. His account vividly demonstrates that domestic space is in fact not as solid and inert as it so often seems. Rather, houses are complexes of forces and flows, and are connected to the wider world in myriad ways. Crucially, dispelling the illusion of a house's discreteness and immobility helps to combat the widespread and profoundly ideological conceptualisation of space as a neutral container whose only purpose is to receive and maintain whatever has been placed within it. (Such a view, of course, makes impossible an understanding of space as socially produced, and works against an appreciation of the ways spatial forms engender social relations.) On the other hand, Lefebvre acknowledges that the mode of analysis he has exemplified risks substituting a place's practical character with a fetishised abstraction in which 'users' cannot recognise themselves, and against which it is impossible to 'conceive of adopting a critical stance'.[2] Indeed, Lefebvre contends that most forms of representation, and visual modes in particular, trade in the same kinds of abstraction, which entail the detachment of 'pure form from its impure content – from lived time, everyday time'.[3] But as my discussion of Waldie's memoir in the previous chapter demonstrated, suburban narrative is capable of examining in a nuanced and self-conscious manner the imbrication of the abstract and the ordinary. In this chapter I examine a visual form, comics, which registers the complexity and ongoing production of domestic space while providing scope for self-recognition. By harnessing the formal properties of their chosen medium, many comics artists have managed to produce critical spatial analyses of suburban houses of the kind outlined by Lefebvre, without resorting to alienating technocratic abstraction. In fact, the examples of comics that I examine below are less likely to consider the suburban house as a purely abstract 'nexus of [. . .] conduits' than they are to conceive of it as being produced by a convergence of ongoing narratives. These comics describe not only historical and material processes, but also the materiality and temporality of everyday life.

Consider for instance Heide Solbrig's ongoing transmedia graphic memoir, *Dandelion King: Love and Loss Waiting in the Gas Line*, whose first two chapters were published in one volume in 2015. In the second chapter, Solbrig meditates upon her grandparents' sprawling bungalow in Whittier, California, where she spent three years of her early childhood at the beginning of the 1970s. Solbrig supplies her readers with several perspectives of the house. One is a detailed plan view, which reveals each room and its furnishings, and the surrounding yard space. But it seems that the plan on its own fails to get the measure of the place, for Solbrig comments that her grandparents' house was in fact 'more of a complex; a million small places, cultivated and overgrown'.[4] She then proceeds to depict a series of these interior and exterior spaces in a grid of small numbered panels, and provides corresponding micro-stories on the facing page (Figure 4.1). Then, over the page, the house is reconstituted in a two-point perspective sketch populated by members of Solbrig's extended family and a number of visitors. This scene is positioned above, and appears to nest within, a lengthy textual account of her grandparents' house and the wider social environment of Whittier (Figure 4.2). Indeed, Solbrig seems keen to situate her experience of her grandparents' 'suburban homestead' (35) within broader social developments, for instance, the dissemination of West Coast alternative lifestyles and the resurgence of Christian conservative politics in Southern California. Picking up the horticultural theme that runs throughout *Dandelion King* – her father was a plant population geneticist of some renown – Solbrig drolly adds that out of 'Whittier's jumbled mix of utopian aesthetics and religious backlash grew some troubled varietals' (36). In the following chapter, using another motif derived from botanical science, Solbrig further expands her historical frame of reference when she describes California bungalows as being successful 'hybrids', 'born of colonialism and good factory jobs'.[5] Thus, *Dandelion King* sketches the complex narrative ecology of the suburban home, which is both parsed into highly localised and personal stories, and enmeshed within a series of larger ones.

Solbrig's graphic narrative is not concerned purely with the experience of growing up suburban. She refers to *Dandelion King* as a 'divorce biography' (rear cover), and is equally preoccupied with a number of developments taking place in the 1970s, including the rise of the encounter group, the effects of changes to mental health policy and, as the memoir's subtitle indicates, the decade's oil shocks. But my reason for beginning this chapter with an account of Solbrig's work is because it illustrates very well some of the techniques particular to graphic narrative for depicting and, especially, framing suburban space and history. *Dandelion King* is, however, no conventional comic book. Its wilfully uneven style veers between a scuffed, *faux naïf* manner and documentary-like precision. The organisation of the memoir's pages is similarly chaotic: irregularly framed panels, unframed scenes and large sections of text collide variously; reproductions of photographs, advertisements and legal

It was more of a complex, a million small places, cultivated but overgrown. My grandmother's saccharine smile was reserved for children and adults she found boring or slow while with me she read difficult stories and told family secrets.

I was the favorite child of my grandmother's eldest. I knew this was unfair and I basked in it. She saved me.

1. THE DODGE DART: (page 30) Our car. We drove our powder blue Dodge wagon across country. It carried us through the 1970s. Our new little family began with conversations while driving around in this car.

2. LIVING ROOM: Grown ups talked politics. Grandma taught all the kids to read in this room. No rough housing was allowed in here-- we still did it.

3. DINING ROOM: My grandpa sat on one end of the long formica table eating simple foods-- no sugar! When I bite strawberries-- they bite me back"

4. KITCHEN: The kids ate in the narrow yellow and white formica kitchen, away from the adults & politics. We ate lettuce sandwiches and Chinese noodles.

5. PLAYROOM: Grandma's classroom "See Jane Run" books in the toy chest, wooden blocks, legos & an old fashioned school desk. My brother slept here.

6. THE SEWING ROOM: My grandmother's sewing room held a closet with my mom's clothes, home-made polyester pants suits, slacks and dresses. I slept here next to piles of quilting squares and sewing patterns.

7. GRANDPA'S BATHROOM: The yellow bathroom. Here Grandpa treated various ailment, snorted vitamin C and salt water or rubbed on Epson salts.

8. THE GUEST ROOM: My mom's room when she was a child and when she returned. Otherwise, the nearby from the church stayed here, or when it was empty, grandchildren jumped on the bed.

9. GRANDMA'S ROOM: We would peek surreptitiously through the crack in the door, as my grandmother changed her expensive bathing suit. Small girls were allowed inside, but my grandmother hide her cushiony folds from most.

10. STUDY: Great grandfather White built the lockroom to work and live in after he was widowed and moved in with his daughter. It became Grandpa's study. Here, he wrote his final 1600 page treatise: "Ecstasy in Reaching Out."

11. HALLWAY: The hallway was a critical causeway in the house. We played there and many small plastic animals and soldiers were forced to dodge my grandpa's Epson covered calves & daily jogs up and down the royal blue berber.

12. THE SWIMMING POOL: We were not allowed to swim in the high sun. We waited impatiently until 4:00pm. Squeezing into one of dozens of hand-me-down suits in the closet. We burned easily and swam mightily around the pool.

13. TOMATOES: We were gardeners of farming descent. My mother had excelled at the victory garden during WWII--the quality and quantity of the tomatoes was no small concern, providing neighborhood AND church prestige.

14. THE PATIO: My grandma's garden was here. we, were paid in quarters and knickknacks to dig dirt and pull weeds. We played with ancient, rusty toy trucks and filled spring-loaded missile launchers with sharpened sticks and dull pencils.

15. BAMBOO: An invasive weed which also seemed romantic, linking our family history in China with many line outdoor games and props including ten-foot bamboo swords, dart guns and building supplies for tiny villages.

16. THE LAWN: The St. Augustine grass housed bees, clover and was good for playing Red Light, Green Light, Red Rover and Ring around the Rosie.

17. THE RUBBER TREE: Cut into a rubber tree, and it bleeds white sap which turns into rubbery substance which can be shaped. Rolling sap into balls we build tiny soldiers or animals in battle, with an afternoon's lifespan.

2. LIVING ROOM: 3. DINING ROOM: 4. KITCHEN: 5. PLAYROOM:

4. SEWING ROOM: 7. GRANDPA'S BATH: 8. GUEST ROOM: 9. GRANDMA'S ROOM:

10. THE STUDY: 11. THE HALLWAY: 12. SWIMMING POOL: 13. TOMATOES:

14. THE PATIO: 15. THE LAWN: 16. BAMBOO: 17. RUBBER TREE:

Figure 4.1 Heide Solbrig, *Dandelion King: Life and Love Waiting in the Gas Line*, 33–4

Whittier is a small, conservative city near the southeastern edge of Los Angeles county. Founded by Quakers, folks mostly eschewed West Coast alternative lifestyles. Despite this, the self-help movements of the early 1970s dovetailed nicely with cathartic and anti-establishment elements of a new evangelical movement in Southern California. For a time, it became difficult to distinguish between the hippies and the Jesus Freaks in the hinterlands of L.A. county-suburbs like Whittier, Bell Gardens, or La Mirada. At the time my mom returned home, Whittier was near the epicenter of a reawakening Christian conservative politics. Just as my mom, Roberta was hoping to join the counter-culture, she found herself back in a community with no fewer than three churches on every block when you drove into town. In addition to Quakers, Protestant escape artists of all stripes populated the small city. Methodists, Baptists, Seventh Day Adventists, Nazarenes, Jehovah's Witnesses and Mormons, Catholics, lived there too. The papists represented the class and race divide between Okie migrants & Mexican immigrants—at one time both worked the Orange Groves but now they were divided between owners and laborers.

My grandparents' suburban homestead was a way station for a lot of folks. The house on Floral drive thrived on church ladies armed with garden vegetables coming over for a dip in the pool. There were folks beholden to Joe or Frances for some past kindness, who came by to chat, others currently in need found temporary lodgings in their extra rooms. My grandpa mowed the St. Augustine grass with devotion, my cousins played neon light green lint, someone from the Credit Union on Pickering dropped by for a chat and to pick a few

35.

peaches.

It was no secret that my grandparents were FDR liberals, though, my grandpa once confessed to me in a conspiratorial tone that he had not voted for FDR in 1932. He had voted for socialist candidate Norman Thomas, not something he might have admitted openly in the pews of the Methodist church. However serene Floral Drive seemed to a small child there was a culture war happening in Whittier. The Unitarian church on Pickering was mostly attended by Whittier College students, hosting naked body painting, and stories of Jesus the revolutionary. Across town, folks listened to Billy Graham as he invigorated several generations with new kinds of resistance to the encroaching social revolutions of the 1960s.

The Kibbutzes along with various back-to-the-land movements were what inspired my mom. She fantasized about life on a commune, but she had little patience for the community of which we were already members, run by her politically liberal but socially conservative parents. Floral Drive was like most traditional societies: doubt and apostasy—the stock and trade of divorcees and scorned women as a class—were frowned upon.

Whittier's jumbled mix of utopian aesthetics and religious backlash grew some troubled varietals. Skipping ahead in that decade, when Christian sex-fiend and mass-murdering cult-leader Jim Jones, moved to Guyana, followers fell hard to a disillusioned utopia and the messianic figure's own paranoia. My grandmother was saddened to find out some young people from Whittier—Jesus dilettantes in their search for utopia than my mom—were caught up in that terrible configuration.

36.

Figure 4.2 Heide Solbrig, *Dandelion King: Life and Love Waiting in the Gas Line*, 35–6

judgements jostle for space with fantasy scenes and the domestic everyday. Solbrig is also currently developing animations and an interactive comic/film smartphone app to accompany the printed narrative; the project's website indicates how users will be able to project historic documentary footage through cutaways in fold-out sections of the graphic memoir. All this serves to highlight, once again, the embeddedness of suburban space and experience within multiple unfolding histories.[6] But Solbrig's eclecticism also underscores the requirement for a different kind of reading practice – one that is not wholly reliant on linear sequence – to facilitate comprehension of these interactions. Noticeably, the grid of sixteen panels that depict spaces within the Whittier house is the only part of the entire narrative that resembles the layout of a conventional comic strip. Of course, this composition does not function in the manner of most comics. The individual panels fail to produce meaning if they are read sequentially; instead, rather like webpage hyperlinks, they index other narratives. The suburban home is, in this way – and in a similar fashion to Lefebvre's projected analysis of an ordinary house built in the 1950s – shown to be a networked space. Furthermore, the apprehension of the intersecting personal and historical narratives that constitute it is predicated on the interruption of linear narrative modes.

These preoccupations and techniques are by no means unique to Solbrig's work. Indeed, in this chapter I will demonstrate that her approach to the framing of suburban and domestic space is shared by more established contemporary comics artists, namely Alison Bechdel, Richard McGuire and Chris Ware. But while, as I have suggested, Solbrig's multipartite narrative enables an appreciation of the complex genealogies of everyday spaces, the formal innovations of McGuire and Ware in particular are more closely attuned to matters of temporality, to the ways we experience, as it were, the time of place. In doing so these comics potentially help temper a Lefebvrian pessimism about the capacity of visual art to represent time and space without resorting to abstractions wholly divorced from everyday rhythms.[7] In the sections that follow, I consider how the disorientating effects generated by the work of McGuire and Ware oblige readers to reappraise their temporal understanding of suburban and domestic spaces.

It is, though, easy to overstate the originality of any contemporary comics artist. I want to preface my discussion of the work of McGuire and Ware by qualifying my claims about their innovativeness in two ways. The first has to do with the defining formal attributes of comics as well as the experience of reading them. The second relates to the wider transformations that have taken place within comics cultures over the last fifty years. In other words, I seek to contextualise McGuire's and Ware's apparent distinctiveness by, on the one hand, foregrounding the peculiar properties of comics generally and, on the other, indicating that their inventiveness has not simply come out of nowhere. Both qualifications, I will show, bear significantly upon any consideration of the representation of suburban environments in comics.

Time/Frames: Comics, Temporality and Periodisation

As many theorists of comics have observed, even the most conventional of comic strips are constituted by a set of spatio-temporal relationships that have the capacity to produce all kinds of ambivalence. A defining attribute of the comic strip is the manner in which units of time – present moments, typically – are apportioned units of space in the form of individual panels. A sense of narrative progression is normally produced when these temporal segments are 'read' in sequence. By no means is this the inevitable result of a seamless process, however. What Scott McCloud terms 'closure', the translation by the reader of a series of words and images into a meaningful sequence, relies on a set of learned competencies and, in the case of more complex or disjointed compositions, may only be achieved with considerable interpretive effort. Further, as McCloud observes, a peculiar quality of comics is that, even when one focuses on the present moment of an individual frame, prior and subsequent panels remain in view. Uniquely amongst narrative forms, the comic strip's past, present and future are simultaneously visible.[8] Consequently, even the most orderly, conventional layouts invite, or at least allow for, a disorderly manner of reading. As numerous formal analyses propose, the reader's engagement with the comic-book page is characterised by a tension between 'sequence and surface'; in the words of narratologist Gérard

Genette, 'a successive or diachronic reading' of comics often clashes with 'a kind of global or synchronic look'.[9] And then, as Hillary Chute comments, the manner in which comic strips are broken into fragments of time invites us 'to look and look again' at the detail of panels. Such recursivity has proven especially interesting to comics artists and theorists concerned with memory work and, in particular, the effects of trauma.[10] Thus, in even the most seemingly straightforward-looking comics, the spatial and temporal co-ordinates of narrative may interact in unpredictable yet also productive ways. Perhaps more than any other narrative form, then, comics are a potentially extremely useful platform for examining spaces whose temporal dimensions are ordinarily conceived in predictable and reductive ways.

Most of the book-length formal analyses published in the last three decades do not merely provide accounts of the way comics 'work'. As is clear from their subtitles – for example, *The Invisible Art, An Emerging Literature, Comics as Literature* – these studies advance arguments for the artistic and literary merits of (certain) comics.[11] Few though would have been written were it not for the recent cultural transformations that have helped foster the talents of McGuire and Ware. Indeed, the rapid expansion of comics scholarship (in the English-speaking world at least) follows in the wake of two discrete though related periods of remarkable innovation and diversification: the underground comix of late 1960s and early 1970s US counterculture; and the post-underground 'alternative comics' scene that gained momentum in North America and beyond in the 1980s. Enormously varied in subject matter and style, much of the material produced during these two waves demonstrates not only a sophisticated understanding of the longer history of comics, but also a willingness to explore and transgress their formal conventions. Even before academics began to write their legitimating accounts, these successive cultural revolutions helped loosen widespread and firmly held associations between the form and a narrow range of low-brow popular genres – crime, horror, science fiction and, above all, superheroics – and with immature, predominantly male readers content with formulaic pleasures.[12] But arguably, more than any other development, it is the rise of the 'graphic novel' from the late 1980s onwards that has helped materialise a distinction between comics as serious literature and as juvenile diversion. Despite the notorious imprecision of the term – which designates not only fictional material in cartoon form produced as a single, standalone publication but also memoir, travelogue, documentary, history, and collections of short stories – the graphic novel has become ubiquitous within mainstream publishing and bookselling. Famously, while some creators of comics quickly embraced the term, others have continued to treat it with suspicion, judging it to be at best unhelpful and pretentious, and at worst merely a cynical ploy to sell comics in fancier, more expensive formats.[13]

Evidently, many comics artists are uncomfortable with the form's new-found respectability, and have little desire to see comics become entirely divorced from their pop-cultural roots. For one thing, failure to maintain dialogue with more commercial manners and means may render comic 'art' abstruse, leaving it a solipsistic irrelevance.[14] Anyway, just as the formal distinctions between 'conventional' and 'alternative' comics may be exaggerated, so too can the cultural distance between them. Despite affording comics increased cultural recognition, alternative material – whether produced in serial form or packaged as graphic novels – has hardly supplanted more mainstream, commercial fare: the former remains a decidedly minority interest amongst readers of comics.[15] Moreover, the rise of alternative comics owes a great deal to a distinctly commercial development, the direct-market comic-book shop. These specialist emporia, which emerged in the 1970s in response to increasingly organised forms of fandom centred on the collecting of old comics, soon became a significant outlet through which mainstream publishers sold their (mostly superhero-oriented) comics. The direct-market business model entails individual stores purchasing consignments of comic books at discount directly from publishers on a non-returnable basis. This arrangement benefited publishers considerably by minimising the costs incurred by overproduction. Being relatively insulated from economic risk encouraged mainstream publishers to experiment with new products. More significantly, however, the direct market, with its extensive network of dedicated comic-book stores and loyal and discerning customer base, helped sustain an array of small-scale, innovative publishers, as well as a considerable number of self-publishing artists. Of course, risk was shouldered disproportionately by the owners of comic-book shops, who became reliant on the more predictable returns of established genres. Thus alternative comics owe their existence to a commercial institution; their viability has always been dependent on the continued health of the very genres and publishing structures against which they are defined.[16]

Comics Go Home

This brief account of the emergence of alternative comics, and the continuing tensions around claims regarding the artistic and literary credentials of certain productions and the status of more popular genres, provides a useful grounding for considering comics' portrayal of suburban domesticity. After all, a principal reason for the vilification of comics has to do with their origins in urban mass culture. As Jörn Ahrens and Arno Meteling insist, comics are 'inseparably tied to the notion of the "city"'. The earliest comic strips in the US, which appeared in newspapers around 1900, were shaped by, and keenly articulated, the speed and rhythms of daily life in the modern metropolis, as well as its disorderliness and diversity. Many of the protagonists – and readers – of these strips were denizens of the city; familiar urban types, from poor immigrants to the nouveau riche, were both satirised and courted in the pages that quickly became known as the 'comics'. The popularity of these entertainments bolstered the circulation figures of a number of new, tabloid-style newspapers, whose questionable reputation was hardly improved by the inclusion of material judged in many quarters to depict – and promote – the unruly exploits of the semi-literate.[17] The proliferation in the second decade of the twentieth century of the domestic comedy and strips with small-town and suburban settings represented a turn towards respectability, and the situations and concerns of middle-class readers became ubiquitous.[18] The domestic comedy has long since been a mainstay of newspaper comics pages. The rise of the stand-alone comic book in the 1930s, however, marked the growing independence of comics from newspapers. In this mode the city continued to provide comics a principal setting, and in the burgeoning popular genres of crime and superheroic adventure it often took spectacular form.

Why was the superhero genre resolutely urban? One the one hand, the crime-fighting superhero provided compensatory fantasies of perception, mobility and control regarding the supposedly impenetrable, ungovernable metropolis; on the other, the city, whether real or imaginary, sustained the comic book's serial form, by constituting an ideal narrative generator that provided a never-ending supply of antagonists, perilous scenarios and mystery.[19]

The more recent 'revolutions' that I have described above also confirm a close relationship, in terms of production and consumption, between comics and the city. The comix underground emerged out of a distinctly urban countercultural scene centring on San Francisco. Famously, the first issue of Robert Crumb's *Zap Comix* was hawked by his pregnant wife Dana and friends from a pram which they pushed around the district of Haight-Ashbury; subsequently underground comix would be distributed largely through a network of head shops located in more alternative-leaning city neighbourhoods. But these new comics cultures also developed an often more politically engaged or historically aware rendering of urban life. Crumb's 1979 strip 'A Short History of America', for instance, charts the development of an imaginary US city from its agrarian beginnings to its congested, corrupted present day. In a later version, a range of utopian or post-apocalyptic scenarios are presented as possible futures.[20] By providing a sequence of single frames that depict the same site at different historical moments, Crumb prefigures McGuire's later work, though 'A Short History' maintains a chronological presentation of its material. Some productions obviously engage with and subvert the longer tradition of comic-book crime-fighters. Spain Rodriguez's anarcho-Marxist superhero Trashman (1968–85), who fights for left-wing causes in the sprawling urban agglomerations of a near-future American police state, appeared very much to be in concert with the political sensibilities of the counterculture. Most of the strips in underground publications, however, took for settings the everyday urban present in which their contributing artists lived and worked.

Much of the material produced in the wake of comix, such as Will Eisner's short story cycle *A Contract with God and other Tenement Stories* (1978), constituted a more conscious turning away from genre comics. The successes of the comix underground encouraged

Eisner to realise long-held ambitions for producing more serious material than his signature strip 'The Spirit' (1940–52). Noticeably, though, *A Contract with God* demonstrates a formal playfulness similar to his earlier crime-fighting title; in both, for instance, elements of the urban landscape are frequently employed as framing devices. But the weightiness of the later work – one of the earliest publications to declare itself a graphic novel – becomes more apparent after Eisner's next two instalments in what would become a trilogy that narrates a century-long history of Jewish American life centring on one street in the Bronx.[21] A different mode of historicity is evident in more recent comics that interrogate the urban environment. Ben Katchor's Julius Knipl series follows the operations of the eponymous 'real estate photographer', whose accompanying narrator is rather more preoccupied with documenting ephemeral and redundant artefacts and locations embedded within the buildings and streetscapes of New York City. Katchor's characters are urban archaeologists or archivists who hover within a historically liminal space; as Jared Gardner puts it, they 'live delicately (often painfully) poised between yesterday and today, between history and the experience, attempting to serve as emissaries of soon-to-be-lost truths, beachcombers of the gray sands between past and present'.[22] Other contemporary comics artists have documented urban conflicts from around the world, for example Joe Sacco, whose journalism provides graphic accounts of flashpoints such as Sarajevo, or Khan Yunis in the Occupied Territories; Sophie Yanow's response to the 2012 student protests in Montreal, *The War of Streets and Houses* (2014), reflects on longer histories of population management and urban protest.

While comic books have then largely maintained their urban orientation during the cultural transformations of the last fifty years, the same period has also seen comics artists increasingly focus on suburban and domestic scenarios. Some of this material parodies the well-worn genre of the domestic comedy. Many of these satires push in directions which meant that they could never be published within the pages of newspapers, the domestic comedy's principal home. They were either too outrageous, as in the case of Crumb's 'Joe Blow', the titular head of an incestuous white-bread household, or else they were too gloomy and cerebral, for instance, Jerry

Moriarty's strip 'Jack Survives', which first appeared in the flagship publication for alternative comics in the 1980s, *Raw*.[23] A number of luminaries of the comix underground contributed to a single-shot title published in 1978, *Lemme outa Here!*, which explores the trials and tribulations of growing up suburban. One contributor, Bill Griffith, went on to become best known for a syndicated newspaper strip, 'Zippy', which would occasionally revisit and offer wry observations about the author's hometown, Levittown, New York.[24] But most evidence for comics' domestic turn can be found perusing the shelves of the graphic-novel sections of mainstream bookstores and specialist comics shops. Many bestselling, critically acclaimed titles by US artists published since 2000 focus, at least in significant part, on domestic experience at a remove from the city: consider for instance Craig Thompson's *Blankets* (2003), Alison Bechdel's *Fun Home: A Family Tragicomic* (2006), David Small's *Stiches: A Memoir* (2009) and Adrian Tomine's *Killing and Dying: Six Stories* (2015).

To a considerable extent this shift is simply part of a much-remarked-upon broader turn toward autobiographical modes in comics that began in the early 1970s. Being independent from corporate publishers enabled artists of the comix underground to have creative control, and to maintain copyright, over their own productions. The drawing on lived experience for inspiration for their comics creations was thus perhaps inevitable. The year zero for autobiographical comics was 1972, which saw the publication of Justin Green's startling confessional *Binky Brown Meets the Holy Virgin Mary*, and Robert Crumb's and Alice Kominsky's pioneering autobiographical strips, which appeared in, respectively, the underground titles *People's Comics* and *Wimmin's Comics*. Harvey Pekar's ongoing saga of his everyday travails, *American Splendor* (1976–2008), written by Pekar but with artwork provided by a variety of artists, is probably one of the most influential and certainly one of the longest-running autobiographical comic strips. According to Hatfield, Pekar's achievement is to have established a new mode in comics: 'the quotidian autobiographical series, focused on the events and textures of everyday existence'.[25] Pekar's famous justification for the unremitting attention to the ordinary in his work is that he sought 'to write literature that pushed people into their lives [. . .] rather than helping people to escape from them'.[26]

The escapism from which Pekar wishes to distance his own artistic endeavours obviously corresponds to the fantasy worlds of mainstream comics. This argument – that creators of comics could and should produce material sourced from real life in order to enrich the lives of others – would become a recurrent rationalisation for alternative comics in the 1980s and 90s. In fact, on the whole the growth of autobiographical comics stimulated a response that was quite opposite to the critical fallout from the contemporaneous memoir boom. Whereas the latter, as I discussed in the previous chapter, precipitated concerns about the genre's debasement, as well as its debasing effects, the rise of graphic memoir – with its emphasis on ordinary, personal experience as opposed to the fantastical – has helped further distinguish alternative comics from less reputable, industrially produced material. Equally, while anxieties about the proliferation of memoir have frequently had to do with its being a distinctly feminine genre, especially in terms of its readership, the number of graphic memoirs penned by women has brought alternative comics further approval; these cultural products are no longer merely boys' toys.[27]

Domestic interiors and banal suburban streetscapes have increasingly come to articulate and frame private experience – most frequently memories of childhood – in graphic narrative. And, just as the memoir in comic strip form requires its creator and its readers to have multiple encounters with embodied selves, so too are those selves repeatedly defined by everyday architectural spaces. But whereas graphic narrative's 'pictorial embodiment', to use Elisabeth El Refaie's term, can facilitate an understanding of the self as mutable and manifold, the equivalent pictorialisation of architectural space may seem to work in a contrary direction.[28] Take for example Alison Bechdel's celebrated memoir *Fun Home*. Its opening chapter certainly seems to present the Gothic revival house in which Bechdel grew up from a variety of aspects. Its history is charted: grand beginnings during Bechdel's small Pennsylvania hometown's brief period of wealth in the 1860s preface steady decline; after her parents purchase the shell of the building in 1962 it is slowly restored and returned to its former glory. Bechdel provides numerous views of the house over a period of eighteen years that show the transforming effects of the obsessive attentions of her father, Bruce Bechdel. She also adeptly articulates, sometimes with the help of dramatic shifts in composition, the brittle moods that defined her household: scenes of intimacy and contentment are swiftly succeeded by embarrassment or confusion; moments of sharp tension or flashes of violence erupt unpredictably. But despite all of these closely observed changes, the house is understood first and foremost to reflect her father's inauthenticity and inflexibility. While Bechdel is sure to depict ordinary family life carrying on in their home's carefully curated period rooms, she suspects her father's main investment in his family had to do with its lending an air of credibility to his 'exhibit', which resembled 'a sort of still life with children'.[29] Moreover, she comes to understand that his love of useless adornment corresponds to embellishment 'in the worst sense', that is, lying (16). Bechdel contends that the house, with its labyrinth of meticulously composed facades, provided her father both a mask and a diversion from the self-loathing that stemmed from his inability to come to terms with his homosexuality. Father and daughter are shown in numerous ways to be polar opposites of one another: Bruce dies a closeted homosexual in the small provincial town in which he was born; Alison departs for New York City in her late adolescence, comes out as a lesbian and goes on to become the successful artist that she suspects her father had always longed to be.

Yet Bechdel's own autobiographical endeavours closely correspond to her father's monomaniacal restoration of their family home. Bechdel contends that the impressive materiality of its interiors helped her father believe in the life he had fabricated: 'perhaps affectation can be so thoroughgoing, so authentic in its details, that it stops being pretense // and becomes, for all practical purposes, real' (60). The same observation though might well describe Bechdel's own project, her own urge for authentication. At the very least it cannot help but draw attention to the extensive collection of archival materials, all painstakingly reproduced by hand, to be found, as it were, loading the pages of Fun Home. Further, the memoir's highly convoluted structure inevitably echoes the labyrinthine qualities of Bruce Bechdel's 'greatest achievement' (4). Indeed, in the very last panel of the memoir, Bechdel announces what has already become apparent: that Fun Home's complexity is a consequence of her narration of their 'entwined stories' (232). The accompanying image shows the young Alison seemingly about to be caught in an embrace by her father. It is a fitting conclusion in many ways: it invokes not only their physical entwinement – or, perhaps rather, a yearning for contact – but also their intellectual relationship. After all, Bruce Bechdel was instrumental in encouraging Alison, at the age of ten, to begin a diary, an enterprise which ultimately leads to the publication of *Fun Home*. (Indeed, the final image comes in the wake of a series of suggestive comparisons with Joyce's *Ulysses* that underscore her father's role in fostering her own artistic development.) The concluding image also loops back to the memoir's opening panels, which depict father and daughter's awkward tumbling apart. This sequence shows a different side of their relationship: a moment of physical closeness is interrupted when her father notices imperfections in the living room's decor that require attention; a disgruntled Alison is shown being sent away to fetch appropriate tools. The problem with her father's obsessiveness is not just that it denies his children loving attention. His is a restorative aesthetic that seeks to fix everything in place and in time. Early on Bechdel complains that her father lacked a 'vital [. . .] elasticity'. Thus the house, his life's work, is unsuited to the requirements of living. Indeed, more than once it is compared to the Bechdels' family business, a funeral home, whose heavily draped showroom – also decorated by Alison's father – yields the 'sensation that time was at a standstill' (38). 'Fun Home', indeed, is the family's facetious abbreviation for the funeral home; Bechdel's choice of title for her memoir is also an obvious ironic invocation of the predominantly frigid, solipsistic environment that she at one point refers to as an 'autistic colony' (139). But as complex and moving as Bechdel's depiction of her relationship with her father is, the house functions within the narrative primarily as an expression of, and an extended metaphor for, one individual; secondarily it stands as a foil to her own emotional and artistic development. In its preoccupation with the materialisation of her father's failings, his affectations and evasions, which in turn define Bechdel's *Künstlerroman*, *Fun Home* trades in the central concerns of graphic memoir, that is, in questions of authenticity and the representation of selves.[30]

Bechdel does however situate her familial home within a network of intersecting physical and literary geographies. Her memories of the house and its surroundings are shaped by an understanding of the effects of environmental degradation: the beautiful sunsets Alison and her family once enjoyed from their porch were produced by high levels of particulates from the pre-Clean Air Act paper mill a few miles away; mine run-off gave the nearby creek admirably clear but lifeless waters (128). Bechdel contends that the difference between her life's trajectory and that of her father was determined in part by the history of highway building. Interstate 80 was completed during her childhood, providing easy access across the Appalachian Ridges that had long inhibited cultural exchange; Bechdel comments pointedly that 'on its way from Christopher Street to the Castro, it passed only four miles from our house' (127). And then, texts like *The Wind in the Willows*, *The Addams Family*, *The Great Gatsby* and the myth of Daedalus and Icarus each provide, at different moments in Bechdel's life, a narrative or set of images that help her interpret her family's habitat. Bechdel reproduces a series of maps which explain why as a young child she took for granted the parallels between her hometown and the landscape of Kenneth Grahame's children's story (146–7). For instance, the showy edifice that is Toad Hall is situated in roughly the same position relative to the rivers and roads of its fictional world as the Bechdel home is to the equivalent physical features of Beech Creek, Pennsylvania. And in one of *Fun Home*'s many self-reflexive moments, Bechdel marvels at the way the illustrated map from her *Wind in the Willows* colouring book constituted a 'mystical bridging of the symbolic and the real, of the label and the thing itself. It was a chart, but also a vivid, almost animated picture' (147). These words, evidently, correspond with the art form that will become her chosen medium, one that charts space and time by means of 'almost animated' pictures – pictures with labels, moreover – that can better articulate past experience than the purely lexical methods of which she becomes increasingly sceptical.

In these ways, Bechdel's memoir develops the kind of 'narrative ecology' of the home that I see being advanced in the other recent graphic narratives under discussion in this chapter. By narrative ecology, I mean once again a conception of a spatiality as a series of interacting, ongoing material processes and narratives situated within broader geographical and historical developments. But as sophisticated and self-aware as Bechdel's memoir is, what it does not do is require its readers to consider the position from which they are reading, to reflect on how they are placed in relation to the unfolding story. The plotting of *Fun Home* may be far from linear; indeed, it presents itself as an intricate puzzle requiring solution. Hillary Chute usefully describes the memoir's tortuous narrative, with its many repetitions and ellipses, as a 'counterarchitecture' to Bruce Bechdel's stultifying perfectionism. Chute contends that *Fun Home* is less concerned in 'fixing and preserving' its material than it is in releasing it 'into timelessness through the open gaps of its word an image form' (216). Bechdel's ambition to animate the archive in this manner should be seen as wholly salutary. Yet I would argue that readers of *Fun Home* rarely find their own temporal co-ordinates being called into question. In part this is a consequence of the relatively consistent and conventional layout of the book's pages.[31] Virtually every panel, moreover, is accompanied by the words of a reassuringly even-toned, analeptic narrator.[32] The book's diegesis, in this respect, is entirely linear; the temporal locus of the narrator – the putative present in which she is narrating – is never encroached upon by the narrated material. Throughout the book, readers are coupled to the narrator in the same present moment. By contrast, even though they are even more obviously centred on particular buildings, the graphic narratives of McGuire and Ware discussed below are more clearly *de*centred in a number of ways. Their stories are dispersed across time and space and are shared between various human and non-human agents. Certain framing techniques produce temporal disruption, which renders the stories' narrative time uncertain. An important effect of these disturbances and confusions is to encourage readers to reappraise a building's relationship to its environment, its longer history and its possible futures.

Shifting Baselines, Framing Futures: Anticipatory Histories in Richard McGuire's *Here*

For many activists and educators concerned with ecological change – particularly in relation to the management of natural resources and heritage landscapes – the concept of the 'shifting baseline' has proven to be a useful device through which to frame their interventions. An appreciation of change within one's local environment is often limited to the time frame of one's own life, which can lead to a kind of generational amnesia. Transformations taking place over longer periods of time thus frequently become indiscernible. On the other hand, against an erroneous sense of a locality's permanence, recent developments, when they do occur, are typically perceived as unnatural ruptures. Relocating the baseline from which change is measured to an earlier historical moment, and thereby resituating places, both natural and man-made, within much broader temporal frames, may help promote an understanding of place as characterised by flux rather than stasis. Such a move is central to 'anticipatory history', an interdisciplinary mode of enquiry encompassing diverse strategies that attempt to connect past, present and future environmental change. Indeed, articulations of the mutable nature of place are understood to have particular utility in relation to habitats threatened by loss or that are undergoing rapid transformation. As the editors of the 2010 volume *Anticipatory History* suggest, 'history that calls attention to process rather than permanence may [. . .] help us to be more prepared for future change [and] to respond thoughtfully and proactively, rather than in a mode of retreat [. . .] or regret'.[33]

The invention of the term 'shifting baseline' is usually attributed to the fisheries scientist Daniel Pauly. In a short article published in 1995, Pauly describes as a syndrome the tendency of fisheries scientists to employ measurements of fish stocks and species variety made at the beginning of their careers as the baseline from which to evaluate change within their own lifetimes. When the next generation starts its career, says Pauly, 'the stocks have further declined, but it is the stocks at that time that serve as a new baseline. The result obviously is a gradual shift of the baseline, a gradual accommodation of the creeping disappearance of resource species'.[34]

The acceptance of shifting baselines is so prevalent in part because scientists are liable to distrust and dismiss historical sources of information, for example, anecdotes describing fishing bonanzas in the nineteenth and early twentieth centuries, or the extirpation of species of marine megafauna by coast-dwelling Native American peoples in earlier times. Such stories do not accord with the protocols that define reputable research, such as scientific methods of observation. It is easy to see why the term has had much traction in fisheries science and marine ecology. Other branches of science possess extensive records: astronomers for example are able to draw on 2,000-year-old Chinese and Babylonian observations of celestial phenomena in order to develop and test new hypotheses. By contrast, marine environments have existed for a much longer period of human history in relative obscurity. Unsurprisingly, then, it is marine conservationists who have taken the lead in attempts to draw attention to the problem of the shifting baseline syndrome.[35] In the last decade, however, the concept has proliferated, and has featured in scholarship that engages with a range of environmental concerns, including water resource management, light pollution, rewilding and the conservation of heritage landscapes.[36] However, before I return to the work of anticipatory historians, for whom the latter issue is a central preoccupation, I consider the work of architect and regional planner Ian McHarg, which appears to articulate the concept of shifting baseline syndrome *avant la lettre*, and is centrally concerned with suburbanisation in the US.

McHarg founded the world's first department of landscape architecture, at the University of Pennsylvania, and authored the classic study on ecology and planning *Design with Nature*, published in 1969. Like many of his contemporaries, McHarg was profoundly disturbed by suburban sprawl. But rather than campaigning for the preservation of open space, which was the dominant paradigm for anti-sprawl activism in the post-war years, he instead argued for new developments to be informed by greater sensitivity to ecological conditions, for a new way of planning that respected natural processes.[37] Like many of his contemporaries, McHarg was a vociferous critic of planners who had little understanding of the workings of the natural environment. He repeatedly rebuked the mainstream of the profession for its unquestioning 'economic determinism':

in other words, the presumption that the value of any piece of land may be realised through financial calculation alone. But McHarg was also dismissive of conservationists who determined man-made habitats and the natural world to be anathema. Their preoccupation with preserving 'unspoilt' landscapes, which often lay distant from urban centres, did little for large swathes of the nation's population. Meanwhile, unplanned development would continue to destroy the character and amenity of areas on the margins of cities. Nothing was to be achieved in opposing urban expansion; growth was inevitable. What was needed was a planning methodology that carefully considered 'the place of nature in the metropolis'.[38] Analysis of the complex of natural processes particular to a region would identify specific opportunities and constraints and ultimately the optimum pattern for development. McHarg's celebrated 'Plan for the Valleys', a proposal for a large-scale housing development on the rural fringe of Baltimore, and his Philadelphia open space study, are reproduced in detail in *Design with Nature*; his later plan for The Woodlands, thirty miles outside Houston, Texas was realised in the 1970s.[39]

One reason why some commentators have suggested McHarg's work predicted the term shifting baselines has to do with his comment that scientists suffer 'a certain professional myopia'; like Pauly he asserts that 'they are thoroughly irresolute in the absence of impeccable evidence', which, he adds, is 'a profound weakness in a world which is finally unknowable'.[40] McHarg's response was to develop a method that dissolves the conventional boundaries that define scientific endeavour by combining various optics that might be employed to analyse a particular locality. In short, this is the overlay technique now so widely used in regional planning and which was critical to the development of Geographical Information Systems (GIS) from the 1960s onwards. (McHarg's techniques were, however, entirely analogue; unlike the pioneers of GIS he did not exploit the computational power of new information technologies to collate, analyse and display complex geographical data.) The most detailed example in *Design with Nature* that employs this method is a study of Staten Island that was commissioned by the City of New York to discern suitable future land use. McHarg provides over thirty separate maps of Staten Island, each detailing a specific aspect: geology, hydrology, topography and so on. Each map was reproduced as a transparency. Compiling them enabled McHarg to construct a composite image that indicated areas best suited for conservation, recreation and/or development.

Echoes of McHarg's method can be found in graphic narratives with domestic settings. As I illustrated at the beginning of this chapter, Heide Solbrig splits her grandparents' home across multiple frames, with each recalling discrete habits and pleasures; subsequently the house is reassembled in the manner of McHarg's final composite image of Staten Island. McGuire's *Here* uses a similar technique, by repeatedly showing the same site in order to reflect on the different processes – including forms of labour – that have shaped it: Figures 4.3 and 4.4 both depict different kinds of layering (floorboards, carpets, wallpapers) involved in place creation and, as I discuss in more detail below, demonstrate the book's method of layering images in order to articulate change. And the notion of process is key for McHarg, who stresses the importance of recognising how any place is the sum of ongoing historical, physical and biological processes and, further, that 'these affect man and are affected by his intervention'.[41] Only by reframing places within these dynamic processes, argues McHarg, can the destructive amnesia and myopia of economic determinism be combatted; the plan for Staten Island, he declares, 'was an attempt to reveal the alternatives for the future destiny of the beleaguered island'.[42] Only a radical reconceptualisation of the baselines from which we assess spatial change will bring into focus a range of more responsible future courses.

McHarg's approach also accords with the work of scholars keen to explore the potential applications of anticipatory history. The slim volume *Anticipatory History*, which brings together writers from across disciplinary divides in a fashion that would have appealed to McHarg, considers how, in the face of an increase in the rate and scale of environmental change in our lifetimes, 'the stories we tell about ecological and landscape histories can help shape our perceptions of plausible environmental futures'.[43] The book takes the form of a glossary, with each entry offering reflections and accounts of concepts and cultural practices that relate to the diverse and sometimes conflicting ways in which people know the 'past in place'.[44] There is a section on shifting baseline syndrome, which is determined to be 'just as relevant to the built environment' as it is to natural ones, not least because man-made structures are just as likely to be threatened by radical change even while they are thought of as being permanent, timeless fixtures.[45] Taking up these considerations elsewhere, Caitlin DeSilvey asks 'what kind of cultural work might be required to give *time* back to a timeless landscape, and to open up an appreciation of the past not as static and settled, but as open and active?'[46] Echoing McHarg, she speculates: 'might it be possible to experiment with other ways of storying landscape, framing histories around movement rather than stasis, and drawing connections between past dynamism and future process?'[47] DeSilvey experiments with reverse chronology and montage to retell the history of a Cornish fishing harbour. The picturesque harbour, a popular tourist attraction, is a landscape which faces significant alteration, indeed likely destruction, in the near future, due to environmental change. The deployment of these narrative techniques, DeSilvey asserts, 'allows us to imagine the history of this place [as] an assemblage of "past presents" which remain open to addition and subtraction, [with] the process of making sense and assembling story exposed'.[48] Such storying may help to activate the past, rendering it less fixed and more useable.[49]

Richard McGuire's 2014 graphic narrative *Here* would appear to answer DeSilvey's call for new ways of historicising familiar landscapes. McGuire's book indeed constitutes a self-reflexive assemblage of past presents that frames histories around change not stasis. This description may seem counter-intuitive, for at first glance McGuire's narrative seems entirely static. *Here* tells the history of a house built in 1907 by focusing entirely on one corner of what appears to be its living room. Each double-page spread comprises a single unframed panel. Most of the book's pages depict the room at a particular moment in time; the year is always detailed in a caption in the top left-hand corner. A succession of occupants, furnishings and decor is presented to the reader, though not in chronological order. The essential geometry of the room, however – the intersection of ceiling, walls and floor, a large sash window visible on the left, a fireplace with mantelpiece situated to the right – remains unchanged. But neither the room nor the house

Figure 4.3 From Richard McGuire, *Here*

Figure 4.4 From Richard McGuire, *Here*

ultimately defines the 'here' of *Here*; rather, a specific vantage point does. It would perhaps be more accurate to say that *Here* relates the history – and pre-history – of not a house but a site. From the same fixed point of view the reader witnesses the construction of a nearby grand colonial-era building, its later conflagration and subsequent restoration. Other pages show that the same area was once forested and made use of, in a variety of ways, by Native American peoples. Readers are also offered glimpses of ice-age landscapes; McGuire even reaches back three billion years into the Earth's Archean eon, the geological period during which the first continents formed. Noticeably, the scene with the earliest date in the book, 3,000,500,000 BCE – a marker of geological time equivalent to 'a year and a day', perhaps – is presented three times. The dramatic shifts in atmospheric colouration across the three views presumably indicate different moments in a single 24-hour period, which helps give a sense of the past – even one as distant as this – as ongoing, in process. McGuire also imagines the site's future prospects. New domestic technologies and fashions come and go. Not one but two apocalypses occur: the house is destined to be destroyed in a catastrophic flood in 2111; two centuries after that, scientists in heavy protective suits are shown monitoring a barren land with their digital instruments. McGuire even imagines a future after humanity: one day, hummingbirds will rule the earth. With its vastly expanded timescale – its radically altered baselines – *Here* emphasises the contingent, impermanent nature of sites that are so often presumed to be inert and unchanging.

But the most distinctive aspect of *Here* is the way it reconfigures that essential unit of comic strips, the panel. McGuire eschews traditional sequential framing; at no point in the book is a succession of discrete panels depicting the progress of specific actors through space and time ever presented on the same page. In other words, *Here* does not feature comic strips in the usual sense. Instead, McGuire deploys frames that often overlap one another; each provides a view onto a particular moment in time. The book's narrative logic is established at its beginning. After a number of pages depicting the empty room at different moments across the twentieth and twenty-first centuries, a young woman in a bright pink dress appears standing in the centre of the room with her back to the reader (Figure 4.5). It is 1957. In what is the first speech act of the book, she asks herself, 'why did I come in here again?' In the foreground of the same double-page spread a small frame is suspended over these proceedings. It depicts a much more purposeful-looking black cat walking across the room's floor. It is 1999. Over the page, the woman is captured again with the same hesitant posture (Figure 4.6). However, the frame, still marked '1957', has contracted around her, and is superimposed over a jarringly different scene. The page is now mostly filled with a blurry woodland landscape; the ground is partially covered with snow. It is 1623. There is an intriguing symmetry between the framed picture of a wooded scene fixed above the mantelpiece in the room in 1957 and the panel containing the woman in the pink dress – now resembling a portrait – that is suspended over the seventeenth-century woods. The equivalence suggests that, in *Here*, the room and its occupant are not primary, are no more significant than scenes in which there is no house or humans at all. Meanwhile, in the second frame marked 1999, which appears slightly to the right of the position occupied by its equivalent on the previous page, the black cat appears to have made some progress, but has stopped to lick its paw. On the following page, it is shown exiting right. From the outset, then, McGuire establishes not only the book's formal logic but also certain animating themes: an insistence on viewing unremarkable spaces through much broader time frames than is usual; and an emphasis on memory and forgetting, on patterns and symmetries, and on repetition and interruption – all of which are signalled by the book's opening line, 'why . . . here again?'

In a way, the three panels depicting the cat do constitute a strip, albeit one distributed across several pages. On numerous occasions in *Here* sequences can be established by turning the page and making connections between scenes designated as contemporaneous. Movement through space is suggested when there is a shift in position between one frame and the next. Indeed, the cat and several other figures – for instance, a boy performing a headstand in in 1933, a man lifting a baby into the air in 1962 – can be animated manually in the manner of a flick book. But usually the interruption of turning the page requires some effort from the reader to establish certain frames as consecutive. Sequences employ differing temporal

Figure 4.5 From Richard McGuire, *Here*

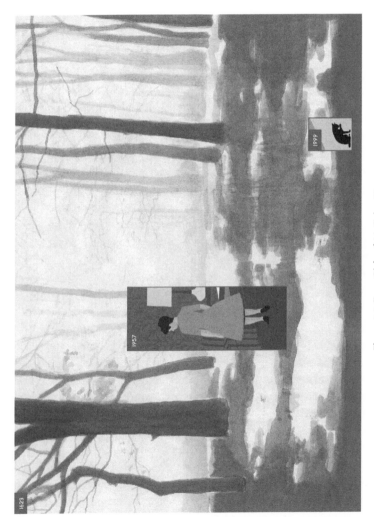

Figure 4.6 From Richard McGuire, *Here*

registers: an arrow shot from the bow of a Lenape tribesperson in 1402 is framed over three successive pages, but it seems to progress much more slowly than the ambulatory cat depicted at the book's opening; thus the missile seems to move in slow motion, even while a blurred background suggests speed. As McGuire's compositions become more complex, the reader is required to negotiate between different temporalities, to deal with multiple unfoldings. The flying arrow, for instance, is superimposed over images of a roiling Archaean Earth. It is almost impossible to assimilate the two frames' cosmically different trajectories. Perhaps that is rather the point: evidently, McGuire is little interested in merely charting time's arrow.[50] A parallel sequence on the left-hand side of the page further emphasises our limited capacity, or unwillingness, to comprehend place across different temporal scales. This set of frames depicts a much more pacific scene from 1870: in a verdant meadow an artist, accompanied by his indolent female muse, prepares to paint a landscape. He is captivated by the view off left – the opposite direction to the one in which the arrow is heading – and observes, 'the line of that ridge looks like a woman's hip'. Such a human-centred appreciation of the landscape is of course ignorant of geological processes, blind to the continent-forming capabilities of immense timescales. (On the other hand, the page's composition renders the artist's limited perception understandable. The impressions of the primordial scenes behind the frame containing the Victorian-era couple are discomfortingly indistinct; they could hardly be said to be beautiful. Suspended in their fragile-looking bucolic oasis, the artist and his companion seem vulnerable, insignificant.)

McGuire does, however, provide numerous, more immediately arresting juxtapositions, which often constitute sight gags. For instance, in 1623 a deer leaps through the forest; superimposed over the room in 1993 the animal seems to be vaulting furniture set up for a game of musical chairs. The waterjet shooting forth from the hose of firefighters who have entered the room in 1996 appears to be aimed at a flame-red bouquet held by a woman in 1934. These and other examples could though be interpreted as having a more serious purpose: they register the limitations of the work's fixed point of view. Further, such compositions reveal the potential of McGuire's reframing of space and time to shock and disorientate, as well as to entertain. Elsewhere, though, single frames and sequences resonate with each other in more ambivalent ways. For instance, the continual tracking of a whole host of creatures across the page – before, during and after the house's existence – suggests a narrative trajectory in which the building, along with much human endeavour, is an irrelevance. Throughout *Here*, objects are continually being lost and found, individuals are hidden and revealed, sounds echo and go unheard (or are seemingly overheard). Like Bechdel's memoir, *Here* baits its readers with a wealth of possible connections; it seems to promise that some underlying pattern, a complete structure, is waiting to be made out. But there is no such structure. There are, however, echoes and congruencies, many of which can be discerned only if they are attended to carefully. For McGuire, then, the past in place is a constellation of past presents, a multitude of here-and-nows. *Here* shows that such fragments and threads may, with effort, be recombined to tell new stories of a place: stories with new protagonists, or none; stories defined not by beginnings and endings but by the possibilities presented by multiple *in media res* happenings.

Here repeatedly draws attention to its own materiality, but not in order to bring closure to its narrative. Rather, *Here*'s many self-reflexive gestures communicate how the book's physical properties may help elaborate a suitably multifaceted account of a physical location. The book – a remarkably beautiful object – reproduces the interior and exterior of the house through its internal and external surfaces: its covers imitate the building's outer walls; an external view of the sash window in close up is provided on the front cover, which corresponds to its position on the left-hand interior wall when the book is opened. (And the open 'V' of the book, which replicates the perpendicularity of the interior walls, has the effect of placing the reader within the room.) The final 'E' of the title on the front cover appears to be partially obscured by the window's curtain, which lends a sense of depth to the black space behind the open lower half of the window, suggesting that the 'there' of *Here* is indeed to be located within the building's interior. Closer examination, however, reveals this to be a visual trick: the edge of the curtain in fact stops just short of the title's final letter. The upper half of the window similarly plays with perceptions of surface and depth. The glazing is reflective and therefore opaque. Yet the window is bifurcated into clearly defined, uniform areas, one illuminated, the other in shadow; the dividing line, which runs at an angle down the window pane from the top-left-corner of the frame, resembles the meeting of an interior wall and ceiling. The multipartite window frame pictured on the front cover thus artfully predicts not only how the room's interior will be viewed through multiple panels, but also the manner in which the surfaces of its pages articulate differing depths of field simultaneously. The same kind of self-conscious equivocation can also be found between the book's covers. Noticeably, the corner of the room, which provides a constant defining axis, is always just out of sight, lost in the book's gutter. This seems marvellously apposite. *Here* lacks the traditional gutters of most comic strips. True, its smaller superimposed frames all feature uniform fine grey borders, but these do not function in the same way as the white space between the panels of conventional comic strips; they do not designate intervals or promise sequentiality. Instead, the book's sole gutter – which is also its basic mechanism, its hinge – obscures and articulates, in both senses of the word, the room's situation in space and its journey through time.

The room's temporalisation thus seems to be quite literally bound up with the book's materiality. However, McGuire has developed other versions of *Here* that organise the same material in quite different ways.[51] Further, the book has its origins in a six-page black-and-white strip drawn by McGuire, titled 'Here', which was published twenty-five years earlier in *Raw* magazine. Thus the book's opening line, 'Now why did I come in here again', seems even more appropriate. The setting and formal logic of 'Here' and *Here* are similar, though only in the latter is the operation of turning the page critical to the sense of time passing. The house's identity, however, becomes more definite in the later publication. As McGuire has declared, the setting of the 1989 strip was meant to be 'Anyplace USA'.[52] The subsequent death of his sister and parents led to the later project becoming much more personal. The living room depicted in *Here* represents the heart of what was once McGuire's family home, in which his parents had lived for some fifty years. Several pages show family members present in the room. A sequence towards the end of the book even appears to represent McGuire himself in conversation with his ailing father. However, no announcement makes clear the identity of these figures or the relationship between house and the book's author. Like Waldie's *Holy Land*, then, *Here* enacts a continual 'turning away' from personal experience; his family's occupation of the home does not provide the book its core narrative or affective centre. McGuire has said that after the house was sold he came into possession of a wealth of family photos, which provide reference points for many of the images in *Here*. But while the book became 'mixed with [his] own past', McGuire insists that 'it wasn't meant to be a memoir'.[53]

Even without any awareness of McGuire's biography, though, the book's precise setting may still be discerned. The colonial-era building across the way is the Proprietary House, situated in Perth Amboy, New Jersey, which lies just across the Arthur Kill from the southern end of Staten Island. The building was briefly occupied by William Franklin, the last Royal Governor of New Jersey and acknowledged illegitimate son of Benjamin Franklin. McGuire represents the meeting of both men in 1775, during which their political differences boil over into heated argument. (The younger man's steadfast loyalism would precipitate, in the aftermath of the Revolutionary War, his permanent exile to London.) McGuire has admitted to being intrigued by his family home's historical connections, and by the possibility that a luminary such as Benjamin Franklin might have passed through the very space that it would one day occupy. The Founding Father is indeed shown in the foreground of one of the pages, arriving in a carriage. The strangeness – the ghostliness – of this historic presence, the sense of his passing through the walls of the house, is rather confirmed by his subsequent apparent return, albeit in the form of a man dressed as Franklin at a costume party being held in the living room in 1990. Again like Waldie, McGuire attempts to orientate the house within wider geographical and political histories (which includes the declining fortunes of the Proprietary House, whose grounds are seen being subdivided for housing in the early twentieth century). But equally, both writers seek to articulate a *feeling* of historicity, specifically that haunting sense of repetition and replication produced by the ordinary geometries – and materialities – of domestic space. In McGuire's book this feeling is not equivalent to an apprehension of timelessness, of fixity; rather the historic corresponds to a sense of latency, of the capacity of the past, and therefore the present, to touch the future. (Certain pasts, however, are excluded from McGuire's expanded history. *Here* makes no direct reference to the racist housing policies and practices of the twentieth century, for instance.)

One sequence in *Here* captures very well what is at stake in McGuire's anticipatory history. In 1986 the house's elderly female resident – presumably McGuire's mother – is visited upon by members of the Archaeological Society. The location's historic value is outlined in quite predictable ways: the archaeologists are interested in Native American culture, and hope above all to find a burial site; their host admits the historic nature of the building across the street is one of the reasons she and her husband bought the house. But the sequence demonstrates the characters' disinterest in the archaeological riches of the home itself. The young students, who are left to their own devices while the senior archaeologist pokes around the backyard, seem unaware of other histories of settlement within their immediate vicinity. One superimposition shows them awkwardly staring into space, blind to the more comfortable surroundings of the room of three decades ago. Indeed, the only 'future archaeology' they seem able to contemplate is entirely self-centred. The slogan blazoned on the T-shirt of one of the students, 'future transitional fossil', anticipates the discovery and interpretation of its wearer's remains by a future species as an evolutionary 'link'. But as well as being laughably hubristic the slogan is a reminder that such taxonomic categories are man-made, and are applied retrospectively to a continuum to which we have limited access. Of course, this is all reminiscent of McGuire's technique which provides his readers very limited views of a place across time. Actually, McGuire does depict a future society examining archaeological evidence from the twentieth-century home, and their taxonomies suggest they understand the technologies of pre-colonial-era Native American life and twentieth-century suburban life as being very closely related. It could be said, then, that McGuire's work is characterised not only by past presents, but also future pasts. *Here*, then, is an anticipatory history par excellence; its central project is, as DeSilvey says, to 'unsettle the narrative foundations that stabilize landscape and block reflection on future change'. Its innovative framing technique is crucial to its unsettling of the narrative foundations of the suburban home, and demands from its reader a continual baseline shifting, a continual repositioning and reorganisation of the way we perceive the past – and imagine the future – in place.

Intersections of Loss and Belonging: Chris Ware's Storied Buildings

Several comics artists and scholars have identified McGuire's six-page strip 'Here', originally published in *Raw* magazine in 1989, as being both innovative and influential.[54] No-one, however, has been more insistent about McGuire's significance than Chris Ware. In an appreciative essay on 'Here', Ware admits that no other single piece of work has had a greater impact on his own comics. More boldly, he declares that this 'deceptively modest strip' has 'revolutionized the narrative possibilities of comic[s]'.[55] What Ware sees as most significant about 'Here' is McGuire's experimentation with the 'narrative tense' of comics, that is, how the reader is placed with regard to the strip's temporality. As Ware has it, 'Here' asks 'where exactly it is that the reader's consciousness "is" in a strip'.[56] Evidence of McGuire's influence can be found across Ware's *oeuvre*, much of which shares with *Here* a concern with the experience of domestic spaces through time. A distinguishing mark of Ware's work, though, is a continually discernible self-conscious impulse to delineate and transcend the limitations of conventional comic strips in order to provide more complex and compelling accounts of the interactions between the built environment, narrative and memory. I begin this section with an examination of two examples from Ware's work that evidently take inspiration from McGuire. In each instance, however, I show how Ware's manipulations of form – in particular, his adoption of diagrammatic modes of composition – are motivated by a desire to examine the relationships within and between spaces. Conventional sequential narrative, it would seem, has only a limited capacity to achieve this end. I conclude the section with a discussion of Ware's graphic narrative

Building Stories, whose fragmented narrative structure and material composition constitutes an appropriate analogue to lives dispersed across urban and suburban locations.

In one section of Ware's *Building Stories* (2012), a three-storey townhouse, which Ware grants sentience, is presented as musing upon its various occupants, past and present (Figure 4.7). A cutaway of the building's front elevation affords a view of the interiors of its three apartments; the present-day residents – to be precise, those who called the walk-up home on 23 September 2000 – are all

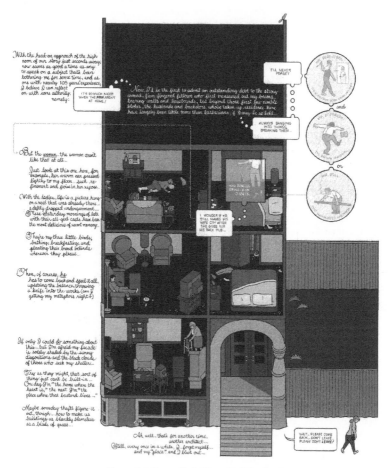

Figure 4.7 From Chris Ware, *Building Stories*

visible going about their lives. But the building also recalls, among others, Mr Bell, 'that ham-handed handyman / who bungled up all my closets'.[57] In the same manner as McGuire's redecorators, Mr Bell's labours are shown in progress in a panel overlaying the top-floor apartment bedroom. (As elsewhere, Ware marks the 'pastness' of this scene, its status as a memory, with a pale blue wash.) The proportions of the superimposed panel are similar to the framing of the building's rooms in the cutaway view. Indeed, organised into storeys as they are, the rooms resemble the tiers and panels of a comic strip. This similarity is reinforced by the uniformity of the spaces representing the walls and floors that separate the rooms; in other words, these spaces appear just like the gutters between comic-strip panels. But it makes no sense to read these panels sequentially, taking each tier in turn from top to bottom and reading each one from left to right. Instead, the page's organisation directs the reader on a different, more complex route, with long, thin blue arrows threading around and through the building's past and present spaces. Thus it would seem that stories about this building – and, perhaps, about inhabited structures generally – are liable to be less interesting and meaningful if told through the sequences of present-tense moments that comics normally provide. Ware's punning title seems to indicate this: stories of buildings need not be built in storeys. Further, the comic-strip-style gutters in Ware's cutaway pictures obscure various kinds of connectivity. Indeed, this section of the graphic narrative is greatly concerned with elements of the building not visible in the cutaway portraits – plumbing, fire escapes, interstices – and with how these components help bring the isolated occupants of the building, both former and present, into each other's lives. *Building Stories*, then, constitutes what might reasonably be described as an 'expanded' comic strip. Rather like the designer's exploded-view drawing that clarifies the arrangement of a mechanical assemblage, Ware's use of superimposition provides a more expansive perspective than that offered by the conventional comic strip. His diagrammatic approach makes better sense of a building's inner workings, its human and physical processes and interactions across time and space.

Another example of Ware's harnessing of McGuire's methods can be found in his earlier graphic narrative *Jimmy Corrigan, The*

Smartest Kid on Earth (2000). In this instance, superimposition has a disruptive effect on the reading experience of the comic strip and, in conjunction with other techniques, draws attention to its own narrativising of the built environment, whose temporality is rendered ambiguous and strange. Halfway through *Corrigan*, one whole page depicts three children playing hide-and-seek in a recently constructed housing development in Chicago's Southside in 1892 (Figure 4.8). The page is organised as a polyptych, Scott McCloud's term for a composition in which 'a moving figure or [set of] figures is imposed over a continuous background'. The polyptych in *Corrigan* also constitutes a 'split panel' – in other words, its single scene is divided across several smaller panels.[58] The young James Corrigan (grandfather to the eponymous Jimmy) is visible in five out of twelve of the page's panels as he progresses around various buildings in search of his playmates. But, in a manner not dissimilar to 'Here', three panels visualise prior moments of the same locality. The narrator remarks that, fifty years before, the only places to hide might have been 'in a depression in the ground' or 'behind an indian on horseback'; in separate panels James's Italian friend is depicted attempting both. And, in one of the central panels, James can be seen running behind a house whose skeletal frame is revealed, an allusion to the building's having been a construction site only a short time ago. The recent addition of houses, trees and telegraph poles has facilitated this game of hide-and-seek; the narrator concludes, a touch ominously, that 'with the inevitable forward march of progress / come new ways of hiding things, / and new things to hide'.

This single page, which so manifestly dwells on the temporality of place and its representation, realises many of the 'narrative possibilities' opened up by McGuire's earlier innovative work. True, the narrator's commentary invokes and, by being arranged sequentially across the page's tiers and panels in the conventional manner, rather demonstrates the inevitability of progress. Almost everything else about the page's organisation and content, however, seems to undermine such an assumption, indicating instead that the 'inevitability of progress' is but a matter of convention. Despite its regular arrangement of panels, the page does not merely produce the 'linear present' of most comic strips, that is, a storying comprised

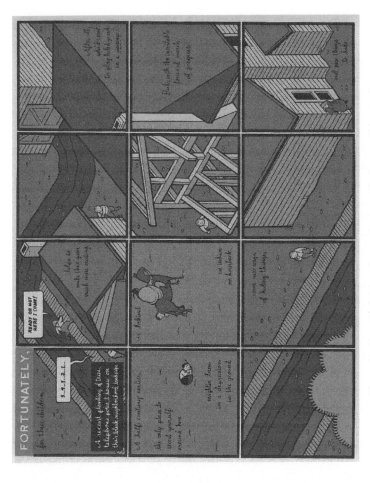

Figure 4.8 From Chris Ware, Jimmy Corrigan, *The Smartest Kid on Earth*

of an orderly sequence of present-tense moments. For one thing, by including children at play within their frames, the three panels that represent earlier moments actually synthesise temporalities. They demonstrate that peculiar power of comic strips for synchronic representation, which Hatfield has described as 'an impossible and provocative at-onceness'.[59] And then, Jimmy's progress is eccentric. He begins straightforwardly enough, being visible in each of the first three of the top tier's panels. But subsequently he appears to proceed down the page; his course thus diverges from the narrator's. At this juncture, the reader is obliged to choose to attend first to Jimmy or to the narrator; they cannot be followed simultaneously. Most likely, the reader will need to consider the page in its entirety in order to make a decision about who to 'follow'.

Ware's elaborate composition thus requires both a scanning and a peripatetic eye in order to make sense of its content. In this way, it exploits the tension that characterises the experience of reading comic strips, which demands apprehension of both the individual panels in sequence and of the overall arrangement of the page. Ware would be the first to recognise, however, that there is nothing new about this. Indeed, there are countless examples of comics from across the twentieth century that demand heightened levels of reader involvement as a result of their manipulation of the tension between what some scholars have called the 'linear' and 'tabular' dimensions of the comic strip.[60] And, as Hatfield observes, because they inevitably draw attention to the ways comics negotiate time and space, polyptychs 'tend to be used when time and space become the thematic concerns of narrative itself'.[61] What is distinct about Ware's self-conscious technique is the way it is made to relate to the built environment. Ware's histories of houses and habitation are characterised by a productive ambivalence. The narrator's conclusion, which equates progress with secrecy, implies that conventional narrative obscures more than it reveals. An alternative, seemingly more playful, narrative mode, presents the reader with a series of distractions and dilemmas, but also, the chance to make meaningful connections across time and space. Thus Ware's framing techniques have the potential to call into question authoritative, progressivist (or indeed lapsarian) histories of urban and suburban development.

In depicting children's games, Ware joins the ranks of poets, memoirists, fiction writers and filmmakers intrigued by the opportunities for play afforded by incomplete urban and suburban developments.[62] As I have argued elsewhere, such narratives focus on the potential of these terrains for new connections and relationalities; being incomplete such sites are volatile, dangerous even, but they are also places of possibility and sources of new stories.[63] Ware's page seems to demonstrate much the same, but the arrangement of the strip's content foregrounds one more tension, between rigid formalism and free play. Its axonometric projection, which lacks the foreshortening of a perspective view, invokes the formal technical drawings of architects and designers. On the other hand, it is also reminiscent of the three-dimensional video games that became popular in the 1990s, such as *Populous* and *SimCity 2000*, in which the designing of cities or civilisations is entirely a matter of play. The axonometric view of the housing development thus gestures towards how these habitats are both made for and remade by children. Of course, the same could be said of the relationship between architects and residents generally, or for that matter, comics artists and readers. For Isaac Cates, the primary function of the diagrams that proliferate across Ware's work is to extend the reader's awareness; typically they articulate an authorial perspective or one that is at least external to the principal characters.[64] I concur with this view. However, my two examples show how diagrams also have the potential to articulate conflicting conceptualisations of and ambitions for certain spaces and, therefore, for disputing authorial judgement. Ware's diagrams are thus at once instructive and playfully disruptive.

These examples from *Building Stories* and *Corrigan* arguably represent some of the clearest evidence of McGuire's influence. Ware has admitted to being embarrassed by what he perceives as the extent to which the six pages of 'Here' have shaped his own work.[65] Certainly, a deep preoccupation with the relationship between architecture and narrative dominates Ware's *oeuvre*. From early melancholic sequences reflecting on the loss of his grandmother that depict nothing but empty rooms, to several of his playful Quimby the Mouse strips, whose composition presumes architectural form, and from *Lost Buildings* (2003), his collaborative work with Ira Glass that explores the legacies of the father of modern architecture, Louis

Sullivan, to the banal suburban landscapes of his socially awkward male protagonists in 'The Last Saturday' (2015) and *Rusty Brown* (2019), Ware's material inhabits a range of emotional registers and social and cultural milieus.

Ware's fascination with built form has not gone unnoticed. Scholars have frequently relayed his suggestion that Goethe's dictum, 'architecture is frozen music', provides 'the aesthetic key to the development of cartoons as an art form'.[66] But his analogies between architecture and comics have led some to interpret Ware's complex architectural motifs as evidence of his artistry and sophistication, of his elevation of the comics form, or otherwise to reduce his interest in the built environment entirely to concerns about the experience of reading comics. The significance of buildings, the manner in which they are experienced and represented, is rather lacking in some of these explanations.[67] More helpful, from my perspective at least, is Jared Gardner's assertion that a primary objective of Ware's *Building Stories* is its demonstration of how the ability to see 'layers of architectural history in a single glance depends on attending to buildings, to the lived spaces we so often take for granted'.[68] Daniel Worden notes, further, that '"Building Stories" contrasts the possibilities embedded within architectural space in the early twentieth century with the archival fantasies about the same space that provide comfort in late twentieth-century America'.[69] Both Gardner and Worden also contend, quite reasonably, that Ware's work, along with the productions of several other contemporary comics artists, more closely resembles a database or an archive than a conventionally linear narrative. But while Worden sees in Ware's depictions of architecture an 'archival fantasy', an unrealisable desire to make the past total, to experience it as a designed whole, Gardner emphasises the ongoing nature of Ware's archival project. Indeed, Gardner argues, the vital project of 'making the present aware of its own "archive", the past that is always in the process of becoming' is facilitated by the form of comics, which 'is forever troubled by that which cannot be reconciled, synthesised, unified, contained within the frame'. Even as the narrative progresses forward in time, excess data is always left behind, which constitutes 'a visual archive for the reader's necessary work of rereading, resorting, and reframing'.[70]

Gardner's focus on what he brilliantly refers to as comics' yielding up of 'the remains of the everyday' helps clarify the potential for suburban history, whose archives, as Roger Webster has it, are so often 'presumed empty'.[71] What I want to pursue in the remainder of this chapter is how a sense of suburban space – and temporality – defines the sprawling and fragmented graphic narrative that is *Building Stories*. Ware's fascination with the architectural history of the city of Chicago is evident across much of his work, but *Building Stories*, uniquely, reflects upon its suburban dimension. Much of the narrative's action, after all, is played out in Oak Park, the suburb in which Frank Lloyd Wright lived and worked in the years around the turn of the twentieth century. Oak Park is also the location of Wright's most celebrated early buildings, some of which are depicted in *Building Stories*: his combined home and studio; Unity Temple; and several private residences, including a number in the modern 'prairie style'. Oak Park's architectural heritage was officially recognised in 1972 with the creation of the Frank Lloyd Wright-Prairie School of Architecture Historic District, which The National Register of Historic Places notes as having 'undoubtedly the largest concentration of early modern architecture to be found anywhere in the world'.[72] Oak Park's reputation is acknowledged in *Building Stories*, though usually in ironic ways: one of the annoyances of living in a suburb famous for its architecture, discovers Ware's female protagonist shortly after relocating from the city with her family, is getting snarled up in dawdling tour groups. On the other hand, the principal factor that convinces her to make the move is the house itself – which she reports is 'sort of prairie style'; later her husband, an architect, will superciliously instruct her not to forget their neighbourhood's architectural significance. But while mildly satirising middle-class attitudes towards property and architectural prestige, Ware's invocation of Wright's legacy acknowledges longer histories of suburbanisation. Indeed, Wright's initial arrival in Oak Park was representative of a broader suburbanising tendency, which his contributions to the neighbourhood only helped accelerate.[73] If works such as *Jimmy Corrigan* and *Lost Buildings* focus entirely on the city of Chicago's vanished architectural masterpieces – respectively, the enormous edifices of the Columbian Exposition of 1893 or Sullivan's Chicago Stock Exchange and Schiller Theater buildings – *Building Stories'* architectural history straddles the city limits and scrutinises more modest structures. Indeed, *Building Stories* rather confirms a key tenet of the New Suburban History – that it is impossible to properly explain the development of the twentieth-century American suburbs without reference to the transformations of cities, and vice versa.

Equally, *Building Stories* demonstrates that our memories of buildings are most frequently about just that: buildings plural, which involve reflections on and feelings about multiple sites. In its very title Ware's graphic narrative gestures toward a multiplicity of stories about the buildings in which our lives are made; it refuses, however, to offer a sense of completion or totality. As the present continuous of 'Building' indicates, these stories are always incomplete, in process. The title also suggests a mode of narration that requires the participation of others in the act of the story's construction, which, as many have remarked, is a quality of comics generally: a sense of narrative is built by the reader bridging, or achieving 'closure' between, the strip's discrete panels. But managing closure seems an especially hard task given the grand scale and dispersed nature of *Building Stories*. Originally appearing in sections from 2002 across a range of publications, the graphic narrative was published in complete form only in 2012. Even in this form, *Building Stories* retains the diffuseness of its original serialisation, being issued not as a single bound book but as a box containing fourteen separate printed elements in a variety of formats. The idiosyncratic nature of its formatting contributes considerably to a sense of *Building Stories* being a decentred or, at the very least, a non-linear narrative.[74]

Virtually all of the extant scholarship on *Building Stories*, however, centres on one site in particular: the townhouse in the Chicago neighbourhood of Humboldt Park. This is unsurprising: the material focusing on suburban Oak Park was produced more recently, after many commentators put pen to paper. And, in different ways, the walk-up does seem central to *Building Stories*. The majority of its fourteen sections are predominantly focused on the intersecting stories of those living under its roof: the rather lonely young woman on the top floor who has a prosthetic leg, the tempestuous heterosexual couple on the floor below, and the elderly landlady on the ground floor who has lived in the building all her life. Additionally, two sections provide maudlin accounts of the Branford the Bee, who lives, works and dies in the building's vicinity. And then, unlike any other structure depicted within the collection, the townhouse is a thinking being; it is a central, if passive, character in these proceedings.

Approaching the boxed collection of ephemera-like materials is, however, a daunting prospect. It is not clear where one should begin. I started by attending to the largest object in the box, a comic strip printed on papers resembling a broadsheet newspaper that relates the experiences of the female protagonist shortly after she has moved to Oak Park. Despite being more numerous, because I came to them afterwards all of the materials focusing on events in the townhouse seemed like memories. In this fashion the dislocated constitution of *Building Stories* has the potential to destabilise the 'perpetual present' of the traditional comic strip. At the same time, as Gardner would have it, Ware's work demonstrates the historicity of the everyday, the continual production of a visual archive of the present. But in whichever order the collection is approached, the reader will encounter several domestic locations situated across time and space, the majority of which are suburban: the protagonist's Oak Park home; her parental home, situated in an unremarkable mid-twentieth-century subdivision in a small town several hours' drive from Chicago; or the grand house in Oak Park of a family for whom she works as an au pair after completing art school. What may appear to be narrative digressions effectively operate like more expansive versions of Ware's numerous inserted sequences that can be found right across his *oeuvre*. (These numerous parenthetic insertions express, in diagrammatic fashion, developments across time frames that intersect with the present sequence – for example, the life stages, from foetus to death, of a given character depicted at a particular moment in an individual panel.) But while it is clear enough that the fourteen sections of *Building Stories* are loosely interconnected, it is impossible to decide their precise and final arrangement. The collection's structure prevents the reader from determining which sequences are to be inserted into which and, therefore, which sequences are primary, constituting the collection's present tense. By the same token, no single location can be presumed to be central. Rather, the fourteen components of *Building Stories*, and the places they represent, seem simultaneously to nest within one another. Ware contributes further to the sense of the collection's *mise-en-abyme* structure by offering directions to the reader on the box's underside. However, these instructions say nothing about in which order the contents are to be read, but only how the individual elements might be (mis)placed within 'the walls of an average well-appointed home'. Again, then, there is a suggestion that reader participation is essential, inevitable: the collection's sections are quite literally to be inserted into the quotidian lives of readers. But, also, Ware nods to the impossibility of a single, total reading and, through the dispersal and loss of the material components of *Building Stories*, how difficult it can be, from the perspective of everyday life, to establish meaningful connections across space and time.

Like McGuire's *Here*, Ware's *Building Stories* attends to the historicity of suburban domestic space. In both artists' work this feeling for history is achieved by disrupting the linear proceedings and the presumed present tense of comic strips. Once again, Ware's work is the more determinedly self-reflexive. While at art school the young woman – who is seemingly at the centre of the story, even while she feels herself to have no centre – describes an abstract painting she has produced as being 'about the intersection of loss and belonging and the spaces we create to negotiate these'. While she doubts what she says (she finds the 'critique' element of her classes both pretentious and cruel), her statement rather corresponds to a principal project of *Building Stories*. Noticeably, her own creative output – mostly short stories and paintings – fails to achieve this aim. Echoing the artistic progress of Alison in *Fun Home*, *Building Stories* argues that comics, with their capacity to bring together words and images in loose but complex arrangements, are better able than other forms to explicate our emotional investments in the places we inhabit. Indeed, one section shows the protagonist in middle age having dreamt about discovering a book about herself in a big chain-bookstore. The book resembles *Building Stories* in almost every way: 'all of the illustrations [. . .] were so precise and clean it was like an architect had drawn them'; and 'it wasn't really a book either . . . it was in . . . pieces, like, books falling apart out of a carton, maybe'. Potentially this sequence, which would appear to provide *Building Stories* a poioumenon-shaped navel, comes across as a piece of self-aggrandisement on Ware's part: it suggests the architect-cartoonist alone has the power to make meaningful a personal history.[75] The revelation of the dream, though, is that the fragmented materials of her life do indeed constitute something worthy of aesthetic reflection.[76] *Building Stories* constitutes an archive of the ephemera of an ordinary life. It promises not a revelation of coherence; the precision and cleanness that the protagonist appreciates – and which characterises Ware's visual style – is compensatory, the stuff of wish-fulfilling dreams. Rather, *Building Stories* provides a resource for finding value and meaning in messily dispersed lives. Far from merely providing another vehicle for promulgating the sentimental dispossession of the suburbanised middle classes, then, *Building Stories'* rich narrative ecology is concerned with both loss and belonging. Its fragmented composition may indeed reflect increased social atomisation, but it also demonstrates myriad actual and potential connections and attachments.

CHAPTER 5

Devolved Authorship, Suburban
Literacies and the Short Story Cycle

Of all the literary forms considered in this book, the one most closely associated with the narration of community and place is the short story cycle, which may be defined as a single-authored volume comprising a complex – as opposed to a loosely arranged collection – of stories that are linked in various ways, most often by setting. Due to its composite structure the short story cycle is especially well suited to the task of providing diverse perspectives on particular localities. Indeed, there are numerous twentieth-century examples of the form which provide multifaceted accounts of real or imaginary American places. Typically the setting that unites a cycle's diverse views or voices is proclaimed in its title: consider for instance Sherwood Anderson's *Winesburg, Ohio* (1919), John Cheever's *The Housebreaker of Shady Hill* (1958) or Gloria Naylor's *The Women of Brewster Place* (1982). Until only relatively recently, however, short story cycles written by American authors have received scant attention from literary critics. Anderson's volume of tales of small-town Ohio life and a handful of modernist composite narratives – for example, Ernest Hemingway's *in our time* (1924) and William Faulkner's *Go Down, Moses* (1942) – received acclaim for their innovation upon publication. Otherwise, the formal characteristics and capacities of the short story cycle, and its development as a distinct mode of writing, have generally been overlooked. The form's marginalisation owes much to the superior status of the novel, which is still widely presumed to demand from authors greater artistic vision and endeavour than do short stories.

If the short story cycle is thought to have a role to play, then, it is to provide aspiring young writers with a looser, and therefore more forgiving, form so that they may hone their craft before graduating to the more complex challenges of novel-writing.

Such attitudes, however, ignore the fact that the short story cycle has long served as a principal literary form for telling stories about situated communities. Indeed, in many ways it is an eminently suitable vehicle for realising the complexities of place. For, along with its obvious plural aspect, the short story cycle is defined by a vital tension between cohesion and fragmentation. Unlike the individual chapters of most novels, the constituent stories of a cycle make sense when read separately from one another. (Indeed, it is often the case that cyclical volumes are assembled in part out of previously published standalone short stories.) Yet, a successful cycle is always more than the sum of its parts: gaps, echoes and inconsistencies – none of which are apparent when its individual stories are read in isolation – are all crucial to the cycle's overall effect. But this outcome does not necessarily entail the provision of a complete or clear picture. Lacunae and dislocations between stories, as well as discrepancies between retellings, are as likely to be disruptive as they are generative of a coherent sense of place. In short story cycles, then, place is produced tenuously through a set of relationships between narrative elements that are at once autonomous and interdependent. The short story cycle thus bespeaks the inability of narrative to fully pin down place; even after turning the final page of a cycle's concluding story, readers are typically left with a partial, conflicted view of a fictional world.

The form of the short story cycle also facilitates complex temporalisations of place. The same could be not be so confidently said about the standalone short story. Indeed, as Kasia Boddy notes, the widely made claim about Americans being the greatest short story writers in the world has its basis in commonalities about the nation's essentially footloose condition, its freedom from the encumbrances of history. As Julian Hawthorne – son of Nathaniel – once explained, the short story, 'needing no historical perspective, nor caring for any', is a perfect, always-new and therefore quintessentially American form.[1] By contrast, short story cycles that are unified by place frequently do bring to bear a historical perspective on their settings, though such a view is often complex. Indeed, in many cycles, linear time does not provide an organising principle. But even those cycles whose stories are arranged in a more straightforwardly chronological fashion are liable – in part because of the echoes across and the gaps between individual stories – to dwell on the equivocal interactions between time, space and memory. Further, while many cycles are linked by a unity of place, others are comparatively decentred and emphasise instead the manifold connections between geographically distant localities. In these various ways, then, the short story cycle might well be the literary form which best realises geographer Doreen Massey's imperative, which I outlined in this book's introduction, that space be conceived in ways that emphasise its heterogeneity, its incompleteness and its interrelatedness. The short story cycle would thus appear to be an ideal form through which to articulate suburban spatiality in a suitably nuanced fashion.

In this chapter, I attend to the ways short story cycles register suburban complexity. I show that engagements with spatiality in these narratives typically have a metafictional aspect: the short story cycles that I discuss regularly feature suburbanites who write stories, and who seek to develop new techniques and new kinds of collaboration in order to make sense of suburban change. I contend that this devolution of authorship marks not only a repudiation of enduring master narratives of suburban life and an attempt to give voice to diverse experiences, but also an understanding that suburbanites need to take on responsibility over the long term for the narration and memorialisation of their own environments. These short story cycles demonstrate that the fostering and maintenance of suburban literacies is required to counter the persistence of authoritative external narratives that only ever banalise and ossify their subject. Further, the ongoing promotion of such literacy demonstrates an appreciation that, while the dominant story is unlikely ever to change, suburban environments are in flux; their future forms are far from certain. Thus, as well as encouraging an appreciation of the rich historicity of the suburbs, there is an anticipatory quality about suburban short story cycles: these narratives comprehend, and in some instances even instruct, that suburban communities will forever be needing to develop the requisite skills to read and authorise their own environments, in order to triangulate between a spatiality that is continuously changing and a corrosive master narrative which remains constant.

Before I provide a necessarily brief outline of the suburban short story cycle's development in the US, a note on nomenclature. One of the main controversies that has dominated scholarly discussion of this literary form – seemingly a hybrid of the novel and the short story – is what to call it. I have stuck with the most widely used term in criticism, though the two closest contenders for that accolade – short story sequence and short story composite – seem to me to be perfectly acceptable alternatives.[2] 'Sequence' I have passed over mainly because I have employed it already in Chapter 1; the term seems to me better suited to a series of novels published at regular intervals and whose characters and their milieus develop in synchrony with the real world. As well as sounding somewhat technical, 'composite', like 'sequence', unhelpfully suggests rigidity. On the other hand, its connotations of materiality and manufacture arguably make 'composite' a suitable descriptor for collections of stories about suburban housing developments. Ultimately, I favour 'cycle' precisely for its ambivalence. While some critics allege that the term's imputation of circularity is misleading, I find that 'cycle' usefully suggests both sequentiality and recursivity.[3] Indeed, as Jennifer M. Smith demonstrates, it makes sense to describe the organisation of short story cycles as helical: 'stories circle around a common framework without exact repetition. The linking structures – of place, time, and family – serve as axes around which the stories curve.' Smith adds: 'The cycle's spiralling structure disorients, creating a kind of vertigo offset by sharp moments of insight.'[4] I would add that the word cycle also invokes radically different timescales, and these differences too may have vertiginous effects. Many have suggested that, while it has strong associations with modernity (and indeed literary modernism), the short story cycle has its roots in oral tradition.[5] Further, as well as invoking primordial time, 'cycle' is redolent of the quotidian; the word collocates with not only 'epic', but also 'washing'. This duality – a coupling of indisputable historicity with the utter ordinariness of everyday life – may provide a useful counterweight to abstract visions of suburbias that emphasise their timelessness, or critiques of suburbanisation that dismiss the process as a mere historical anomaly.

Cycling through History

The employment of story cycles to write about suburban localities in fact has a surprisingly long history in the US. William Dean Howells's *Suburban Sketches* (1871), may be the first such publication. Drawing on a nineteenth-century tradition of 'local-color' literature, whose customary form was the sketch series, Howells's volume describes everyday life in the emergent suburb of 'Charlesbridge', a thinly disguised version of Cambridge, Massachusetts, where Howells had settled in 1865. While each of the sketches is narrated by and focalised through Howells's unnamed alter ego, they provide a rather ambivalent portrait of the suburb. This ambivalence owes partly to the narrator's tone, which wavers between self-satisfaction and self-irony, but it also has to do with certain qualities of the new suburb's spatiality. Howells's narrator declares that the 'neighbourhood was in all things a frontier between city and country'. Similarly, life in Charlesbridge marks a peculiar convergence of different eras: 'we learned, like innocent pastoral people of the golden age, to know several voices of the cows pastured in the vacant lots, and, like engine-drivers of the iron age, to distinguish the different whistles of the locomotives passing on the neighbouring railroad'.[6] Indeed, the collection is defined by multiple mobilities and the continuous interpenetration of city and suburb. The opening story, for instance, sees the narrator obliged to make an excursion into Boston's black neighbourhood – which provides much pleasurable spectacle – in order to recruit a new domestic. By contrast, the following story, 'Doorstep Acquaintance', gives account of the Italian and Irish immigrants – of various class backgrounds and temperaments – who visit the narrator's Charlesbridge home. Later chapters describe pedestrian tours beginning and ending in Charlesbridge but which traverse various ethnic enclaves and industrial suburbs, and the travails of the commute to Boston by horse-car, a mode of transportation the narrator describes as being 'full of imposture, discomfort, and sublime possibility' (13). This earliest of suburban narratives then defines its principal setting –

a landscape of 'half-finished wooden houses [and] empty mortar beds' (11) – as distinct from the city and countryside, yet still in formation, and a dynamic component within a complexly imbricated metropolis. The American short story writer most closely associated with suburban settlement is without doubt John Cheever. The tales of the 'Ovid of Ossining' are more familiar to twenty-first-century readers either as single stories or collected in recently published voluminous compilations. Cheever did, however, publish one volume of short stories that arguably constitutes a cycle, his 1958 collection *The Housebreaker of Shady Hill and Other Stories*. (However, in stark contrast to Cheever's early novels, *Housebreaker* reviewed poorly.) Despite the appendage 'and other stories', which suggests a loose collection, the cycle's constituent tales are united by their setting, the eponymous upper-middle-class suburb of Shady Hill. While it features some of Cheever's most celebrated short stories – 'O Youth and Beauty!' and 'The Country Husband' – the volume does not dwell solely on the transgressions and disenchantments of the country-club set. Indeed, as Scott Donaldson suggests, in *Housebreaker* Cheever stages the ironic possibility of middle-class contentment alongside the 'sorry spectacle' of suburbanites deceiving themselves.[7] The volume's multipartite form helps produce this tonal dissonance and thereby its ambivalent portrait of suburban life.

Not all short story cycles render their suburban settings in complex or ambivalent fashion, however. By extension, the cyclical form does not preclude narrowly based, predictable or even conservative accounts of suburban places and people. Kelly Cherry's *The Society of Friends* (1999) is a cycle of thirteen interlinked stories about the residents of an upscale suburb of Madison, Wisconsin which emphasises both the transience and the homogeneity of the American upper-middle classes. The volume's setting is dominated by academics and writers (Cherry is herself a distinguished professor of English Literature.) One character feels that university towns are 'all the same: intellectually homogenous no matter how ethnically diverse, one big reading list'.[8] In this fictional universe, conflict does not seem to be a significant dimension of either university or suburban life. Perhaps more usefully, the cycle is attuned to the risks of neighbourly estrangement; according to Jeff Birkenstein, 'characters in *Friends* try to advance their own lives independently on some kind of positive trajectory, but fail to account for the unavoidable change that comes from interaction, petty or otherwise, with others'.[9] On the other hand, the volume seems little inclined to countenance suburban spatiality or society as having any significant capacity for transformation; at most, characters can detect 'a contained, neighborly turbulence'.[10] In the collection's final story, 'Block Party', which assembles the previous stories' principal characters, there is a keen sense of the relative insignificance of each neighbour, of their interchangeability. As the narrator muses:

> In this town, there will be events to mark births and marriages and deaths. There will be graduation parties and retirement parties. People will enter your life, but some of them will stay in it and others will merely visit for a longer or shorter weekend.

And, she concludes, 'there will be block parties'.[11] This statement of inevitability, which comprises a paragraph all to itself, insists on the definitively enduring quality of suburbanity. Birkenstein commends this as revelatory: 'Like the clichéd march of time, everything and nothing changes in Madison.'[12] I prefer to see *Friends'* central vision as merely clichéd, an outcome that is all the more disappointing given in its use of the cycle form.

Diaspora Stories

The short story cycle does not of course only take privileged communities for its subject. Consider for instance Russell Banks's *Trailerpark* (1981), which is set in a mobile home community situated outside a small, down-at-heel New Hampshire town, or Cathy Day's *The Circus in Winter* (2004), which focuses on the everyday lives of members of a travelling circus troupe while it overwinters in a small Indiana town. Smith remarks that many recent collections of short stories dwell on 'a certain economic underbelly' defined by a limited locality.[13] Several scholars, including Smith, have noted the short story cycle's further affinity with ethnic American literatures. James Nagel asserts that the form is 'patently multicultural', a condition that derives 'both from ethnic cross-fertilization within the literary community and from a shared legacy reaching back to ancient oral traditions in virtually every society throughout the world'.[14] Moreover, since the early 1980s the short story cycle has become the 'genre of choice for emerging writers from a variety of ethnic and economic backgrounds' whose principal preoccupation has been the 'situation of the ethnic community as a whole'.[15] Examples of breakthrough publications from this period include Louise Erdrich's *Love Medicine* (1984), Amy Tan's *The Joy Luck Club* (1989) and Julia Alvarez's *How the Garcia Girls Lost their Accents* (1991). Rocio Davis qualifies this frequently articulated periodisation by drawing attention to the fact that cycles have existed in the Asian American canon 'since Toshio Mori published *Yokohama, California* in 1949'.[16] Davis accords with other scholars, though, when she acknowledges how the cycle's formal properties and location within American literary culture have made it an attractive proposition for ethnic-minority writers. Its relative marginality as a genre fosters self-critical and sometimes subversively ironic material, while its hybridity 'becomes both the means and the embodiment of modifying and reshaping [. . .] personal and collective identity'.[17] Further, the short story cycle's rejection of linear narrative, its resistance to teleology and closure, challenges the sense that meaningful experience is that which is plotted. Short story cycles that focus on immigrant and ethnic American communities thus typically demand a different kind of engagement from readers. Indeed, Michael Fischer suggests that using fragments or incompleteness to force readers to make connections 'is not merely descriptive of how ethnicity is experienced, but more importantly is an ethical device attempting to activate in the reader a desire for *communitas* with others, while preserving rather than effacing differences'.[18]

As I outlined in Chapter 2, suburbanisation has frequently been associated with the 'twilight' of ethnic identity and, more specifically, with the cultural assimilation of populations associated with earlier waves of immigration from Europe between the 1880s and 1920s. The apparent readiness of some 'white ethnics' to exchange community affiliations for the material benefits of suburban life attracted the attention of satirists in the post-war years, most notably Philip Roth. The title novella which dominates Roth's 1959 collection of fiction *Goodbye, Columbus and Other Stories* tells of the paradisal existence of the Patimkins, a wealthy Jewish family who have recently moved to the upscale New Jersey suburb of Short Hills. The Patimkins' self-satisfaction is not purely a target of scorn, however: the novella's Newark-based young narrator, who becomes a guest of the Patimkins while dating their self-assured daughter, is by turns captivated, spurred to cynicism and made to feel insecure by the prodigal lifestyle of his host family. Among ethnic-minority communities associated with immigration to the US since the Hart-Celler Act of 1965, suburban settlement is far less likely to carry connotations of either assimilation or luxury. Suburbs increasingly serve as immigrant gateways, a role formerly monopolised by large cities; numerous suburban municipalities, from North California's Silicon Valley to the sprawl of New Jersey, are now minority-majority.[19] It is hardly surprising then that suburban settings feature frequently in recent short story cycles by non-white American writers. More interesting, though, are the ways these narratives understand suburban sites to be defined by various transnational relationships and trajectories, an understanding which in turn informs these cycles' complex organisation.

The stories that comprise Jhumpa Lahiri's 1999 collection *Interpreter of Maladies* are not, as in many short story cycles, unified by a single locality. Rather, they navigate two very different geographical regions on separate continents: West Bengal in India and the suburban north-east of the US. (The volume's final story in addition triangulates through London.) *Interpreter of Maladies* shuttles between the two regions, with several of its constituent stories describing various kinds of movement and relocation, from deportation to holidaymaking. Lahiri's multifocal, multidirectional account of the Bengali diaspora dwells, predictably enough, on feelings of exile and displacement. As its title indicates, however, one of the collection's central themes is the drive to mediate between cultures and to mitigate dislocation. On the other hand, many of its stories foreground failures of communication between married heterosexual couples as they attempt to negotiate different cultural models of privacy and community. Throughout the cycle, various domestic arrangements appear to plot a trajectory from social cohesion to suburban atomisation. But several stories confound such expectations: consider for instance the decidedly modest but sociable Calcutta apartment building of 'A Real Durwan', whose residents stop caring for their caretaker in their quest for gentility, or the well-appointed, frigid suburban home in 'A Temporary Matter', whose regular power cuts facilitate intimate disclosure. Further, despite the recentness of their settlement by Indian immigrants, American suburbs are not shown to be without historical depth. Rather, Lahiri's stories scrutinise how the past is contested by different parties who compete to secure their own vision of the suburban present and future.

This dynamic is most apparent in the story 'This Blessed House', in which married couple Sanjeev and Twinkle discover various items of 'Christian paraphernalia' – mostly kitsch statues and portraits of Christ and Mary – secreted around their new home in a Connecticut suburb.[20] The artefacts are presumably the legacy of former Catholic residents; their presence is suggestive of a refusal to relinquish a claim to place and to accommodate difference. Twinkle's eager adoption of the found objects in turn frustrates Sanjeev's desire to have the house confirm a narrative of his personal achievements, a version of reality in which Twinkle behaves in a much more house-proud fashion than is her wont. Noelle Brada-Williams registers the ambivalence of the conclusion of 'This Blessed House': it is unclear whether Sanjeev's final balancing act as he holds up an enormous silver bust of Christ while following behind Twinkle will in fact be his last act of pleasing his wife, or whether it is, in stark contrast, 'indicative of the balancing of their character differences and Sanjeev's following of Twinkle into a more spontaneous and playful approach to life'.[21] The same refusal to provide closure recurs in other stories and across the cycle as a whole. Thus *Interpreter of Maladies* not only stresses the diversity of the Indian diasporic experience, but also refuses to project suburbs purely as a kind of narrative terminus, or as locations characterised wholly by loss and displacement. Instead Lahiri's short story cycle recognises suburbia to be open, contested and a principal site in a still unfolding imagined diasporic geography.

The prevalence of affluent suburban locations in *Interpreter of Maladies* is indicative of the relatively narrow class constituency of

Lahiri's US-based characters, almost all of whom are academics. Not every short story cycle that explores diasporic experience indexes suburban living with material success, however. In Junot Díaz's 1996 collection of short stories *Drown*, for example, suburban settings underscore the relative failure of young Dominican men burdened by economic precarity, toxic models of masculinity, and the discordancy of immigrant identity. In the manner of *Interpreter of Maladies*, the stories in *Drown* are split between the Dominican Republic and the US. But unlike Lahiri's stories, many of Díaz's are linked by recurring characters. The most salient of these is Ramón de las Casas, or 'Yunior', who departs the Dominican Republic with his mother and siblings in the late 1970s to settle in central New Jersey, where the family is reunited with Yunior's father, who arrived in the US nine years earlier. Yunior narrates several of *Drown*'s stories, in which he recalls a childhood in the Dominican Republic shaped by family estrangement and poverty, and an adolescence in the US overshadowed by his domineering, philandering father. Two stories feature Ysrael, who sustained a horrific facial injury as an infant, and who has been left behind in the Dominican campo where Yunior spent summers as a child. Yunior is haunted by Ysrael's disfigurement but ultimately appears to identify with the boy nicknamed 'No Face'. Ysrael's need to wear a mask, his always being on the run, and his apparent incompleteness all seem to resonate with Yunior's immigrant condition. Indeed, in the cycle's final story, Yunior responds to a photograph of his American-born half-brother and namesake by declaring: 'we were brothers alright, though his face respected symmetry'.[22] The implication of his comment is clear: Yunior perceives himself to be visibly scarred or deformed by his experience of displacement, and by the asymmetry between his third-world upbringing and his life in the US. At the same time, the cycle establishes all kinds of discomforting symmetries between the situations of those who have failed to make it across to the US and those whose passage has ended in failure. For instance, Ysrael's abandonment in a rural backwater is paralleled by the suburban oblivion endured by several of *Drown*'s narrators. In 'No Face', the always-roving Ysrael is an object of ridicule in his local community. In 'Edison, New Jersey', the similarly peripatetic narrator also provides entertainment to unsympathetic neighbours:

his dead-end job involves delivering luxury pool and card tables to wealthy suburbanites, whose ranks pointedly include immigrants who have 'made it'.

While *Drown* presents a decidedly bleak account of the Dominican diaspora, a pessimism that has drawn criticism from some quarters, the collection retains an open and indeterminate quality.[23] Noticeably, several of the stories' male narrators are unnamed. An exception is the drug-dealing narrator of 'Aurora', whose present-tense voice differs from Yunior's melancholic retrospection. He is identified as Lucero, though his eponymous girlfriend's ambition to name her unborn child after him echoes Yunior's own patronymic inheritance. The other narrators mostly share very similar domestic circumstances – cramped apartment, taciturn mother, absent father – and range across the same anonymous New Jersey suburbs. Thus there is little in the cycle that negates the possibility of its being unified by the perspective of one individual. On the other hand, readers cannot be certain that *Drown* is not in fact narrated by several different speakers. In this way the short story cycle proves itself to be an apt vehicle for exploring the ambivalence of immigrant identity. As David Cowart suggests, the ambiguousness of Díaz's narrator(s) yields a further conundrum: by asserting a single narrative voice are we trying to create unity where there is really none, or do the stories' similarities show that the immigrant condition, while defined by fracture and fragmentation, nonetheless produces recognisable patterns, a consequence of shared experiences of poverty, dislocation and loss?[24] Some of the collection's individual stories articulate this simultaneous fracturing and coalescence of identity. In 'How to Date a Browngirl, Blackgirl, Whitegirl, or Halfie' for instance, the narrator ostensibly provides young Dominican heterosexual males a guide to navigating the fraught racial and class dynamics of dating women in his local area. But the instructional second-person voice thinly disguises the narrator's feelings inadequacy and shame: 'take down any embarrassing photos of your family in the campo, especially the one with the half-naked kids dragging a goat on a rope leash' (111); 'Tell [the whitegirl] that you love her skin, her lips, because, in truth, you love them more than you love your own' (115). At the same time that impersonal 'you' seems to diagnose a condition shared by young Dominican men living in the US. Thus *Drown*'s anonymous narrators simultaneously speak for themselves and for a wider, though decidedly marginalised constituency.

An even more pessimistic reading of 'How to Date' and of the cycle as a whole might foreground the apparently deleterious effects of conventional Dominican machismo. This is indeed how Cowart responds to the cycle's title story. I think it is important, though, to register that 'Drown' is ambivalent in a similar fashion to Lahiri's 'This Blessed House'. The story concludes with its narrator – quite possibly, but not definitely Yunior – promising his mother that he will lock the windows of their apartment after they have spent a long evening together watching old movies dubbed into Spanish. It is, contends Cowart, a vision of inertia and suffocation, a state predicted by the story's title. The narrator's responsibility for security follows his assumption, in his father's absence, of the role of family patriarch. His domestic confinement also follows on from his homophobic rejection of his best friend Beto, who has departed for college and better things. In ignoring his gay friend's advice, 'you need to learn how to walk the world' (81), and by throwing away unopened Beto's parting gift of a book, the narrator seems to be consigning himself to a life of poor prospects. Yet the story's conclusion is nuanced. When the narrator regards his slumbering mother – the woman he has made a habit of silencing – he sees, and seems finally to appreciate, her attempts to communicate. Recognising her trembling eyelashes to be 'a quiet semaphore', he surmises that 'she is dreaming, dreaming of Boca Raton, of strolling under the Jacarandas with my father' (85). This is, then, a different kind of 'walking the world': not his former friend's project of self-advancement, but a sympathetic attempt to imagine another's memories and desires. The story's final lines then suggest both a retreat from the world but also something much more outward-looking. The narrator's domestic seclusion is echoed by Yunior's surname; equally, its plurality ('of the houses') is suggestive of more ambivalent and wide-ranging attachments. In any case, the narrator's act of discarding the book does not entail his rejection of the future or of literature. The narrator of 'Drown' takes pride in his sophisticated vocabulary and his reading. (In doing so he reveals another affinity with Ysrael, who has a penchant for using power words derived from comics.) The cycle's narrators may feel their atrophied Spanish as a loss of authenticity, and that their own misadventures in scrappy suburban neighbourhoods make for unrewarding narrative material compared to the more heroic endeavours of their immigrant fathers. (The cycle's concluding story, 'Negocios', in which Yunior narrates his father's earlier travails, is noticeably twice as long as any other.) And yet, seemingly against all the odds, these young men still manage to tell their stories – stories which are indubitably their own but, curiously, also each other's.

Vernacular Adaptations: Commemorating Suburban Change

The final two suburban-set short story cycles I discuss in this chapter share with Díaz's *Drown* a preoccupation with literacy and devolved authorship. That is to say, these cycles underline the need for suburbanites to take on responsibility for narrating their own environments. Such storifying, I argue, entails not only an attentiveness to spatial change but also new kinds of collaboration. The engagements of suburban communities with their own environments depicted in these short story cycles accord with the arguments of humanistic geographers and scholars of cultural landscapes who are concerned precisely with the phenomenology of habitats undergoing change. For instance, in *What Time is this Place?* (1972) Kevin Lynch defines a 'humane environment' as one which 'commemorates recent events quickly and allows people to mark out their own growth'.[25] This capacity for commemoration is predicated on one of forgetting, or the fading of 'these marks as they recede in time or lose connections with present peoples'. To be properly habitable, local landscapes must facilitate personal narratives of the lived past; they must enable people to transform their experiences through 'dramatic recital'.[26] In his work on American vernacular landscapes, John Brinckerhoff Jackson argues that far from being 'timeless', as is commonly presumed, vernacular building has not only undergone a long and complicated evolution, it is inherently responsive to the changing physical, social and economic needs of its inhabitants.[27] In an essay on the suburban garage, Jackson asserts that 'the garage as a family center half outdoors, part work area, part play area, is a family invention, not the invention of designers'.[28] It is suburban inhabitants who design and redesign their homes; the homebuilder merely provides the structure. For Jackson, such adaptation defines the vernacular. Jackson, it must be admitted, is little concerned with the possibility of conflict – either within or between households – arising from ongoing adaptation, perhaps presuming that suburbanites are only concerned with developments occurring within the boundaries of their own properties. There would also appear to be less scope for those who do not own their own homes to engage in and benefit from such adaptative practices. However, suburban short story cycles pay particular attention to the impacts of adaptations to both the home and the wider environment on various parties; regardless of who is the agent of change, such adaptation provides opportunities for commemorating the past and for anticipating future developments.

The two short story cycles I examine below were written by admittedly very different authors: children's author Pam Conrad and avowed postmodernist John Barth. The pairing is less eccentric than might first seem. Both writers employ metafictional techniques to break from the static tradition of suburban writing and to engage with the changing form of America's suburbs. Both conceive of suburban narrative as a kind of 'dramatic recital' which articulates personal and public attachments to place. Each story cycle focuses on the adaptation of the local environment by its inhabitants, for it is precisely such changes which give sense to their situated lives by providing shape to the stories they tell. But these stories are by no means hermetic: the changes which are registered often index developments taking place within the wider world.

'Keep in Mind that You are Making Memories': Pre-emptive nostalgia in Pam Conrad's *Our House*

Pam Conrad's 1995 short story cycle written for children, *Our House*, is an account of what is probably still the United States' most famous planned suburb, Levittown, New York. Its six stories are each narrated by a different child growing up in its prefabricated environs in consecutive decades following its construction in the late 1940s. Conrad presents each of her child narrators recording significant experiences, an act which always corresponds to the creation and habitation of new spaces as Levittown matures. In the volume's first story, 'Boy Fossil', the young narrator TeeWee Taylor recounts playing in his new home's attic. It is a space his family hopes to transform: the recently installed full staircase is described by his mother as her 'stairway to the stars', which prefigures it as a place of imagination and possibility. Conrad here would seem to be inscribing a Bachelardian vision of the home as a structure which fosters revivifying modes of daydreaming.[29] Indeed, in his celebrated phenomenological expedition through domestic space, Gaston Bachelard remarks on how in the oneiric house – the 'house of dream memory' – the attenuated space of the attic fulfils the daydreamer's requirements for intimacy.[30] The very verticality of the oneiric house also provides for the stowage of memories: says Bachelard, 'memories are motionless, and the more securely they are fixed in space, the sounder they are'.[31] Thus Bachelard's observations have the potential to dignify the Levittown home. Contemporary critics of the post-war American suburbs such as William H. Whyte and Lewis Mumford bridled at what they saw as their relentlessly social – and conformist – nature; Lynn Spigel has since characterised the suburban home as 'a place for looking', with the picture window, open-planned interiors and the television generating increasingly visual and correspondingly less private spaces.[32] Through Bachelard, the suburban home may be appreciated as still having the capacity to foster intimacy; further, despite its inauspicious mass-produced fabrication, it can be seen as an environment which nurtures the imagination and enables memory making.

While she shares a concern about the relationships between domestic spaces and memory, Conrad's project is, however, quite the reverse of Bachelard's. At a very basic level, the act which TeeWee is memorialising is not his ascent to the intimate space of the attic – and Bachelard claims we always remember climbing the attic stairs, but never coming down them – rather, it is a movement from lofty solitude back into society.[33] TeeWee bursts through the ceiling into the middle of a party held by his parents. (Fortunately, his fall is cushioned by a large tomato cake prepared by his mother.) Repeatedly, while Conrad is interested in personal memories and narratives, the experience of domestic space in which they are enmeshed is always shared with others. By contrast, Bachelard seeks to *'desocialize* our important memories' in order to reify a shared, ancestral domestic imaginary.[34] Even though he goes on to claim that 'it is better to live in a state of impermanence than in one of finality', for Bachelard, the oneiric house, mined from childhood experience, is always already complete, ever comforting, and universal in its structure and extent.[35] For Conrad the suburban home, located within a nexus of social relations, is an ongoing project; it is precisely its development which prompts the creation of memory-texts. TeeWee memorialises his fall in another extension of the family's domestic territory: a cement patio. By inscribing his name next to his footprints in the wet cement, an act which recalls his earlier soft landing, TeeWee produces the first of many texts by Levittown children which act as mnemonics for particular experiences of suburban space. As the earliest, TeeWee's is appropriately primitive: a 'boy fossil'. Subsequently, the children's texts become more sophisticated and indeed literate as Levittown matures as an environment.

In the remaining stories, Levittown is shown to be by no means detached from wider historical currents: the effects of war, de facto segregation and environmental degradation are felt by the later child narrators – but always in ways that alter the parameters of their environment and daily routines, and prompt the creation of narrative. For instance, in 'The Longest Summer on Record', a teachers' strike ruptures Levittown's daily and annual rhythms, fostering new rituals and recording methods: storytelling and a diary. The clearing of polluted drainage sumps creates new play spaces and, as readers find in the story 'Writer's Notebook', new narrative possibilities and scope for imagining racial harmony. In the book's final story, 'The Second Bad Thing', the young Katie narrates the events surrounding the death of her younger brother who is killed in a road accident in Levittown. Her story is really about her quest to produce and locate an appropriate memorial. Once again, it is the Levittown house that provides. As her father prepares the foundations for an extension to accommodate Katie's widowed grandfather, TeeWee's 'fossilized' imprint is revealed. Katie leaves her brother's boot prints and name next to those of the unknown child. This is a private, enacted memorialisation (for both sets of prints will be covered over with flooring). Yet, Conrad's *Our House* encourages the view that such private acts have public consequences, that the suburb holds such memories palimpsestically. Katie concludes:

> Maybe that's what neighborhoods are all about. Always changing and growing and sometimes getting worse, but underneath it all, there are invisible footprints pressed into the sidewalks and gardens and wet cement, footprints of all the kids who have ever played there. A kind of remembering that is everywhere. (114–15)

So, what is felt to be in evidence is not so much traces of past lives, but textual traces of memorialising acts, acts of remembering which are embedded in the suburban landscape.

Thus, Conrad's collection rejects suburban literature's traditional insistence on dispossession, and demonstrates instead the ways narrative can performatively create home attachments. Indeed, in the epilogue, the (child) reader is invited to 'keep in mind that you are making memories' (121). The use of the present continuous here is suggestive of the way memories, ever in a dynamic relationship with current experience and emotions, are inevitably and continually remade. As Owain Jones puts it, 'memory is not just a retrieval of the past from the past, it is always a fresh, new creation where memories are retrieved into the conscious realm and something new is created in that context'.[36] The instruction to produce narrative mnemonics, however, invites a confidence in the future fixity of memories of place. With its trust in the capacity of storytelling to safeguard against forgetting, coupled with the presumption of transience – the succession of child narrators suggests that none will experience maturity in Levittown – the appeal 'keep in mind that you are making memories' comes across as a modified, rather peculiar form of nostalgia. One might indeed describe it as 'pre-emptive nostalgia', that is, the anticipation of the future production of the present as remembered past.

But in spite of its frankly odd construction, arguably Conrad's nostalgia is fairly conventional after all. *Our House* determinedly counters the complaint that the suburbs cannot produce homeliness. This move, though, is perhaps indicative of another, frequently articulated variation of nostalgia: less a longing for home that has been lost than for a home one has never had, but for which nevertheless the loss is still felt. Thus the book's insistence on the necessity of generating feelings of home through narrative thus might seem compensatory. Svetlana Boym considers how nostalgia may also take the form of a longing for a lost time as much as a lost place. The period of time in question is of course typically childhood, a constant realm untouched by the conflicts of history and the march of progress. It is the basis for secure, comforting visions, à la Bachelard. But, once again, Conrad seems keen to show that childhood experiences of suburban space are connected to and not divorced from historical time; the stories produced by the child narrators respond to and even critically reflect on events taking place in the wider world. Arguably, Conrad's is a species of what Boym identifies as 'reflective nostalgia'. Unlike the 'restorative' forms that typically lie at the centre of nationalist discourse, 'reflective nostalgia does not follow a single plot but explores different time zones; it loves details, not symbols. At best, reflective nostalgia can present an ethical and creative challenge, not merely a pretext for midnight melancholias.'[37] These comments well describe the fragmented narration of *Our House*, which breaks apart the conventional bi- or tripartite generational narrative of post-war American suburbs – the veteran settlers, then baby boomers, then Generation Xers – and offers a more nuanced account of the post-war nation. And the text's preoccupation with children's attentiveness to detail – and its rejection of panoptic accounts that were so prevalent in the post-war period – is perhaps an encouragement to its readers to leave off tired metanarratives about the suburbs and register instead the complex textures and temporalities of these environments.[38]

'Signs of Deferred Maintenance': New Narrative Collaborations in John Barth's *The Development*

Superficially, the planned residential development which provides the setting to Barth's cycle of nine stories, *The Development* (2008), is a very different kind of habitat from Conrad's Levittown. Situated on a toponymically adjusted version of Maryland's Upper Eastern Shore, the fictional Heron Bay Estates development is hardly the iconic, child-centred American suburb. Rather, it represents the kind of upscale, exurban gated community that has proliferated across the United States since the 1980s. Noticeably, Barth's setting is virtually child-free, being populated in the most part by affluent retired 'empty nesters', who seem all-too conscious that once-close parents and children have become emotionally and geographically distant. Like Conrad's *Our House*, however, Barth's stories focus on the ways individuals produce texts in order to make sense of the evolving residential environments they inhabit. Each of Barth's narrators is a writer: Tim Manning is a retired high school history teacher who has turned 'self-appointed chronicler' of Oyster Cove, one of several contiguous but distinct Heron Bay subdivisions; Gerald Frank pens a weekly opinion piece – *'FRANK OPINIONS'* – for the County newspaper; and George Newett is a self-proclaimed 'Failed Old Fart' 'fictionist' and professor emeritus following several decades of teaching English literature and creative writing at the local liberal-arts college. Each of these writer-narrators grapples with the problem of producing what they consider to be appropriate narratives to account for the exigencies of the environment they inhabit and the lives they lead. As a consequence, many of the stories are not organised in the manner of conventional short stories; indeed, often they are preoccupied first and foremost by the troubled process of narration itself.

For instance, Manning insists that he is not a 'storyteller' but a 'history-teller'.[39] Towards the end of the collection's opening story 'Peeping Tom', about a nocturnal interloper to Oyster Cove whose identity, and indeed very existence, is never established, Manning explains to his putative reader: 'What You're winding up here [. . .] is a history, not a Story, and its "ending" is no duly gratifying Resolution nor even a capital-E Ending, really, just a sort of petering out, like most folks' lives' (22). It would seem that a history of a place and a people does not require, and will likely be hindered by, the conventional components of a story. Indeed, had it been a story, Manning asserts, he would also not have started it where he did. Instead, the narrative would have opened with the comfortable domestic scene that was disturbed by the first sighting of the peeping Tom. The several initial expository pages about the Heron Bay Estates would have been lost. But Manning's historical preamble, and other similar passages elsewhere in the collection, crucially gives account of the Heron Bay Estates' maturation, the development's development: its being 'built out' after the 'raw early years of construction' (5); the remodelling of '"colonial" mini-mansions' (57) by their new owners some two decades after being built; more dramatically, the arrival of 'Mega McMansions' on keyhole plots and following teardowns; and the inescapable signs of 'deferred maintenance' (5). Moreover, Manning's narrative expresses the attachment residents feel for their environment precisely because the landscape is undergoing change; such development seems analogous to shifts taking place in their own lives. Many of the collection's stories, indeed, are narratives of decline and loss: their elderly narrators struggle with bereavement, impotence and dementia. But place attachment does not precipitate simply because human minds and bodies share with bricks-and-mortar structures built-in obsolescence. Their accounts of the Estates' artificially variegated landscape help residents to shape and bring order to their lives. Manning for instance speaks of how movements between the different subdivisions represent upwards, sideways, downwards or terminal transitions, depending on age, health and material circumstances (4), and describes his own progression as his 'phased retirement' (131). Also, while conscious that some of it is absurdly euphemistic, Manning and his wife Margie employ the jargon of the Estate's developer, Tidewater Communities, Inc., regularly and with some affection. Indeed, sometimes the Estate's official names and expressions prove to be surprising apposite, and these felicities generate narrative: few tire of explaining to visitors that 'Doubler Drive' is an appropriate term for a street of 'over-and-under' duplexes – a 'doubler' is a fisherman's term for a catch of a pair of mating crabs (58). And after settling in TCI's 'Assisted Living' development Manning is prompted to create a more able third-person version of himself to provide him with assistance through his increasingly isolated and difficult life.

By contrast, conventionally told stories are liable to misrepresent the unassuming lives of contemporary exurbia. Subsequently almost none of the collection's stories involve characters in high-stakes situations or feature startling denouements – even the freak tornado that destroys the entire development in the penultimate story is, like the peeping Tom, emptied of dramatic potential. Tellingly, one reviewer of *The Development* identified 'Toga Party' as the collection's stand-out story.[40] (Students I taught on a course which focused on the suburbs in American literature almost unfailingly did the same.) Of all the stories this one features proportionally the fewest metafictional interventions, and the most 'action': it concludes with an attempted suicide (in public, and in fancy dress) of a bereaved elderly resident, followed by a successful suicide pact (behind closed doors) of an apparently contented retired married couple who decide that they have, on balance, little to look forward to. The 'satisfying' story elements combine with a depiction of suburban existence as unsatisfying, and a rather familiar account of smug suburban affluence prevails. Clearly, there are certain kinds of stories about suburban life which people still prefer to read.

The collection's numerous metafictional interruptions, which amongst other topics include discussions of counterfactual narrative possibilities and the fabricated nature of the stories' characters, serve as reminders that such familiar, more palatable fare will not be on offer. The collection's fourth story, 'The Bard Award', shows an awareness that there exists a tradition of suburban fiction writing in the United States, but suggests that merely perpetuating it will be unproductive. The eponymous award is the nickname for the Stratford College Shakespeare Prize, which is given annually to the creative writing student whose work shows most promise. The prize is associated with failure. None of its previous winners have gone on to make successful careers out of writing; its over-generous patron, the CEO of Tidewater Communities, Inc., was a budding playwright before lack of success spurred him on to a much more lucrative career in property development; and George Newett admits that the Prize Committee, of which he is member, is made up of second-rate writers. The parallels between literary failure and exurban development are not meant to indicate, however, that the former is an inevitable consequence of the latter. Newett, for instance, insists that his muse would have withered regardless of where he ended up living. The problem seems rather to stem from the entrenched conventionality and earnestness of all parties involved. Newett appears to break the cycle of failure with the aid of the most talented student he has ever taught, the freewheeling 'provocateuse' Cassandra Klause, who has a penchant for all manner of metafictional and performance-art-related high jinks. The wilful young woman provokes little other than eye-rolling from most of her elder instructors; Newett, though, is inspired. Together they conspire to submit a portfolio of Newett's own short stories, edited by Klause, for consideration for the Shakespeare Prize. Newett's stories, which hitherto have been serially rejected by publishers, are fictionalised accounts of the people and environment of Heron Bay Estates. For Klause, they are merely 'pallid rehashes [. . .] of "the 3 Johns" (her dismissive label for Messrs. Cheever, O'Hara, and Updike): the muted epiphanies and petty nuances of upper-middle-class life in a not-all-that-upscale gated community' (89). Thus, the numerous frame-breaking moments that occur in *The Development*'s other stories may be presumed to be the work of Klause, or at least a writer reinvigorated by her demands for freshness and self-aware writing. The interventions are improving: far from being just metafictional ticks, they prevent the work from falling into complacent reiteration of earlier suburban narratives. Moreover, by insisting that his characters are as artificial as their habitat, Barth renders absurd the suburbanised middle class's *cri de coeur* over their own inauthenticity.

The collection's final two stories, which relate the Heron Bay Estates' complete destruction by natural disaster, comprise an interesting thought experiment. How might a community, given the opportunity, re-envisage its own environment? Would residents have ambitions for the development at large, or solely for their own property? How might they negotiate conflicting visions for redevelopment? For sure, the capacity for rebuilding is a measure of the residents' affluence: references to Hurricane Katrina and the South East Asian tsunami acknowledge that the victims of other catastrophic natural events had no such privilege. But rather than merely indicating the freedoms attendant on wealth, this final 'tear-down' illustrates the residents' attachment to their environment and community. While almost every resident desires to rebuild his or her property, each is aware that this would only be meaningful if more or less everyone else were to choose to do the same. Thus, place attachment in this habitat extends beyond the perimeters of personal plot. Decisions about how the Heron Bay Estates at large are to be reconstructed are made collectively: as the leader of the Estate's Community Association reminds residents, 'it's our baby these days, not its original developers' (160), an assertion of design control which echoes Jackson's observations about the suburban home. The only conflict between residents that emerges is over the extent to which the development should be rebuilt with greater sensitivity to the environment. But even the most radical of the residents acknowledge that a 'greener' development must first respect people's place attachments. Thus Barth's collection – like so many short story cycles – drives towards ambivalence, by relating both the desire for and possibility of transformation, but also more conservative feelings towards space and place.

By stopping short of depicting a singular, determined vision of the future for the Heron Bay Estates, Barth seems rather to confirm Kathy Knapp's thesis that it is 'uncertainty that provides a basis for a new suburban literary tradition' in the twenty-first century.[41] The refusal of a number of contemporary writers of suburban fiction to provide determinate endings, Knapp argues, stems from a rejection of the triumphalist accounts propagated by the American media in the wake of 9/11. These media accounts offered comforting but premature closure; the wounds caused by the attacks, however, have had insufficient time to heal. The suburbs provide an appropriate setting for examining such unresolved trauma, for demonstrably they no longer offer a safe retreat from the world made perilous by the very attitudes which fostered them: the desire for security, moral minimalism and compulsive consumption. A consequence of this new metanarrative, though, is that the suburbs are reinstalled to explain once again a national problem, a general malaise. This risks, I would suggest, the obscuration of other kinds of suburban story. For sure, Conrad's and Barth's narratives, which were written either side of 9/11, hardly show the suburbs to be untouched by history or trauma. Yet, neither author presumes to tell a 'national' story, and neither employs a singular 'everyman' figure in order to do so. Indeed, their youthful and elderly narrators are actually unusual voices in suburban narrative, and are all the more welcome for it. The indeterminacy of Conrad's and Barth's short story cycles instead stems from the multiple and sometimes conflicting accounts of, and claims made on, suburban environments. These locales are shown not to be merely symptomatic of economic and social crisis. Neither are suburbs presumed to be merely redundant and residual formations. Rather, they are environments undergoing change; it is by providing accounts of such changes that their inhabitants attempt to make sense of their lives and the world around them.

Conclusion:
Built to Last?
Staging Suburban Historicity in
the Teardown Era

The history of the United States *is* the history of private property.

Steve, in Bruce Norris's Clybourne Park[1]

Contestation is the real story of suburbia.

Dolores Hayden[2]

'The great suburban build-out is over', declares James Howard Kunstler in his scathing indictment of post-war sprawl *The Geography of Nowhere*, published in 1993.[3] Kunstler is just one of a chorus of voices proclaiming the end of the era of the American suburb. Largely inspired by the work of new urbanists Andres Duany and Elizabeth Plater-Zyberk in the early 1990s, Kunstler's invective holds the unchecked suburban growth of recent decades to be economically and environmentally unsustainable, and calls for a return to the traditional, pedestrian-friendly, mixed-used neighbourhoods of pre-war cities. Economists such as Robert J. Shiller have asserted that the massive residential dispersal of the post-war period – stimulated by the Federal Housing Administration and Veterans Administration loan programmes – was historically anomalous; Shiller further argues that there is no long-term future for exurban growth following the collapse of the housing bubble in the mid-2000s and continually escalating fuel prices.[4] A few years earlier, the architectural critic Herbert Muschamp insisted that the post-war mass-produced suburban house was in any case only ever able to remain standing for a few decades before the cheap materials used in its construction, such as plywood, inevitably peeled, buckled and split, with features such as doors and windows 'morph[ing] into trick or treat versions of themselves'.[5] Muschamp outlines some proposals made by planners for the 'recycling' and repurposing of declining 'first-tier' suburbs, and in subsequent years interest in redesigning or 'retrofitting' older suburbs has grown.[6] Over the last three decades, however, individuals have been taking matters into their own hands. The apparent obsolescence of the housing stock of many 'inner-ring' suburbs, coupled with the increasing desirability of living in closer proximity to central cities, has fuelled the 'teardown' phenomenon, which involves older properties being bought with a view to demolishing and replacing them with a structure more suited to the needs or status of the new owners. Teardowns have proven controversial for an assortment of reasons, environmental, socio-economic and aesthetic. Indeed, 'historic character' is an attribute frequently mobilised to bolster competing claims about what constitutes appropriate architectural form in suburban and urban neighbourhoods across the United States that have been affected by teardowns.[7]

Critics who have called time on the suburbs show little willingness to countenance longer histories of suburbanisation; typically, their accounts begin in the post-war moment. Neither are they much interested in recent instantiations of suburban diversity, such as the consequences of changing patterns of immigration across metropolitan areas. For sure, the question of how suburbanites conceive of the historicity of their own habitats hardly registers as a significant matter. Why after all would it: the post-war suburbs are understood to be a temporary aberration and thus without historical content. *The Literature of Suburban Change* offers a challenge to such terminal diagnoses: throughout this book I have shown how writers across a range of forms and genres have sought to situate suburbs within wider, continually unfolding histories. This concluding section considers some recent plays which appraise suburban histories in a period during which the continued existence of suburbs is in question. Against a backdrop of teardowns and revanchist urbanism these plays emphasise that suburban histories are nevertheless still being produced and contested; these histories, moreover, attempt to navigate a present moment and near future defined by uncertainty.

Three recently produced plays engage with histories of post-war suburbanisation: Marc Palmieri's *Levittown* (2006), Lisa D'Amour's *Detroit* (2010) and Bruce Norris's *Clybourne Park* (2010).[8] The latter two plays contemplate or enact the destruction of a single-family home in neighbourhoods where teardowns are taking place. All three depict post-war suburban settlers as well as members of a younger generation seeking a home in the present. Each production literally stages changes to the conditions that have shaped attitudes to property and community over a span of five decades. While all three plays construct suburban histories, each historicises the suburbs very differently, with important consequences for thinking about present-day life in urban and suburban environments. D'Amour's play takes a distinctly Kuntslerian line. In her vision, the suburbs have run their course, and no longer offer, if they ever did, a model for community, security and freedom. But by indicting first-generation suburbanites for the current malaise while denying them the opportunity to speak for themselves, I would suggest that *Detroit* is ultimately unable to offer meaningful answers to the current problems experienced by many American cities and suburbs. By contrast, Palmieri's *Levittown*, which I consider briefly, presents the post-war mass-produced home as a veritable archive, a vital resource from which later generations might learn important lessons. Norris's *Clybourne Park* takes a different approach again. By devoting each of its two acts to the exchange of a single house – first in 1959 and again in 2009 – Norris's play articulates how such environments continue to be deeply desired places, but also sites of conflict. *Clybourne Park* meditates on the ways residents are liable to assert alternative histories in order to consolidate competing claims over places. As the geographer Doreen Massey has argued, 'the identity of places is very much bound up with the *histories* which are told of them, *how* these histories are told, and which history turns out to be dominant'. Yet such histories are never final and fixed, but continually in process. Indeed, contends Massey, 'what are at issue are competing histories of the present, wielded as arguments over what should be the future'.[9] Whereas D'Amour and the New Urbanists are preoccupied by suburbia's supersession, Norris seems exercised by more straightforwardly political questions: who benefits from the articulation of particular urban and suburban histories, and which voices and arguments carry the most authority. According to its production notes, D'Amour's play is not set in Detroit, but in a declining inner suburb of an unnamed Midwestern city. Presumably the play is so-titled because of Detroit's undoubted metonymic power: more than any other rust-belt city, Detroit has come to epitomise the abject wreckage of post-industrial collapse. Late twentieth-century Detroit's extensive portfolio of ruins – a selection of which Camilo José Vergara has provocatively argued might be preserved as 'an American Acropolis' so as to monumentalise the hubris of industrialists – is now a staple of documentary photography.[10] The hulking shells of the city's vast auto-industry plants and civic buildings have been hauntingly – but also lavishly – portrayed in numerous publications, such as Dan Austin and Sean Doerr's *Lost Detroit*, Andrew Moore's *Detroit Disassembled*, and Yves Marchand and Romain Meffre's *The Ruins of Detroit*, all of which were published within a year of the first performance of D'Amour's play. Just as ubiquitous are photos of the abandoned residential homes that are a common feature of many Detroit neighbourhoods. Several websites – for example, '100 Abandoned Houses' and the prominent Detroit blog 'Sweet Juniper!' – provide a visual record of these apparently more human-scale ruins. Much of this photographic material has proven controversial, especially with local residents. Detroiters rarely feature in these often highly aestheticised images, and when they do appear they are at most peripheral, incidental figures. Dwarfed by the majesty of the ruins, local people are depicted as having no influence over their environment, which, in many instances, is being reclaimed by nature. Certainly, some photographers show little interest in engaging with the complex historical reasons for the ruins' existence or with the ongoing social and economic challenges faced by the city's majority-black population. Indeed, as Rebecca Kinney argues, the invocation of Detroit's lost grandeur in these photographs naturalises a racist narrative that equates blackness with moribundity and which suggests the city is waiting to be saved.[11] For its sensationalism as well as its superficiality, this proliferating genre has been dismissed locally as 'Detroitsploitation', and more widely as 'ruin porn'.

In this context D'Amour's choice of title seems, at the very least, an act of appropriation – and perhaps all the more so after the playwright admitted to having first visited Detroit only in 2012, two years after the play's first performance. However, after runs in Chicago, New York and London, the next city to host the play was in fact Detroit. Some Detroit-based reviewers celebrated the Hilberry Theatre Company's 2013 production as a homecoming of sorts. Others, however, were more sceptical. John Monaghan, for instance, was not convinced that the play captured or spoke to the city in any meaningful way. Others still were intrigued by the production's complex dynamics of place, which involved a Detroit-based company putting on an outsider's play that was titled 'Detroit' despite not being explicitly set in the city or one of its suburbs. Carolyn Hawes applauded the production design's subtle rendering of locality: rather than attempting verisimilitude, she found 'the surroundings [to be] loaded with approximations of the city', a strategy she saw as consciously addressing the tension that defines the 'urge to *claim* Detroit without being *of* Detroit'.[12] A sense that the principal aims of the production were to address the very question of who gets to represent the city and to promote ongoing dialogue was affirmed by a special collection of photographs put on display during the play's run. The exhibition, produced by the Hilberry Theatre in co-operation with The Detroit Institute of Arts and with the collaboration of community organisations and local businesses, was titled 'Reveal Your Detroit'; its many contributors helped showcase the city's diversity. The multiplicity of responses generated by the Hilberry Theatre production suggests then that the play's relationship with its namesake city need not be exploitative; indeed, in contrast to photography of Andrew Moore et al., which tends to marginalise and even disempower Detroiters, the production appeared to foster engagement.

Detroit emblematises not only the failures of America's industrial past: increasingly it also conjures up more optimistic impressions of the possibilities of a post-industrial present and future. Boosterish commentators point to the dynamism of Detroit's flourishing arts scene, a new entrepreneurialism, as well as various projects around food sustainability, which have led to the establishment of a number of urban farms, many of which are community run. These various scenes and schemes have though been much criticised from several quarters. The social scientist Jackson Bartlett for instance has complained about how media coverage of the endeavours of recently arrived whites has occulted those of established black residents.[13] Others are less than impressed about the projects themselves. Says John Patrick Leary, who teaches at Wayne State University and lives within the city, 'if Detroit is really so full of possibilities, why do so many of [them] so closely resemble a cut-rate version of what western Brooklyn already looks like?'[14] In his study of the gentrification of American cities, journalist Peter Moskowitz writes that the recently regenerated area of downtown Detroit is 'a nearly closed loop'; indeed, 'it is possible to live in this new Detroit and essentially never set foot in the old one'.[15] And Patrick Sheehan, another Detroit resident, links plans for revitalisation to the evictions of thousands of poor black residents, whose homes are being repossessed and resold due to tax delinquency. These tax foreclosures resemble the racist housing practices of the post-war years, especially urban renewal schemes that relied on slum clearance: while long-time black residents are being shown the door, Sheehan contends the city 'is simultaneously preparing the ground for a new Motor City, with a lighter complexion'.[16]

D'Amour's play is interested not only in the bleak prospects afforded by post-industrial landscapes and economies, but also with how new forms of collective activism might help to re-envisage urban or indeed suburban life. In a post-performance Q&A session at London's National Theatre, she declared that the play is about the experience of 'waking up in a machine' – presumably one that is malfunctioning – and the course of action required to make it work, or to escape from it. The play focuses on the developing friendship between two young heterosexual white couples. They live in neighbouring modest suburban tract houses; most of the action takes place in their adjoining backyards. In an early scene, the slightly older Ben and Mary are entertaining the younger newcomers Sharon and Kenny over a barbeque dinner; the gathering provides each of them opportunity to voice their frustrations with their unrewarding and insecure service-sector jobs, the lack of community spirit in their neighbourhood, as well as the flimsiness of their suburban homes. (Much is made of the fact that the sliding glass door which communicates with the interior of Mary and Ben's house continually gets stuck on its runners.) Various neuroses are disclosed, as is the fact that the younger pair are recovering drug addicts. Despite anxieties felt on both sides about their differences in class and status, the four pair off for some homosocial bonding activities off-stage, though all of their adventures are aborted. It seems that no-one has the imaginative resources to escape the machine. Their final act together is a drunken nocturnal party, which brings out latent sexual and violent urges. After some almost orgiastic couplings, the younger couple burn down their new friends' home and then disappear, never to be seen again. In the play's final scene, during which Ben and Mary are sitting in bewilderment in the smoking ruins of their home, a stranger appears who declares himself to be a relative of one of the absconders. The late middle-aged Frank relates that he was a pioneer of the subdivision – promoted as 'Bright Homes' – when it was developed back the 1960s, and he nostalgically recounts its egalitarian and sociable heyday. He even vows to create an archive of oral testimonies of early settlers. His suggestion though has little impact on the couple, who abandon their ruined home, despite being unsure of their next destination.

The significance for me of this odd historicising coda became more complicated after I was commissioned to write a short contextualising essay for the National Theatre production's programme. I was encouraged to discuss the historical bases for suburbanisation in the US and to talk about some of the more recent problems that have beset many suburbs, including the 'teardown' phenomenon, to which the play alludes in its notes about its own setting. Initially I asserted that one of the boldest moves made by the play was its recognition that the much-maligned post-war suburbs are historical spaces; I had taken Frank's proposals seriously. D'Amour, however, demurred, declaring that she did not think that her play 'is saying the postwar suburbs are historic'.[17] Consequently, my revised version of the essay made no mention of the play. In a subsequent Q&A session, the playwright insisted that Frank's plans for a physical archive are patently silly.

One the one hand, D'Amour's resistance to the idea of suburb's historicity makes sense. Mary tries to organise her lifestyle as though she were a suburban housewife from an earlier era. But the bases for such a way of life have been superseded. Thus Mary's obsessive hostessing is as inappropriate and unhelpful as her husband's addiction to 'Brit-Land', a role-playing website 'designed especially for non-Brits who want to be British'.[18] What is required is a preparedness and a capacity – something these suburbanites appear to lack entirely – to comprehend and grapple with the conditions of the here and now. Frank's nostalgic appeal to the suburb's bright dawn is then just another way of avoiding having to take purposeful action in the present.

On the other hand, I would argue that the impasse at the play's conclusion is a missed opportunity for potentially productive dialogue about the successes and failures of suburban life. Discussion between the generations might have provided a forum for sharing stories about how solidarity has been achieved in the past, about aspirations realised and thwarted, and about protest and struggle. Dolores Hayden notes the example of the Park Forest Public Library digital archive, which covers the history of that post-war suburb's development and its progress towards racial integration. Oral history interviews, Hayden contends, 'offer rich materials for both scholars and the general public'.[19] Hayden suggests further that:

> residents, old and new, can also use local economic history to understand who has been involved in the transformation of the suburban landscape over the decades. They may become curious about which contractors built the local tracts. Who graded and paved the highways? Who owned the earliest strip malls and highways?[20]

Such endeavours could very well constitute the kinds of collective action that D'Amour has suggested might help people better understand and operate the estranging 'machine' that is the contemporary American metropolis. *Detroit* shows that the suburbs have a past, but not one that can speak to the present in any meaningful way. D'Amour's motivation for using an aphorism of Heraclitus – 'Dogs bark [at] what they cannot understand' – for an epigraph is then clear. And if it is not, the same phrase's superimposition on an image of post-war suburban tranquillity in the National Theatre production's programme clinches the matter. The early pioneers were in bad faith or suffered from a kind of false consciousness by believing in this unsustainable vision of the good life. As implied by the play's second epigraph – Herbert Muschamp's report about the corruption of plywood quoted at the beginning of this chapter – this formation had only a very limited lifespan. The time of the suburbs is over; the only thing to do, the play suggests, is to burn them down and walk away. But providing yet another potential photographic subject for the website '100 Abandoned Houses' might not be the most useful contribution to continuing discussions about the future of rust-belt suburbia.

Marc Palmieri's play *Levittown*, first performed in New York in 2006, takes quite the opposite view to D'Amour with regard to the historicity of the post-war suburbs. With its action unfolding in 1999, the play's principal setting is described as 'the living room of a classic Levitt house on Long Island'.[21] The adjective 'classic' indicates that the house has been little altered throughout its existence. Indeed, as the time-worn furniture and the family photographs that date back to World War II suggest, the house has had a single owner-occupier since its construction: Edmund Maddigan, World War II veteran, retired fireman and widower. But not only has the Levittown house endured resolutely into the present, it has also been rediscovered by a new generation. The play opens with siblings Kevin and Colleen, who are both in their twenties, entering their grandfather's home. Kevin tells his sister that he has recently learnt about Levittown's history in college. Despite having grown up in the neighbourhood, his studies have brought home to him that he knows little about either Levittown's development or his own family history.[22] Palmieri shows that the two are closely entwined. Whereas D'Amour insists suburban oral history to be a pointless endeavour, Palmieri presents the Levittown house as a literal archive: Kevin spends much of the time he is off-stage going through boxes of his grandfather's diaries and ephemera. From these, he discovers details of a traumatic family history, but also the means – in the form of a revolver, his grandfather's guilty spoils of war – to confront his estranged father and neutralise his malign influence over the Maddigan family. Meanwhile, his sister harnesses another aspect of the Levittown home to get her life back on track. Years earlier Edmund planted a sapling next to his house which he intended would one day provide the upper bedrooms with a fire escape. Colleen does not resort to using the tree in real life, though it is transfigured into an imaginative resource enabling her to free herself from her father's all-consuming contempt and to allow herself to dream of a future of domestic contentment with her new partner. Meanwhile Kevin, a serial college-dropout, contemplates following his grandfather's footsteps to become a fireman. Palmieri's play would perhaps have made less sense had it been set a decade later, in the wake of the financial crisis. Certainly, the chance of inheriting an occupation is a pipe dream for the characters of *Detroit*. Indeed, the contrast between the two plays' concern with fire – which in the one marks an end to a suburban way of life and, in the other, its continuation – could not be starker.

When asked if there were any suburban narratives her play was indebted to or in dialogue with, D'Amour mentioned the TV drama *Weeds* (Showtime, 2005–12). The show, whose episodes open with Malvina Reynolds's famous song 'Little Boxes', satirises false suburban surfaces, and so has some things in common with *Detroit*. There is, however, a long tradition of suburbanites complaining about the flimsiness of their homes. Consider, for instance, Harry Angstrom in Updike's *Rabbit Redux*, who berates the fact that America has got the technological wherewithal to get a man to the moon but not, it seems, to make a modern kitchen that functions properly. Then there is the crack in the living room that takes the form of a question mark which so torments the Raths in Sloan Wilson's *Man in the Grey Flannel Suit*. It seems that suburban homes were always already falling down. These complaints also correspond with the warnings of post-war critics who predicted the rapid and inevitable degeneration of these new residential communities into suburban slums. Mary and Ben may be in more difficult circumstances than their literary forebears, but their discontentment is realised in much the same way.

By contrast, Norris's play is more explicitly invested in the literary history of suburbanisation. Indeed, *Clybourne Park* is a sequel of sorts to Lorraine Hansberry's 1959 famous play *A Raisin in the Sun*, which centres on an African American family's struggle to leave their cramped apartment in Chicago's South Side and claim their piece of the American Dream by purchasing a modest free-standing house in a more affluent, but wholly white neighbourhood. (The imaginary locality of Clybourne Park is not a suburb as such, as it still lies within the city limits of Chicago. In both plays, however, the neighbourhood is imbricated within different suburban trajectories.) Across its two acts, Norris's play provides an expanded account of this same house by attending to the white folk who owned it both before and after its occupation by Hansberry's African American family, the Youngers. Act 1, set in 1959, focuses on Bev and Russ, who, with the help of their black maid Francine and her husband Albert, are packing up their belongings on the eve of their departure for the suburbs, having sold up to the pioneering Youngers. Later their endeavours are interrupted by Karl Lindner, the leader of the Clybourne Park Residents' Association, who features also in Hansberry's play. Lindner hopes to protect the neighbourhood from black incursion, and just as he was unsuccessful in persuading the Youngers to abandon their plans to occupy their property, he fails to prevent Bev and Russ from leaving. Act 2 revisits the same house fifty years later. In the intervening years Clybourne Park has become a black neighbourhood. In the present moment, however, its housing stock is in the process of being bought up by affluent whites from the suburbs attracted by cheap property prices and the area's proximity to the Loop. The second act depicts discussions and arguments between three parties: the purchasers, Lindsey and Steve, a white couple who wish to tear down the property and replace it with something more commodious in order to house their planned family; a representative of the local property owners' association, whose preoccupation with the preservation of the neighbourhood's 'architectural integrity' cuts across the interests of recently arrived gentrifiers; and a local middle-class black couple, Lena and Kevin, who challenge the new owners' right to replace their home with a new structure by asserting the historical significance of black settlement in Clybourne Park.

Much of the play's satiric power derives from its intricate duplication and transfiguration of situations and themes across its two acts, almost all of which have to do with race, ethnicity, community and property. The desire to maintain the neighbourhood's racial exclusivity in 1959 becomes a matter of protecting Clybourne Park's architectural character fifty years later, but for the spokesmen of both associations, maintaining property values is a principal underlying motive. Whereas in *A Raisin in the Sun* the Youngers and the Clybourne Park Residents Association are at loggerheads, in the second act of Norris's play the black characters are in alliance with the property owners' association, even though their respective appreciation of the area's 'value' differs markedly. And despite being a blood relative of her namesake in Hansberry's play, Lena's anxiety about incursions into the neighbourhood aligns her with Lindner. In particular, her warning that white gentrification happens 'one house at a time' echoes Lindner's prediction made fifty years previously that black encroachment will lead to a stream of white families leaving one after the other.[23] But rather than asserting a moral equivalence between these territorial claims in order to delegitimise African American demands for official recognition of historic black neighbourhoods (or, perhaps worse, to legitimise Lindner's justifications for racially exclusive communities), these parallels underscore instead the persistence of a political imbalance. Rather like the conversation between Frank Bascombe and Ms Pines discussed at the end of Chapter 1, Lena's patience is sorely tested by her distracted and prolix white interlocutors, who continually interrupt her to assert their own claims and concerns. They simply do not take her or her arguments seriously; certainly, they refuse to countenance the racial dynamics of gentrification.

In any case, the white purchasers in 2009 attempt to trump African American claims by asserting an even earlier white ethnic heritage; the area, they are pleased to find out, was once inhabited by German and Irish families. (Their lawyer chooses this moment to reveal that her father was in fact Karl Lindner, which helps consolidate white claims to the neighbourhood.) Lindsey and Steve also exploit Clybourne Park's officially recognised designation as a historic neighbourhood with a distinctive collection of 'low-rise single-family homes' (94): 'Aren't we a single family?' asks Lindsey. This is grotesque because the white couple as yet only have ambitions for children, ambitions which in Lindsey's mind require the complete reconstruction of their property, an outcome which would of course be inconsonant with that other historical marker, 'low rise'. Her appeal also parallels Lindner's earlier reinforcement of his neighbourhood's right to self-determination with the assertion that it is 'a community with *soon-to-be-children*' (47).

Perhaps the play's many echoes encourage only cynicism about the racial politics of housing in the US: nothing much seems to have changed. And the play's coda, which sees the unearthing of a trunk that once belonged to the Bev and Russ's son, a suicide, arguably constitutes a disappointing retreat into humanist sentiment. The never-ending ruckus about race and property, the conclusion seems to suggest, obscures real human tragedy. But more productively, Norris's play helps demonstrate Massey's observations about 'the continuing struggle over the delineation and characterisation of space-time', about how 'the description, definition and identification of a place is [. . .] always inevitably an intervention not only into geography but also, at least implicitly, into the (re) telling of the historical constitution of the present'.[24] Norris, like Massey, is exercised about how one claim about a place's identity may be outmanoeuvred by those of other, better resourced parties: Lindsey for instance connects a narrative about Clybourne Park's past with one about its projected future that she hopes to inhabit; simultaneously, she disavows the need for historical continuity in order to invalidate the rival claim of Lena: 'communities change', is her breathtaking declaration, which is made the instant after she has asserted her family's connection with earlier inhabitants of Clybourne Park. Norris also shows how official recognition of a place's historic character does not finalise or close down debate but rather provides yet another stage on which to contest that place's identity. A place's history, the play shows, is multi-stranded and continually in process. It is this insistence that makes *Clybourne Park* politically more useful than its counterpart *Detroit*, which sees the history of its suburban setting as unilinear and complete. Indeed, *Clybourne Park* constructs something that rather corresponds with Massey's ideas about what might comprise 'a really "radical" history of a place', that is, one which does not 'try to seal a place up into one neat and tidy "envelope of space-time" but which recognise[s] that what has come together, in this place, now, is a conjunction of many histories and many spaces'.[25]

What seems to be one of the more frivolous discussions in the play helps establish the ongoing struggle to define places as its central preoccupation. I am referring to the opening discussion of demonyms (or, more specifically, exonyms), which is inspired by Russ's consumption of a tub of Neapolitan ice cream that will not survive the move.[26] Surely, insists Bev, the term 'Neapolitan' refers not to Naples, but to inhabitants of a new city. She is of course both mistaken and absolutely correct: Naples was founded as Neapolis – in Greek, 'new city'. Bev is disconcerted by the absence of rules for demonyms – Grecians but not Nicians, Congolese not Mongolese – and she is especially upset by her and Russ's inability to decide upon a name for the people from the city of Brussels. A reasonable answer, which the characters do not alight on, would be 'Brusselian'. But their preoccupation with the Belgian capital is apposite. Historically Dutch-speaking, Brussels experienced a language shift from Dutch to French following the influx of Walloons in the late nineteenth century. In recent years Brussels has become more international and multilingual. As the de facto capital of the EU the city-region houses expatriates from across the European continent as well as large concentrations of immigrants of Turkish and African origin. In this polyglot city, the demonym employed often depends on the language being spoken, or on the identity of the individual in question, in other words, whether he or she speaks French, Dutch, Brabantian or some other language. (One unacclimatised American in Brussels complains in a recent blog post of 'Rude Brusselites . . . Brusselians . . . Brussellers . . . whatever you call them!'[27]) As the second act of Norris's play clearly demonstrates, identity and belonging in Chicago have been similarly shaped by regional and global population movements.

Perhaps Bev's pondering of demonyms indicates a contentedness to simply marvel at the world's complexity, its irreducible differences. Her ignorance certainly contrasts with the urbanity of her twenty-first-century counterparts, who joust with one another over their appreciation of the European capitals to which they have recently travelled while on holiday. And Bev's imaginary peregrinations are set against the fact that Russ derives his knowledge from the *National Geographic*, a publication which now recognises that its anthropological eye was, for most of its history, unambiguously racist. But Bev's naivety is far from innocent. When a house visitor reasonably suggests that knowledge is power, her petulant response is 'then I choose to remain powerless' (14). Her desire for a systemised nomenclature of exonyms suggests, however, a refusal to countenance either the power of naming, or the manner in which places are shaped by multiple, unfolding and, often, contested identities. Bev's Brussels conundrum foreshadows the way many of the characters in the play's second act – particularly the white gentrifiers – attempt to fix a place's historical identity to facilitate a narrowly based vision of its future habitability. Norris's play may not provide much in the way of analysis of the historical mechanisms – for instance, the influence of public policy decisions on housing patterns – that have entrenched racial inequality across metropolitan America. What it does do, though, is illuminate and problematise a particular mode of historicising place. *Clybourne Park* demonstrates that internalist historical narratives of places that insist on an essentialist continuity can only ever operate within a zero-sum game. While offering no obvious solutions to live issues such as the preservation and gentrification of urban neighbourhoods, the play refuses to present its setting as sealed and complete. With its contested histories and its innumerable relationships extending beyond its frontiers – to nearby suburbs and faraway cities – the neighbourhood of Clybourne Park is shown to be both an open site and unfinished business.

This book thus closes with an assertion of the openness of the suburbs. In so doing, *The Literature of Suburban Change* does not, in its final analysis, provide a paean to suburban life, nor has it ever been my intention to write an apology for the many shortcomings of and injustices arising from low-density living in the US; the development of swathes of mid-twentieth-century suburbia was after all predicated on its being closed to peoples of certain racial, ethnic and class backgrounds. Rather, my argument has been that for at least the last six decades suburbs have generated, and continue to inspire, narratives that respond to their spatial complexity. An appreciation of such complexity – that is, the interconnected, incomplete and heterogenous qualities of suburbia – may well be precisely what enables more informed and responsible consideration of some of the challenges faced in metropolitan regions across the US, and be the quality that provides scope to imagine and make possible better futures. The suburbs, this study suggests, are here to stay, but they are not static or hermetic, and neither are the stories we continue to tell about them. The suburban story has expanded and proliferated across diverse forms. Indeed, it makes little sense to speak of a singular suburban story; if there is anything that the narratives examined in this book have in common it is their engagement with the contested historicity of the suburbs and their articulation of spatial change.

NOTES

Introduction: The Time of the Suburb

1. On 'technoburbs' see Robert Fishman, *Bourgeois Utopias: The Rise and Fall of Suburbia* (New York: Basic, 1987), 182–208; on 'edge cities' see Joel Garreau, *Edge City: Life on the New Frontier* (New York: Anchor, 1991); on ethnoburbs, see Wei Li, 'Anatomy of a New Ethnic Settlement: The Chinese *Ethnoburb* in Los Angeles', *Urban Studies*, 35(3) (March 1998), 479–501; on 'post-suburban regions' see Rob Kling, Spencer C. Olin and Mark Poster (eds), *Postsuburban California: the Transformation of Orange County since WWII* (Berkeley: University of California Press, 1995); on the post-metropolis, see Edward Soja, *Postmetropolis: Critical Studies of Cities and Regions* (Malden, MA: Blackwell, 2000); on social activism in the suburbs, see for instance Genevieve Carpio, Clara Irzábal and Laura Polido, 'Right to the Suburb? Rethinking Lefebvre and Immigrant Activism', *Journal of Urban Affairs*, 33(2) (May 2011), 185–208.

2. Following the 2000 census, the US Census Bureau reported: 'From 1940 onward, suburbs experienced more population growth than central cities, and by 1960 the proportion of the total U.S. population living in suburbs (territory within metropolitan areas but outside central cities) was 31 percent, almost equal to the proportion of the population living in central cities (32 percent). In 2000, half of the entire population lived in the suburbs of metropolitan areas.' United States Census Bureau, *Census Atlas of the United States*, Chapter 2: 'Population Distribution', 3. Available at <www.census.gov/population/www/cen2000/censusatlas/pdf/2_Population-Distribution.pdf> (last accessed 11 March 2019). The 2010 census showed that the rate of growth of central cities just overtook that of suburbs, a reversal which for many indicated the beginning of an urban renaissance. William H. Frey's analysis of newly released census data, however, suggests such celebrations are premature: in 2016 and 2017, suburban growth once again exceeded urban growth. William H. Frey, 'Early Decade Big City Growth Continues to Fall Off, Census Shows', *The Avenue*,

29 May 2018. Available at <www.brookings.edu/blog/the-avenue/2018/05/25/
early-decade-big-city-growth-continues-to-fall-off-census-shows/?utm_camp
aign=Metropolitan%20Policy%20Program&utm_source=hs_email&utm_med
ium=email&utm_content=63594951> (last accessed 11 March 2011).

3. Two trenchant and illuminating studies delineate how contemporary American authors have grappled with post-suburban forms: Pippa Eldridge, 'The Poetics of Sprawl: Literary and Filmic Engagements with American Suburbia, 1990–2017' (unpublished PhD thesis, Birkbeck, University of London, 2018), and Tim Foster, 'Escaping the Split-Level Trap: Postsuburban Narratives in Recent American Fiction' (unpublished PhD thesis, University of Nottingham, 2012). By contrast, in *American Unexceptionalism: The Everyman and the Suburban Novel after 9/11* (Iowa City: University of Iowa Press, 2014), Kathy Knapp makes the case that 9/11 triggered a dramatic shift in the way suburban environments and inhabitants are depicted in American fiction.

4. On suburban diversity, see Jon C. Teaford, *The American Suburb: The Basics* (New York: Routledge, 2008), 43–86, and Matthew D. Lassiter and Christopher Niedt, 'Suburban Diversity in Postwar America', *Journal of Urban History*, 39(1) (January 2013), 3–14.

5. My search was made with <www.google.co.uk> on 13 October 2018. Websites that feature 'best of' lists are likely to rank highly in search engine results pages because they are liable to repeat the terms of the search multiple times and thereby be judged to be more relevant.

6. See for example Virginia Savage McAlester, *A Field Guide to American Houses* (New York: Alfred J. Knopf, 2015).

7. Edward Relph, *Place and Placelessness* (London: Pion, 1976), 29–30, 83, 82. A similar argument is made by William H. Whyte in his landmark 1956 study *The Organization Man*. Whyte identifies a shift of allegiance from local community to national corporation, which has led to a willingness to relocate at the behest of one's employer. The new 'package suburbs' such as Park Forest, Illinois provide the ideal staging posts for members of this expanded managerial class, whom Whyte repeatedly refers to as 'transients'. The interchangeability of suburbs and residents is facilitated by an increasingly national, unifying culture that 'is part of the momentum of mobility': 'The more people move about, the more similar the American environments become, and the more similar they become, the easier it is to move about' (Philadelphia: University of Philadelphia Press, [1956] 2002, 276). More recently, Robert D. Putnam has argued that transience itself is not to blame for a reduction in civic engagement across the nation, since there has in fact been a slight reduction in the frequency with which Americans move home since the 1950s. Rather, it is the privatised lifestyles associated with sprawl, and in particular the requirement to spend more and more time commuting alone by car, that has eroded feelings of social connectedness. Noticeably, however, Putnam's own bar charts show that rates of community involvement in the 1990s were higher in suburbs than in central cities. (Putnam, *Bowling Alone: The Collapse and Revival of American Community*, New York: Simon & Schuster, 2000: 204–15.)

8. Ibid. 33.

9. Yi-Fu Tuan, *Topophilia: A Study of Environmental Perceptions, Attitudes, and Values* (Englewood Cliffs, NJ: Prentice Hall, 1974), 238.

10. Ibid. 236. See also Andrew Wiese, *Places of Their Own: African American Suburbanization in the Twentieth Century* (Chicago: University of Chicago Press, 2005), 5; and Martin Dines, *Gay Suburban Narratives in American and British Culture: Homecoming Queens* (Basingstoke: Palgrave Macmillan, 2010), 32–3.

11. The editors of *Making Suburbia* begin their introduction with a similar observation. See John Archer, Paul J. P. Sandul and Katherine Solomonson, 'Introduction: Making, Performing, Living Suburbia', in Archer, Sandul and Solomonson, (eds), *Making Suburbia: New Histories of Everyday America* (Minnesota: University of Minneapolis Press, 2015), vii–xxv, vii.

12. D. J. Waldie, 'Beautiful and Terrible: Aeriality and the Image of Suburbia', *Places*, February 2013. Available at <placesjournal.org/article/beautiful-and-terrible-aeriality-and-the-image-of-suburbia/#ref_14> (last accessed 11 March 2019).

13. Whyte, *The Organization Man*, 267, my emphasis.

14. Tuan, *Topophilia*, 233.

15. Several histories have been written that focus on the development on one or other of the Levittowns. See for example Barbara M. Kelly, *Expanding the American Dream: Building and Rebuilding Levittown* (Albany: State University of New York Press, 1993); Rosalyn Baxandall and Elizabeth Ewen, *Picture Windows: How the Suburbs Happened* (New York: Basic, 2001); David Kushner, *Levittown: Two Families, One Tycoon, and the Fight for Civil Rights in America's Legendary Suburb* (New York: Walker & Company: 2009); Dianne Harris (ed.), *Second Suburb: Levittown, Pennsylvania* (Pittsburgh, PA: University of Pittsburgh Press, 2010).

16. Lewis Mumford, *The City in History: Its Origins, Its Transformations and its Prospects* (London: Martin Secker & Warburg, 1961), 554, 553.

17. Mumford is reputed to have described Levittown, New York as an 'instant slum' on an initial visit to the suburb. The phrase has often been recalled by suburban residents and developers to demonstrate how such predictions were misplaced. See for example Michael T. Kaufman, 'Tough Times for Mr Levittown', *New York Times Magazine*, 24 September 1989, 43.

18. For example, Peter Blake's *God's Own Junkyard: The Planned Deterioration of America's Landscape*, declared by its author to be 'written in fury' and a 'deliberate attack upon all those who have already befouled a large portion of this country for private gain, and are engaged in befouling the rest' (New York: Holt, Rinehart and Winston, 1964: 7), features aerial photos of Lakewood, California; several developments on Long Island, including Levittown; and new subdivisions outside Chicago and Oakland, California. Relph labels aerial photographs of sprawling development as 'a placeless geography' (Relph, *Place and Placelessness*, 118–19). In their manifesto for New Urbanism, Andres Duany, Elizabeth Plater-Zyberk and Jeff Speck illustrate the destructiveness and the absurdities of sprawl with several (mostly unidentified) aerial photos (*Suburban Nation: The Rise of Sprawl and the Decline of the American Dream*, New York: North Point, 2000).

19. Bennett M. Berger, *Working-Class Suburb: A Study of Auto Workers in Suburbia* (Berkeley: University of California Press, 1960).

20. Bennett M. Berger, 'The Myth of Suburbia', *Journal of Social Issues*, 17(1) (Winter, 1961), 38–49. In *Class and Suburbia* William M. Dobriner divides students of the suburbs into two camps: on the one hand there are *scientists* like himself and Berger; on the other there are *commentators*, who constitute 'an exuberant band of social impressionists who greatly outnumber the scientists': Dobriner, *Class and Suburbia* (Englewood Cliffs, NJ: Prentice Hall, 1963, 5, emphasis in original). See also Scott Donaldson, *The Suburban Myth* (New York, Columbia University Press, 1969).

21. Herbert Gans, *The Levittowners: Ways of Life and Politics in a New Suburban Community* (London: Allen Lane, 1967), 179.

22. Ibid. 154.

23. Ibid. 165–72.

24. Ibid. 410.

25. Paul H. Mattingly, 'The Suburban Canon over Time', in *Suburban Discipline*, ed. Peter Lang and Tam Miller (New York: Princeton Architectural Press, 1997), 38–51.

26. Another pioneering work from the 1960s is Sam Bass Warner Jr's *Streetcar Suburbs: The Process of Growth in Boston, 1870–1900* (Cambridge, MA: Harvard University Press, 1962).

27. Kenneth T. Jackson, *Crabgrass Frontier: The Suburbanization of the United States* (New York: Oxford University Press), 203–5.

28. Ibid. 208.

29. See Mark Rose, *Interstate: Express Highway Politics, 1939–1989* (Knoxville: University of Tennessee Press, 1990).

30. Jackson, *Crabgrass Frontier*, 217.

31. Robert Fishman, *Bourgeois Utopias: The Rise and Fall of Suburbia* (New York: Basic, 1987); John R. Stilgoe, *Borderland: The Origin of the American Suburb, 1820–1939* (New Haven, CT: Yale University Press, 1990).

32. Delores Hayden, *Building Suburbia: Green Fields and Urban Growth, 1820–2000* (New York: Vintage, 2003), 4–5.

33. Wiese, *Places of Their Own*, 5.

34. Ibid. 3.

35. Kevin M. Kruse and Thomas J. Sugrue, 'Introduction: The New Suburban History', in *The New Suburban History*, ed. Kruse and Sugrue (Chicago: University of Chicago Press, 2006), 1–10, 6, 10.

36. Other important contributions to this second wave of history include: Paul H. Mattingly, *Suburban Landscapes: Culture and Politics in a New York Metropolitan Community* (Baltimore: Johns Hopkins Press, 2001); Becky M. Nicolaides, *Life and Politics in the Working-Class Suburbs of Los Angeles, 1920–1965* (Chicago: University of Chicago Press, 2002); Sylvie Murray, *The Progressive Housewife: Community Activism in Suburban Queens, 1945–1965* (Philadelphia: University of Pennsylvania Press, 2003); Bruce Haynes, *Red Lines, Black Spaces: The Politics of Race and Space in a Middle-Class Suburb* (New Haven, CT: Yale University Press, 2006); Matthew Lassiter, *The Silent Majority: Suburban Politics in the Sunbelt*

South (Princeton: Princeton University Press, 2006); Jerry Gonzalez, '"A Place in the Sun": Mexican Americans, Race, and the Suburbanization of Los Angeles, 1940–1980' (unpublished PhD thesis, University of Southern California, 2009); Charlotte Brooks, *Alien Neighbors, Foreign Friends: Asian Americans, Housing, and the Transformation of Urban California* (Chicago: University of Chicago Press, 2009); Allen Dieterich-Ward, *Beyond Rust: Metropolitan Pittsburgh and the Fate of Industrial America* (Philadelphia: University of Pennsylvania Press, November 2015); Lila Berman, *Metropolitan Jews: Politics, Race, and Religion in Postwar Detroit* (Chicago: University of Chicago Press, 2015).

37. Doreen Massey, *For Space* (London: Sage, 2005), 10.

38. Ibid. 10–11.

39. Jeff Malpas, *Place and Experience* (Cambridge: Cambridge University Press, 1999).

40. Eric Prieto, *Literature, Geography and the Postmodern Poetics of Place* (New York: Palgrave Macmillan, 2013), 90.

41. Nicholas Entrikin, The Betweenness of Place (Baltimore: Johns Hopkins Press, 1991).

42. Michel de Certeau, *The Practice of Everyday Life*, trans. Steven F. Rendall (Berkeley: University of California Press, 1988).

43. Edward Relph, *Place and Placelessness*, 43.

44. Yi-Fu Tuan, *Space and Place: The Perspective of Experience* (Minneapolis: University of Minnesota Press, 1979), 162.

45. de Certeau, *The Practice of Everyday Life*, 92–3.

46. Michel Foucault, 'Of Other Spaces', *Diacritics*, 16(1) (Spring, 1986), 22–7.

47. Henri Lefebvre, *The Production of Space*, trans. Donald Nicholson-Smith (Oxford: Wiley-Blackwell, 1991).

48. Edward Soja, *Thirdspace: Journeys to Los Angeles and Other Real-and-Imagined Places* (Oxford: Wiley-Blackwell, 1996).

49. Massey, *For Space*, 29, 27.

50. Betrand Westphal, *Geocriticsm: Real and Fictional Places*, trans. Robert T. Tally Jr (New York: Palgrave Macmillan, 2011), 73.

51. David Kolb, *Sprawling Places* (Athens: University of Georgia Press, 2008), 172.

52. Ibid. 175.

53. Margaret Crawford, cited by Kolb, *Sprawling Places*, 175.

54. Kolb, *Sprawling Places*, 191.

55. Catherine Jurca, *White Diaspora: The Suburb and the Twentieth-Century Novel* (Princeton: Princeton University Press, 2001), 7, 8–9.

56. Ibid. 160.

57. Ibid.

58. Knapp, *American Unexceptionalism*, xvi.

59. For instance, both John Updike's 1971 novel *Rabbit Redux*, which I discuss in Chapter 1, and Lisa D'Amour's play *Detroit*, which I discuss in Chapter 5, conclude with the conflagration of a suburban home.

60. Joseph George, *Postmodern Suburban Spaces: Philosophy, Ethics, and Community in Post-War American Fiction* (New York: Palgrave Macmillan, 2016), 5.

61. Ibid. 32.
62. Jo Gill, *The Poetics of the American Suburbs* (New York: Palgrave Macmillan, 2013), 3.
63. Ibid. 17, 16.
64. Timotheus Vermeulen, *Scenes from the Suburbs: The Suburb in Contemporary US Film and Television* (Edinburgh: Edinburgh University Press, 2014), 5. Vermeulen probably overstates the historicising proclivities of previous scholarship. While such studies tend to be arranged in broadly chronological fashion, typically their structure is determined by a series of thematic concerns. Noticeably, the organisation of George's study, published after Vermeulen's, eschews conventional historical chronology entirely.
65. Vermeulen, *Scenes from the Suburbs*, 4.

Chapter 1: The Everyman and his Car: Metropolitan Memory and the Novel Sequence

1. John Updike, 'Afterword by Author', in *Rabbit at Rest* (London: Penguin, 2006), 478.
2. Ibid.
3. The fictional Brewer and its suburb of Mt Judge are based on, respectively, the city of Reading and the suburban borough of Shillington, which was Updike's hometown. Haddam is based on Princeton and nearby towns; the obvious main difference between Haddam and its real-world inspiration is the absence of a university.
4. Walter Benjamin, 'Theses on the Philosophy of History', *Illuminations*, trans. Harry Zohn (London: Fontana, 1973), 255–66, 263.
5. Updike, 'Afterword', 478.
6. Benjamin's allegory is though *spatial* to the extent that historical objects are understood to solidify or 'crystallise', as in the case of the pile of accumulating wreckage that appears before the Angel of History. This spatial form, in which the past may be perceived to inhere, constitutes a rupture to the hegemonic, universalising continuum of history. This crystallisation – which can help recover the repressed past from oblivion – provides a crucial imaginative resource for revolutionary struggle. But it makes less sense to conceive of Benjamin's messianic historicism as being concerned with *place*, which arguably is most usefully understood as a specific location made meaningful by ongoing practices. Whereas Benjamin holds that a stilling or a compaction of historical time may constitute the 'shock' that facilitates the 'revolutionary chance', Updike's and Ford's novel sequences suggest that continual movement through and an intense familiarity with places might provide mechanisms for a critical historical consciousness.
7. Lynette Felber, *Gender and Genre in Novels Without End: The British Roman-Fleuve* (Gainsville: University Press of Florida, 1995), 10.
8. Henry James, *Partial Portraits* (London: Macmillan, 1888), 100–1.
9. Felber, *Gender and Genre in Novels without End*, 3.
10. Ibid. 13.

11. Steven Connor, *The English Novel in History: 1950–1995* (London: Routledge, 1996), 136.
12. Ibid. 136–7.
13. Ibid. 139.
14. David Foster Wallace, 'John Updike, Champion Literary Phallocrat, Drops One; Is This Finally the End for Magnificent Narcissists?', *The Observer*, 13 October 1997.
15. Ibid. The expansiveness of Wallace's own fiction is of course legendary. Wallace's exhaustive narratives, and more generally the post-war American 'encyclopaedic novel', have stimulated more critical engagement than has the novel sequence; noticeably, recent scholarship has exhibited a proliferating nomenclature. See for example Stefano Ercolino, *The Maximalist Novel: From Thomas Pynchon's Gravity's Rainbow to Roberto Bolano's 2666* (London: Bloomsbury, 2014) and David Letzler, *The Cruft of Fiction: Mega-Novels and the Science of Paying Attention* (Lincoln: University of Nebraska Press, 2017).
16. Kathy Knapp, 'How did I get here? Roth, Updike and an Embarrassment of Riches', in D. Quentin Miller (ed.), *American Literature in Transition, 1980–1990* (Cambridge: Cambridge University Press, 2018), 115–29, 124.
17. Ibid.
18. Updike, 'Afterword', 477.
19. Knapp, 'How did I get here?', 125.
20. Kathy Knapp, *American Unexceptionalism: The Everyman and the Suburban Novel after 9/11* (Iowa City: University of Iowa Press, 2011), 1–22; Tim Foster, '"A More Interesting Surgery on the Suburbs": Richard Ford's Paean to the New Jersey Suburbs', in Martin Dines and Timotheus Vermeulen (eds), *New Suburban Stories* (London: Bloomsbury, 2013), 141–50.
21. John Updike, 'Rabbit, Run', in *A Rabbit Omnibus* (London: Penguin, 1991), 1–178, 11. Subsequent page references given in parentheses.
22. Michel de Certeau, *The Practice of Everyday Life*, trans. Steven F. Rendall (Berkeley: University of California Press, 1984), 93.
23. Lynn Spigel, *Welcome to the Dreamhouse: Popular Media and Postwar Suburbs* (Durham, NC: Duke University Press, 2001), 2.
24. William Dobriner, *Class in Suburbia* (Englewood Cliffs, NJ: 1963), 9.
25. Daniel Boorstin, *The Image: A Guide to Pseudo-Events in America* (London: Vintage, [1961] 1997), 259.
26. On the history of picture window in the US, see Sandy Isenstadt, *The Modern American House: Spaciousness and Middle-Class Identity* (New York: Cambridge University Press, 2006), 179–214.
27. John Updike, 'Rabbit, Redux', in *A Rabbit Omnibus* (London: Penguin, 1991), 179–414, 187, 309. Subsequent page references given in parentheses.
28. Robert Beuka, *SurburbiaNation: Reading Suburban Landscape in Twentieth Century American Film and Fiction* (New York: Palgrave Macmillan, 2004), 119. See also Mary O'Connell, *Updike and the Patriarchal Dilemma: Masculinity in the Rabbit Novels* (Carbondale and Edwardsville: Southern Illinois University Press, 1996); Sally Robinson, *Marked Men: White Masculinity in Crisis* (New York: Columbia University Press, 2005), 23–51.

29. Beuka, *SururbiaNation*, 127.
30. Lewis Mumford, *The City in History: Its Origins, Its Transformations and its Prospects* (London: Penguin, 1991), 583.
31. Catherine Jurca, *White Diaspora: The Suburb and the Twentieth-Century American Novel* (Princeton, NJ: Princeton University Press, 2001), 139.
32. I am somewhat sceptical of such clear-cut distinctions. After all, in the very next chapter Abbott discusses the linear route taken on foot from East LA to Venice by William Foster (played by Michael Douglas) in the 1993 movie *Falling Down*. Commuting transects of the kind found in *Rabbit Redux* are not uncommon in literary representations of West Coast or Sunbelt cities: though it is true that they are more frequently made by disenfranchised individuals – consider for example the journeys made across metropolitan LA by Mexican immigrants in T. C. Boyle's *The Tortilla Curtain* (1995) and Héctor Tobar's *The Barbarian Nurseries* (2011).
33. Carl Abbott, *Imagined Frontiers: Contemporary America and Beyond* (Norman: University of Oklahoma Press, 2015), 60.
34. Patrick Geddes, *Cities in Evolution* (London: Routledge, [1915] 1998).
35. Abbott, *Imagined Frontiers*, 66.
36. John Updike, 'Rabbit is Rich', in *A Rabbit Omnibus* (London: Penguin, 1991), 415–700, 417. Subsequent page references given in parentheses.
37. Robert Venturi, Denise Scott Brown and Steven Izenour, *Learning from Las Vegas: The Forgotten Symbolism of Architectural Form*, rev. edn (Cambridge, MA: MIT Press, [1972] 1977), 18.
38. Ibid. 6.
39. Peter Blake, *God's Own Junkyard: The Planned Deterioration of America's Landscape* (New York: Holt, Rinehart and Winston, 1964), 11–16.
40. Ibid. 34.
41. John Updike, *Rabbit at Rest* (London: Penguin, [1990] 2006), 77. Subsequent page references given in parentheses.
42. Hermione Lee, 'The Trouble with Harry', *New Republic*, 24 December 1990, 36.
43. Cited in Stacey Olster, 'Introduction: "A Sort of Helplessly 50's Guy"', in Olster (ed.), *The Cambridge Companion to John Updike* (Cambridge: Cambridge University Press, 2006), 1–14, 4.
44. Quoted in Donald J. Greiner, 'Updike, Rabbit and the Myth of American Exceptionalism' in Olster (ed.), *The Cambridge Companion to John Updike*, 149–61, 154.
45. Anita Brookner, 'Ending the Heartache', *Spectator*, 30 April 1990 (27–9), 28; Joyce Carol Oates, 'So Young!', *New York Times Book Review*, 30 September 1990 (1, 43), 43.
46. Josh Getlin, 'Character Assassination', *Los Angeles Times*, 4 November 1990 (E1, E12), E1.
47. Richard Todd, 'Updike and Barthelme: Disengagements', *Atlantic Monthly* (126, 129–32), 129, 126.
48. Olster, 'Introduction: "A sort of helplessly 50's guy"', in Olster (ed.), *The Cambridge Companion to John Updike*, 1–12, 9, 7.
49. Greiner, 'Updike', 149.

50. John Updike, 'Rabbit Remembered', in *Licks of Love* (London: Penguin, 2000), 177–359, 197. Subsequent page references given in parentheses.

51. John Updike, 'Why Rabbit had to go', *New York Times*, 5 August 1990.

52. Deborah Treisman, 'Living with Frank Bascombe: an interview with John Ford', *The New Yorker*, 5 November 2014.

53. Updike, *Rabbit is Rich*, 435.

54. See for instance the review of *Rabbit is Rich* by Pearl Bell, 'Sequels', *Commentary*, October 1981, 72–4.

55. Edward Dupuy, 'The Confessions of an Ex-Suicide: Relenting and Recovering in Richard Ford's *The Sportswriter*', in Huey Guagliardo (ed.) *Perspectives on Richard Ford* (Jackson: University Press of Mississippi, 2000), 71–82; Matthew Guinn, 'Into the Suburbs: Richard Ford's Sportswriter Novels and the Place of Southern Fiction', in Suzanne W. Jones and Sharon Moteith (eds), *South to a New Place: Region, Literature, Culture* (Baton Rouge: Louisiana State University Press, 2002), 196–207.

56. Richard Ford, *The Lay of the Land* (London: Bloomsbury, [2006] 2007), 174.

57. Ibid. 175.

58. Catherine Jurca, *White Diaspora: The Suburb and the Twentieth-Century Novel* (Princeton: Princeton University Press, 2001), 169–71.

59. Foster, 'Richard Ford's Paean to the New Jersey Suburbs', 144.

60. Richard Ford, *The Sportswriter* (London: Bloomsbury, [1986] 2006), 45.

61. Ford, *The Sportswriter*, 45; Ford, *The Lay of the Land*, 129.

62. Ford, *The Sportswriter*, 235.

63. Ibid. 45.

64. Ibid. 50.

65. Ford, *The Lay of the Land*, 26, 30.

66. Richard Ford, *Let Me Be Frank with You* (London: Bloomsbury, [2014] 2015), 225.

67. Ibid. 226.

68. The presumption that *Let Me Be Frank with You* is the last of the Bascombe books may of course be premature. As Frank declared, endings are determined by there being nothing more to say on a subject. Updike returned to muse over the Harry's world ten years after his death and that apparently final 'enough'; and Ford had previously declared *Lay of the Land* to be the last Bascombe book.

69. Ford, *The Sportswriter*, 36, 37. Subsequent page references in parentheses.

70. Knapp, *American Unexceptionalism*, 6.

71. M. P. Baumgartner, *The Moral Order of a Suburb* (Oxford: Oxford University Press, 1988), 11.

72. Richard Ford, *Independence Day* (London: Bloomsbury, [1995] 2006), 25. Subsequent page references given in parentheses.

73. Ford, *The Lay of the Land*, 76. Subsequent page references given in parentheses.

74. Knapp, *American Unexceptionalism*, 20.

75. Foster, 'A More Interesting Surgery on the Suburbs', 150.

76. Ford, *Let Me Be Frank with You*, 24. Subsequent page references given in parentheses.

77. Ford, *Lay of the Land*, 12.

Chapter 2: Suburban Gothic and Banal Unhomeliness

1. Allan Lloyd Smith, *American Gothic Fiction: An Introduction* (London: Continuum, 2004), 118. See also Donald Ringe, *American Gothic: Imagination and Reason in Nineteenth-Century Fiction* (Lexington: University of Kentucky Press, 1982); Peter Kafer, *Charles Brockden Brown's Revolution and the Birth of the American Gothic*, Philadelphia: University of Pennsylvania Press, 2004); Shawn Rosenheim and Stephen Rachman (eds), *The American Face of Edgar Allan Poe* (Philadelphia: University of Pennsylvania Press, 1995).

2. David Punter, *The Literature of Terror: A History of Gothic Fiction from 1765 to the Present Day* (London: Longman, 1980), 421.

3. Anthony Vidler, *The Architectural Uncanny: Essays in the Architectural Uncanny* (Cambridge, MA: MIT Press, 1992), 3–4.

4. Angela Carter, *Fireworks* (London: Quartet, 1974), 122; Fred Botting, 'Aftergothic: Consumption, Machines, and Black Holes', in Jerrold E. Hogle (ed.), *The Cambridge Companion to Gothic Fiction* (Cambridge: Cambridge University Press, 2002), 277–300, 286.

5. Although see Pippa Eldridge's illuminating account of recent horror films set in Detroit, 'The Poetics of Sprawl: Literary and Filmic Engagements with American Suburbia, 1990–2017 (Unpublished PhD thesis, Birkbeck University of London, 2018), and Maisha L. Wester, *African American Gothic: Screams from Shadowed Places* (Basingstoke: Palgrave Macmillan, 2012).

6. David Riesman, *The Lonely Crowd: A Study of the Changing American Character* (New Haven: Yale University Press, 1950); William H. Whyte, *The Organization Man* (New York: Simon & Schuster, 1956); Lewis Mumford, *The City in History* (New York: Harcourt, Brace and World, 1961); Richard E. Gordon, Katherine K. Gordon and Max Gunther, *The Split-Level Trap* (New York: Bernard Geis, 1961); Jane Jacobs, *The Death and Life of Great American Cities* (New York: Random House, 1961); Betty Friedan, *The Feminine Mystique* (New York: Norton, 1963).

7. On the post-war suburbs in science fiction, see David Seed, *American Science Fiction and the Cold War: Literature and Film* (Keele: Keele University Press, 1999), 132–5, and Amy Maria Kenyon, *Dreaming Suburbia: Detroit and the Production of Postwar Space and Culture* (Detroit: Wayne State University Press, 2004), 41–3, 67–8. On noir-ish renderings of suburban Los Angeles see: Eric Avila, 'Popular Culture in the Age of White Flight: Film Noir, Disneyland and the Cold War (Sub)Urban Imaginary', *Journal of Urban History*, 31(1) (November 2004), 3–22; Norman Klein, *The History of Forgetting: Los Angeles and the Erasure of Memory* (New York: Verso, 1997), 295–300; Edward Dimendberg, *Film Noir and the Spaces of Modernity* (Cambridge, MA: Harvard University Press, 2004), 166–206.

8. Bernice Murphy, *The Suburban Gothic in American Popular Culture* (Basingstoke: Palgrave Macmillan, 2009), 200.

9. Ibid.

10. Allan Lloyd Smith, 'Introduction', in Victor Sage and Allan Lloyd Smith (eds), *Modern Gothic: A Reader* (Manchester: Manchester University Press, 1996), 7.

11. Victoria Maddon, '"We Found the Witch, May We Burn Her?"': Suburban Gothic, Witch-Hunting, and Anxiety-Induced Conformity in Stephen King's *Carrie*', *The Journal of American Culture*, 40(1) (March 2017), 7–20, 7.

12. Ibid. 11.

13. Kim Ian Michasiw, 'Some Stations of the Suburban Gothic', in Robert K. Martin and Eric Savoy (eds), *American Gothic: New Interventions in a National Narrative* (Iowa City: University of Iowa Press, 1998, 237–57), 239.

14. Ibid. 250.

15. Sigmund Freud, 'The "Uncanny"', trans. Alix Strachey, *The Standard Edition of the Complete Psychological Works of Sigmund Freud: (1917–1919)*, *Vol. 17: An Infantile Neurosis and Other Works* (London: Vintage, 2001), 217–56, 245.

16. Vidler, *The Architectural Uncanny*, 23.

17. Freud, 'The "Uncanny"', 242.

18. For overviews of readings of Freud's essay, see Nick Royle, *The Uncanny* (Manchester: Manchester University Press, 2003), and Anneleen Masschelein, *Unconcept: The Freudian Uncanny in Late-Twentieth-Century Theory* (New York: SUNY Press, 2011).

19. For example Jane Marie Todd, 'The Veiled Woman in Freud's "Das Unheimlich"', *Signs*, 2(3) (Spring, 1986) 519–28; Kaja Silverman, *The Acoustic Mirror: The Female Voice in Psychoanalysis and Cinema* (Bloomington: Indiana Press, 1988). See also Alexandra Kokoli, *The Feminist Uncanny in Theory and Art Practice* (London: Bloomsbury, 2016).

20. Freud, 'The "Uncanny"', 232, n. 1; Hélène Cixous, 'Fiction and its Phantoms: A Reading of Freud's *Das Unheimlich*', *New Literary History*, 7(3) (Spring, 1976), 525–48, 537.

21. Vidler, *The Architectural Uncanny*, 37, 38.

22. Ibid. 38, 41.

23. Daisy Connon, *Subjects Not-at-Home: Forms of the Uncanny in the Contemporary French Novel* (Amsterdam: Rodopi, 2010), 14.

24. Ibid. 57.

25. I mean 'banal' in the usual sense of the word, that is, obvious to the point of being platitudinous. Interestingly, this sense evolved from earlier meanings associated with domestic routine. In Old French 'banal' referred to public decrees authorising the communal use of facilities such as mills and ovens by serfs. The term became generalised in French to mean 'open to everyone' and subsequently 'petty' and then its current meaning 'trite', which was first recorded in English in 1840 (*OED*). The earlier sense of banal, which designated a requisite public proclamation, is preserved in English in the term banns (of marriage). Through its routine enunciation, the banal unhomely may well seem similarly obligatory. Thanks to Matthew Birchwood for this prompt.

26. Catherine Jurca, *White Diaspora: The Suburb and the Twentieth-Century American Novel* (Princeton: Princeton University Press, 2001).

27. Stephen King, *Danse Macabre* (New York: Everest House, 1981), 168, 167.

28. Sam Cornish, 'Middle-class Souls on Ice', *Christian Science Monitor*, 1 March 1985. Actually, in what I suspect is a slip of the pen, Cornish contrasts *Linden Hills* with *The Bill Cosby Show*, which aired 1969–71. See also Terrence Tucker,

'In the Shadow of *Cosby*: Gloria Naylor's *Linden Hills* and the Postintegration Black Elite', in *Gloria Naylor's Fiction: Contemporary Explorations of Class and Capitalism*, ed. Sharon A. Lewis and Ama S. Wattley (Cambridge: Cambridge Scholars Press, 2017), 77–100.

29. From Matheson's 1959 novel, *Stir of Echoes*. Cited in Murphy, 10. An appreciation of the incongruousness of a gothic response to the American scene has of course much earlier antecedents in the likes of James Fennimore Cooper, Nathaniel Hawthorne and James Paulding, who agreed that there seemed little scope for the production of gothic romance in a country with 'no shadow, no antiquity, no mystery'. Of course, this observation did not prevent them from resorting to the gothic. See Donald Ringe, *American Gothic*, and Teresa E. Goddu, *Gothic America: Narrative, History and Nation* (New York: Columbia University Press, 1997).

30. Renée L. Bergland makes a similar claim while discussing Stephen King's 1983 novel *Pet Sematary*: King's demonic hauntings serve to distract attention from ongoing disputes over land claims by Native American tribes in Maine and to assuage white guilt over histories of Native American dispossession. See Bergland, *The National Uncanny: Indian Ghosts and American Subjects* (Hanover, NH: University of New England Press, 2000), 165–7.

31. Anne Rivers Siddons, *The House Next Door* (London: Fontana, 1979), 118–19. Subsequent page references given in parentheses.

32. Arguably the house, with its extensive plate-glass surfaces, connects with the cultural history of the picture window, discussed in Chapter 1. The architect's complaints about not being able to find suitable occupants for his modernist dreamhouse seems to correspond with the anguish over the massification of the suburban home as emblematised by the picture window.

33. The phrase is usually attributed to George Herbert. Some of the sayings compiled in his 1640 book *Outlandish Proverbs* were inventions of Herbert; most, however, were collected from sources both domestic and foreign (hence 'Outlandish'). Possibly, then, Rivers Siddons means her protagonist to have blundered across the truth.

34. See Christopher J. Walsh, '"Dark Legacy"': Gothic Ruptures in Southern Literature, in Jay Ellis (ed.), *Southern Gothic Literature* (Ipswich, MA: Salem Press, 2013), 19–34, and Ronja Vieth, 'Charles W. Chesnutt's Southern Gothic of Guilt', in *Sothern Gothic Literature*, 75–92.

35. Colquitt, county seat of Miller County, and Colquitt County. Both were named after Walter T. Colquitt (1799–1855), lawyer, popular Methodist preacher, and US Representative and then Senator from Georgia. Thus there seems to be some design behind Rivers Siddons's choice for the name of Colquitt's husband.

36. Freud, 'The "Uncanny"', 248, n. 1.

37. Gloria Naylor, *Linden Hills* (London: Hodder & Stoughton, 1985), 1, 9. Subsequent page references given in parentheses.

38. On the situation of the black middle class in the 1980s, see Bart Landry, *The New Black Middle Class* (Berkeley: University of California Press, 1987), Mary Pattillo-McCoy, *Black Picket Fences: Privilege and Peril among the Black Middle Class* (Chicago: Chicago University Press, 2000), and Cherise A. Harris, *The*

Cosby Cohort: Blessings and Burdens of Growing Up Black Middle Class (Lanham, MD: Rowman and Littlefield, 2013).

39. See Sut Jhally and Justin M. Lewis, *Enlightened Racism: The Cosby Show, Audiences and the Myth of the American Dream* (Boulder, CO: Westview, 1992), Leslie B. Innis and Joe R. Feagin, 'The Cosby Show: The View from the Black Middle Class', *Journal of Black Studies*, 25(2) (July 1995), 692–711, and Michael Eric Dyson, *Is Bill Cosby Right? Or Has the Black Middle Class Lost Its Mind?* (New York: Basic Civitas, 2005).

40. Fred Botting, *Gothic*, 2nd edn (London: Routledge, 2014), 6.

41. By modelling Linden Hills so closely on Dante's depiction of Hell, Naylor of course inverts the traditional topographic organisation of sub/urban settlement, which sees the highest ground occupied by the most prestigious addresses. On the other hand, Linden Hills' unusual arrangement appears to be the outcome of a longer history of black settlement dominated by the need to make the most of marginal land. A similar inversion can be seen in Toni Morrison's 1973 novel *Sula*: the black neighbourhood of the Bottom occupies poor hilltop land.

42. See Margaret Earley Whitt, *Understanding Gloria Naylor* (Columbia: University of South Carolina Press, 1999), 58–9, for an overview.

43. Bruce Haynes, *Red Lines, Black Spaces: The Politics of Race and Space in Black Middle-class Suburb* (New Haven, CT: Yale University Press, 1999); Andrew Wiese, *Places of Their Own: African American Suburbanization in the Twentieth Century* (Chicago: University of Chicago Press, 2004); Todd M. Michney, *Surrogate Suburbs: Black Upward Mobility and Neighborhood Change in Cleveland, 1900–1980* (Chapel Hill: University of North Carolina Press, 2017).

44. Robert Beuka, *SuburbiaNation: Reading Suburban Landscape in Twentieth-Century American Fiction and Film* (New York: Palgrave, 2004), 14.

45. Michael Atkinson, *Blue Velvet* (London: BFI, 1997), 32. Laura Mulvey, 'The Pre-Oedipal Father: The Gothicism of *Blue Velvet*', in Sage and Lloyd Smith (eds), *Modern Gothic: A Reader* (Manchester: Manchester University Press, 1996), 38–57, 55.

46. Debra Shostak, '"A story we could live with": Narrative Voice, the Reader, and Jeffrey Eugenides's *The Virgin Suicides*', *Modern Fiction Studies* 55(4) (Winter, 2009), 808–32, 813. I follow Shostak in referring to the novel's narrative voice as that of 'the narrators'. Strictly speaking, however, it is not choral, but a singular voice speaking anonymously as or for a unified 'we'. Though catachrestic, 'the narrators' usefully draws attention to the narration's fabricated plurality.

47. Similar observations occur elsewhere in Eugenides's fiction. The similarly retrospective narrator of his second novel *Middlesex*, in which a good deal of the historical action also takes place in Grosse Pointe, Michigan, suggests that his family's eponymous modernist house makes an incongruous home for three generations of Greek-Americans. For instance, remembering his grandmother Desdemona – who, like *The Virgin Suicides*' Mrs Karafilis, arrived in the US as a refugee in the early 1920s – the narrator remarks: 'The boxlike room, stripped of all embellishment or parlor fussiness, a room that wished to be timeless or ahistorical, and there, in the middle of it, my deeply historical timeworn grandmother. Everything about Middlesex spoke of forgetting and everything about

Desdemona made plain the inescapability of remembering.' Jeffrey Eugenides, *Middlesex* (London: Bloomsbury, 2002), 273.

48. Jeffrey Eugenides, *The Virgin Suicides* (London: Bloomsbury, [1993] 2002), 43. Subsequent page references given in parentheses.

49. Shostak, 'A Story We Could Live With', 821–3.

50. On white flight in Detroit, see Thomas J. Sugrue, *The Origins of the Urban Crisis: Race and Inequality in Postwar Detroit*, 2nd rev. edn (Princeton, NJ: Princeton University Press, 2005). In *Middlesex*, Eugenides depicts two generations of Greek-Americans relocating further and further from the centre of Detroit, largely in response to the in-migration of the city's expanding black population.

51. In a trenchant eco-critical reading of *The Virgin Suicides*, Christian Long explains that the Dutch elm epidemic, which decimated half the nation's population of *Ulmus America*, was exacerbated by elm trees being planted closely together in suburban neighbourhoods in order to create idyllic arboreal streetscapes. Long argues that the Lisbon girls may be understood as 'nature painfully absenting itself from the suburbs, a "pristine" nature the suburban form simultaneously idealizes and consumes', though noticeably Long's reading relies on the narrators' questionable association between the girls and nature. Christian Long, 'Running out of Gas: The Energy Crisis in the 1970s Suburban Narratives', *Canadian Review of American Studies*, 41(3) (Winter, 2011), 342–69, 360.

52. Studies of third and later generations have modified this view: the emergence of 'symbolic ethnicity' – an identity enacted periodically and by choice – is actually driven by the very same factors that were once held to weaken ethnic identification: social mobility and the relative social isolation experienced in the suburbs. See in particular Mary C. Waters, *Ethnic Options: Choosing Identities in America* (Berkeley: University of California Press, 1990), and Richard D. Alba, *Ethnic Identity: The Transformation of White America* (New Haven: Yale University Press, 1990).

53. Sugrue, *Origins of the Urban Crisis*, 22.

54. James Baldwin, 'On Being "White" . . . and Other Lies', *Essence*, April 1984.

55. Malcolm X, with Alex Haley, *The Autobiography of Malcolm X* (New York: Ballantine, 1984), 399.

56. See for instance Matthew Frye Jacobson, *Roots Too: White Ethnic Revival in Post-Civil Rights America* (Cambridge, MA: Harvard University Press, 2008).

57. Olivier Zunz, *The Changing Face of Inequality: Urbanization, Industrial Development and Immigrants in Detroit, 1880–1920* (Cambridge, MA: Harvard University Press, 1982); David Roediger, *Working toward Whiteness: How America's Immigrants became White – The Strange Journey from Ellis Island to the Suburbs* (New York: Basic, 2004), 161.

58. Historians and writers of fiction alike disagree, however, over whether or not the sacrifices involved in the rush to acquire a first home actually damaged the future prospects of immigrant families. See for instance John Bodnar, *The Transplanted: A History of Immigrants in Urban America* (Bloomington: Indiana University Press, 1985); Pietro di Donato's novel *Christ in Concrete* (1939) concerning the plight of poor immigrant Italians is decidedly less optimistic about the opportunities afforded by homeownership.

59. Roediger, *Working toward Whiteness*, 177.
60. See also Sugrue, *Origins of the Urban Crisis*, 211–18.
61. See Stephen Higley, *Power, Privilege and Place: Geography of the American Upper Class* (Lanham, MD: Rowman & Littlefield, 1995).
62. More broadly, descendants of immigrants were encouraged to invest in their whiteness, but not their ethnicity, through various New Deal housing initiatives from the mid-1930s onwards, such as redlining and steering. These practices deterred for immigrants from developing their own urban neighbourhoods and encouraged to move into areas, usually suburban, which were designated as raceless. See Roediger, 230–1.
63. Alison Landsberg, *Prosthetic Memory: The Transformation of American Remembrance in the Age of Mass Culture* (New York: Columbia University Press, 2004), 49–80.
64. Cathy Davidson, *Revolution and the Word: The Rise of the Novel in America* (New York: Oxford University Press, 1994), 328.

Chapter 3: Some Shared Story: Suburban Memoir

1. David Beers, *Blue Sky Dream: A Memoir of America's Fall from Grace* (New York: Doubleday, 1996), 17.
2. William Merrill Decker's *Kodak Elegy: A Cold War Childhood* (Syracuse, NY: Syracuse University Press, 2012), xiii.
3. D. J. Waldie, *Holy Land: A Suburban Memoir* (New York: Norton, [1996] 2005), 118. Subsequent page references given in parentheses.
4. Rak notes that these figures do not even take into account the considerable circulation of memoirs in library systems. While accepting that fiction is still by far the bestselling and most profitable category in publishing, the increase in production and sales 'indicates that readers continue to purchase' memoirs, a trend 'which shows little sign of abating in the United States'. Julie Rak, *Boom!: Manufacturing Memoir for the Popular Market* (Waterloo, ON: Wilfred Laurier University Press, 2013), 8–9.
5. 'Misery memoir': 'an account, usually by a noncelebrity, of childhood abuse or otherwise painful or difficult circumstances'; 'shtick lit': 'books perpetrated by people who undertook an unusual project with the express purpose of writing about it'. Ben Yagoda, *Memoir: A History* (New York: Riverhead, 2009), 9, 11.
6. While some companies facilitate the on-demand publishing of 'assisted memoirs', most specialise in the production of commissioned or 'as-told-to memoirs' (terms used by Modern Memoirs, Inc. Available at <www.modern-memoirs.com> (last accessed 11 March 2019), whereby the company conducts extensive interviews about the subject(s) in question to enable the 'professional biographer' to craft a life narrative that is unembellished but 'written in a compelling manner' (Real Life Stories, available at <http://realifestories.com/service/story-memoir/> (last accessed 11 March 2019). Typically, companies will offer a range of options relating to formatting, binding and design, with some including e-book distribution as an optional service. Companies recognise and promote a range of reasons for commissioning a memoir; Real Life

Stories helpfully advises that their 'My Story Memoir' product 'is perfect for a holiday, anniversary, or birthday gift. It can also be a tax-deducted expense as a marketing tool for your business' (ibid.).

7. G. Thomas Couser, *Memoir: An Introduction* (Oxford: Oxford University Press, 2012), 26.
8. Yagoda, *Memoir*, 28.
9. Cited by Yagoda, *Memoir*, 238.
10. Friedrich Schlegel (1772–1829), for instance, deemed 'pure autobiographies' to be written by 'born historians who regard themselves only as material for historic art [. . .] or by pedantic minds who want to bring even the most minute things in order before they die and cannot let themselves leave the world without commentaries'. Cited by Yagoda, *Memoir*, 66.
11. For example Evelyn Werner Barkins, *The Doctor has a Family* (New York: Pelegrini and Cudahy, 1950); Hilda Cole Epsy, *Quiet, Yelled Mrs Rabbit* (Philadelphia: Lippincott, 1958); Edith-Jane Bahr, *Everybody Wins, Nobody Loses (Advice from a Mother who Survived)* (New York: McKay, 1968); June Benefield, *Laughing to Keep me from Crying* (Houston, TX: Gulf, 1972). In *Through a Woman's 'I': An Annotated Bibliography of American Women's Autobiographical Writings, 1946–1976* (Metuchen, NJ: Scarecrow, 1983), Patricia K. Addis gives details of over 2,200 titles; only a handful (including those listed above) dwell on suburban life at any time during the twentieth century. See also Penelope Fritzer and Bartholomew Bland, *Merry Wives and Others: A History of Domestic Humour Writing* (Jefferson, NC: McFarland, 2002), especially Chapter 3, 'Midcentury Merry Wives'.
12. Nancy K. Miller, *But Enough about Me: Why We Read Other People's Lives* (New York: Columbia University Press, 2002), 12.
13. Rak, *Boom!*, 13.
14. Malvina Reynolds, 'Little Boxes', 1962. The song was a hit for Reynold's friend Pete Seeger the following year and has frequently been covered since.
15. Lewis Mumford, *The City in History: Its Origins, Its Transformations, Its Prospects* (London: Pelican, [1961] 1966), 553.
16. Catherine Jurca, *White Diaspora The Suburb and the Twentieth-Century American Novel* (Princeton NJ: Princeton University Press, 2001).
17. Or to use a term coined by Lorraine Adams, the 'nobody memoir'. Lorraine Adams, 'Almost Famous: The Rise of the "Nobody" Memoir', *Washington Monthly*, April 2002. Available at <www.washingtonmonthly.com/features/2001/0204.adams.html> (last accessed 11 March 2019).
18. Peter Balakian, 'A Memoir across Generations: Baby-Boom Suburbs, the Armenian Genocide, and Scholarly Corruption in America', *Chronicle of Higher Education*, 40(44) (12 June 1998), B6-B7, B7.
19. Peter Balakian, *Black Dog of Fate: A Memoir: An American Son Uncovers His Armenian Past*, 10th Anniversary edn (New York: Basic, [1997] 2009), 18. Subsequent page references are given in parenthesis.
20. Joanne Jacobson similarly focuses on the sensate 'body in motion' in *Hunger Artist: A Suburban Childhood* (Huron, OH: Bottom Dog, 2007). See Martin Dines, 'A Child in the Suburbs' in Christine Berberich, Neil Campbell and

Robert Hudson (eds), *Affective Landscapes in Literature, Art and Everyday Life* (Farnham: Ashgate, 2015), 99–112.

21. For example: Frank DeCaro's *A Boy Named Phyllis: A Suburban Memoir* (New York: Viking, 1996); Jennifer Baszile's *The Black Girl Next Door: A Memoir* (New York: Touchstone, 2009).

22. See Valerie Saunders, 'Childhood and Life Writing', in Margaretta Jolly, *Encyclopedia of Life Writing: Autobiographical and Biographical Forms*, Vol. 1 (London: Fitzroy Dearborn, 2001), 203–4.

23. Another account of a suburban organisation man can be found in Decker's *Kodak Elegy*, which recounts its author's upbringing in the suburbs of Rochester, New York. Decker's father – who like many a blue sky suburbanite 'took the optimist's view of force available in the Atomic age' (2) – worked all his professional life as an engineer for Kodak Eastman, a firm which required a considerable degree of secrecy from its employees, in part due to its having government contracts, and whose off-limits Rochester plant was imagined by the young Decker to be 'vaguely military' (12). Like Beers's account, Decker's memoir meditates on the contradictory trajectories of the post-war suburbs. Decker's memoir is elegiac in so far as it recalls the dreaming of a child for whom the suburbs provided 'a field of contemplation to imagine a future life' (20), and acknowledges the fading or corruption of an almost official suburban-utopian vision of the 1950s and 60s, the 'Kodak Moment'. On the other hand, it registers how such imagery always seemed jarring: in the shadow of the bomb, 'surmise of something structurally amiss became a perpetual condition' (239). Decker also recognises how he and his siblings have nonetheless reproduced the same family structures as their parents and have sought 'safe harbour in middle-class homes' (ibid.).

24. Joan Didion, 'Notes from a Native Daughter', in Didion, *Slouching Towards Bethlehem* (Harmondsworth: Penguin, [1968] 1974).

25. Mary Helen Ponce's *Hoyt Street: An Autobiography* (Albuquerque: University of New Mexico Press, 1993) provides a more thoroughgoing example of a suburban autoethnography, which she describes as 'a life story, but also a communal history' (x). It recounts her childhood in a wholly Mexican American community in Pacoima, in Los Angeles's San Fernando Valley. Ponce elects not to recount Pacoima's suburbanisation in the post-war years following the expansion of the aviation industry in neighbouring city of Burbank (where Lockheed had a significant presence), instead focusing entirely on a community life she feels has either been maligned or ignored.

26. Koenraad Verboven, Myriam Carlier and Jan Dumolyn, 'A Short Manual to the Art of Prosopography', in K. S. B. Keats-Rohan (ed.), *Prosopography Approaches and Applications: A Handbook* (Oxford: University of Oxford Linacre College Unit for Prosopographical Research, 2007) 35–70, 37.

27. In 1953 Garnett received the first of three Guggenheim Fellowships, which was the first ever given to an aerial photographer. In 1954 he had a portfolio of pictures published in *Fortune* magazine. In 1955, he had a one-man museum exhibition show at the George Eastman House, curated by the photographic historian Beaumont Newhall, and *The New York Times Magazine* published

a portfolio of his work. That same year, he was included in the 'Family of Man' exhibition at the Museum of Modern Art in New York. In 1969 he contributed photographs to Nathaniel Owings's *The American Aesthetic*, an influential critique of twentieth-century urban planning. (Martha A. Sandweiss, 'Introduction', William Garnett, *Aerial Photography* (Berkeley: University of California Press, 1993), xi–xii.) His photography 'defies the stereotype of aerial photography as purely scientific and devoid of artistry' said the Getty Museum in 2004, when it acquired a collection of Garnett's work, which included six photographs of Lakewood. Available at <www.getty.edu/art/collection/artists/1545/william-a-garnett-american-1916-2006/> (last accessed 11 March 2019).

28. D. J. Waldie, 'Beautiful and Terrible: Aerial Views of Suburbia', *Places*, February 2014. Available at <placesjournal.org/article/beautiful-and-terrible-aeriality-and-the-image-of-suburbia/> (last accessed 11 March 2019).

29. Ibid.

30. Ibid.

31. Mumford, *The City in History*, 553

32. James Howard Kunstler, 'Where Evil Dwells: Reflections on the Columbine School Massacre', paper delivered at the Congress for New Urbanism, Milwaukee, June 1999. Available at <kunstler.com/other-stuff/speeches-guest-articles/where-evil-dwells-reflections-on-the-columbine-school-massacre/> (last accessed 11 March 2019).

33. Waldie, 'Beautiful and Terrible'.

34. Ibid.

35. Michel de Certeau, *The Practice of Everyday Life*, trans. Steven F. Rendall (Berkeley: University of California Press, 1984), 92.

36. Ibid. 93.

37. Ibid. 104, 95.

38. Ibid. 108.

39. Neil Campbell, 'Ordinary Geographies: Trajectories of Affect in the Work of Kathleen Stewart and D. J. Waldie', in Martin Dines and Timotheus Vermeulen (eds), *New Suburban Stories* (London: Bloomsbury, 2013), 151–60, 153. De Certeau also invokes Icarus in his discussion of the outlook from the World Trade Center; his descent – and the transition from disembodied sight to blind body – is characterised as an Icarian fall. De Certeau, *The Practice of Everyday Life*, 92.

40. Campbell, 'Ordinary Geographies', 153–4.

41. Jan Campbell and Janet Harbord, 'Introduction', in Jan Campbell and Janet Harbord (eds), *Temporalities, Autobiography and Everyday Life* (Manchester: Manchester University Press, 2002), 1–17, 2.

42. De Certeau, *The Practice of Everyday Life*, 105.

43. Ibid. 107.

44. *Holy Land*'s circuitous, sedimentary narrative is not the only history of Lakewood that Waldie has written. The first, penned in 1978 shortly after he took up a job as a city officer, became something of an official history, and indeed was published by the City of Lakewood with the express purpose of promoting cit-

izenship among its younger inhabitants. Unsurprisingly, given its pedagogical purposes, this earlier historiography seems a more conventional account: the trajectory of Lakewood's development, from a virtually blank landscape to its incorporation as a city, is linear, and Lakewood's triumvirate of developers appear to be its story's only protagonists (61–2).

45. The J. Paul Getty Museum, 'William A. Garnett'. Available at <www.getty. edu/art/collection/artists/1545/william-a-garnett-american-1916-2006/> (last accessed 11 March 2019).

46. Kevin M. Kruse and Thomas J. Sugrue, 'Introduction: The New Suburban History', in Kevin M. Kruse and Thomas J. Sugrue (eds), *The New Suburban History* (Chicago: University of Chicago Press, 2006), 1–10, 5.

47. Kenneth Frampton, 'Towards a Critical Regionalism: Six Points for an Architecture of Resistance', in Hal Foster (ed.), *The Anti-Aesthetic. Essays on Postmodern Culture* (London: Pluto, [1983] 1990), 16–30, 21.

48. Neil Campbell, '"The compass of possibilities": Re-Mapping the Suburbs of Los Angeles in the Writings of D. J. Waldie', *European Journal of American Studies*, (6)3 (2011), doc. 2, para. 9. Available online at <ejas.revues.org/9424> (last accessed 11 March 2019).

49. Campbell, 'Ordinary Geographies', 155.

50. See Spiro Kostof, *The City Shaped: Urban Patterns and Meanings through History* (London: Thames & Hudson, 1991), 102. The grid also of course offered the most efficient way of organising and apportioning land in the new colony, a fact noted by, among others, Mumford in *The City in History*, 224.

51. See Campbell, 'Ordinary Geographies', 151–2, for a sensitive reading of Waldie's meditation on his bathroom door.

52. Carissa Turner Smith, 'D. J. Waldie's *Holy Land*: Redeeming the Spiritual Geography of Suburbia', *Renascence*, 63(4) (Summer, 2011), 307–23, 315.

53. William H. Whyte, *The Organization Man* (London: Jonathan Cape, [1956] 1957), 7.

54. Ibid. 8.

55. Turner Smith, 315.

56. D. J. Waldie, 'Ordinary Time: The Making of a Catholic Imagination', *Spiritus: A Journal of Christian Spirituality*, 7(1) (Spring, 2007), 58–67, 62.

57. De Certeau, *The Practice of Everyday Life*, 108.

58. Waldie, 'Beautiful and Terrible'.

Chapter 4: Houses, Comics, Fish: Graphic Narrative Ecologies of the Suburban Home

1. Henri Lefebvre, *The Production of Space*, trans. Donald Nicholson-Smith (Oxford: Blackwell, 1991), 92–3.

2. Ibid. 93.

3. Ibid. 97.

4. Heide Solbrig, *Dandelion King: Love and Loss Waiting in the Gas Line*, Chapters 1 and 2 (Somerville, MA: Whatever Floats Your Boat Productions, 2015), 33; subsequent page references given in parentheses.

5. Whatever Floats your Boat Productions, <www.hydafloats.com/2016/10/03/753/> (last accessed 11 March 2019).

6. Solbrig has offered a number of explanations for her decisions about form. Regarding the transmediality of her memoir, she claims to have designed each element to be both interconnected and to stand alone. They all need to work independently, she explains, because there is no guarantee that certain platforms will stand the test of time. On the other hand, she imagines her reader to be a 'contemporary version' of herself – 'an alienated smartass teenage girl sitting on a street corner [who is] at least as likely to stare at her phone [as] read a book'. Solbrig declares she is also interested in producing 'different kinds of transitional moments'. Whereas classic studies such as Scott McCloud's *Understanding Comics* have focused on the interpretive work required of readers of comic strips as they progress from one panel to the next, Solbrig's cross-platform approach demands, she implies, a variety of interpretive strategies in order to negotiate the interactions of history, memory and affect. (More recent scholarly investigations into the formal properties of comics, foremost the 'neo-semiotic' studies of Thierry Groensteen, do attempt more complex analyses of the compositional relationships of visual elements within comics than those advanced by Eisner or McCloud. Groensteen's concepts of iconic solidarity and arthrology, for instance, draw attention to the different ways an individual panel inevitably engages with other contiguous and non-contiguous elements (Groensteen, *The System of Comics*, trans. Bart Beaty and Nick Ngyuen, Jackson: University of Mississippi Press, 2007). However, such formalism provides few if any opportunities to appraise reader participation in the production of meaning, or to consider comics as social artefacts.) Solbrig's inclusion of documentary film material also reflects an impulse to collect evidence: 'My comic pages are built from pretty visceral memories. Memories are pretty un-structured, and [. . .] my childhood was chaotic enough that there aren't too many photos or other people remembering.' She adds that houses are such a feature of her narrative because she lived in as many as eleven different ones throughout her childhood; thus 'they seem an apt metaphor for a dislocated childhood'. At the same time, she insists 'I cannot emphasize enough how much home ownership, and the real estate boom "framed" both my childhood and a general consciousness of Southern California' in the 1970s. Once again, then, the suburban home constitutes a crucial site of negotiation between the between the personal and the historical. (In email correspondence with author, 11 July 2017.)

7. Lefebvre, *The Production of Space*, 95–7.

8. Scott McCloud, *Understanding Comics: The Invisible Art* (New York: Harper Collins, 1994), 104.

9. Charles Hatfield, *Alternative Comics: An Emerging Literature* (Jackson: University Press of Mississippi, 2005), 41; Gérard Genette, Narrative Discourse, trans. Jane E. Lewin (Oxford: Blackwell, 1980), 34.

10. Hillary Chute, *Graphic Women: Life Narrative and Contemporary Comics* (New York: Columbia University Press, 2010), 8. See also Davida Pines, 'History, Memory and Trauma: Confronting Dominant Interpretations of 9/11 in Alissa Torres's *American Widow* and Art Spiegelman's *In the Shadow of No Towers*',

in Jane Tolmie Jackson (ed.), *Drawing from Life: Memory and Subjectivity in Art* (Jackson: University of Mississippi Press, 2013), 185–206; Nancy Miller, 'The Trauma of Diagnosis: Picturing Cancer in Graphic Memoir', *Configurations*, 22(2) (March 2014), 207–23; Harriet E. H. Earle, *Comics, Trauma and the New Art of War* (Jackson: University of Mississippi Press, 2017).

11. Respectively, the subtitles correspond to Scott McCloud's *Understanding Comics*, Charles Hatfield's *Alternative Comics* and Rocco Versaci's *This Book Contains Graphic Language* (New York: Continuum, 2007).

12. As Roger Sabin has detailed, however, adults have always comprised a significant section of comics readers in the US. In the post-war years, adult readerships of comic books expanded significantly in large part due to their popularity amongst military personnel. Roger Sabin, *Adult Comics: An Introduction* (London: Routledge, 1993), 147–8.

13. Jan Baetens and Hugo Frey open their *The Graphic Novel: An Introduction* (Cambridge: Cambridge University Press, 2015), 1–4, with the opinions of sceptics Art Spiegelman and Alan Moore, but then proceed to make a case for the formal, material and thematic distinctiveness of the graphic novel. They note, however, that many other comics scholars choose to employ alternative terms. My preferred term, most commonly used by scholars working in transnational contexts, is 'graphic narrative'. Not only is this an evidently more accurate label for the texts under discussion in this chapter, it suits my broader project of analysing suburban narrative in modes other than the novel.

14. See Bart Beaty, *Comics Versus Art: Comics in the Art World* (Toronto: University of Toronto Press, 2012), and Thierry Groensteen, *Comics and Narration*, trans. Ann Miller (Jackson: University of Mississippi Press, 2013), 159–76.

15. See Hatfield, *Alternative Comics*, 30.

16. On the direct market, see Hatfield, *Alternative Comics*, 20–9; Bradford W. Wright, *Comic Book Nation: The Transformation of Youth Culture in America* (Baltimore: Johns Hopkins University Press, 2001), 260–2; Jean-Paul Gabilliet, *Of Comics and Men: A Cultural History of American Comic Books*, trans. Bart Beaty and Nick Nguyen (Jackson: University of Mississippi Press, 2010), 141–7; Paul Lopes, *Demanding Respect: The Evolution of the American Comic Book* (Philadelphia: Temple University Press, 2009), 118–77.

17. Indeed, it is often remarked that comic strips were first included in newspapers as part of a concerted attempt by their proprietors to tap into the potentially huge market of city-dwelling immigrants. With their visual mode of communication and their broad humour, comics were thought to have particular appeal amongst those understood to have a weaker grasp of English and fewer shared cultural references compared with the native-born population. Roger Sabin comments that, despite the sophistication of some strips, 'because newspaper tycoons were using the strips to reach an ever-wider audience (often an immigrant audience), they were branded as "low class" and accused of "dragging the press down". This was closely tied to a religious objection: for many critics it was a point of principle that the Sabbath was not meant for enjoying the Sunday funnies (the fact that many immigrants happened to be non-Christians was not entirely unconnected).' Sabin, *Adult Comics*, 137. On the urbanity of

early cartoon strips see also Ole Frahm, 'Every Window Tells a Story: Remarks on the Urbanity of Early Comic Strips', in Jörn Ahrens and Arno Meteling (eds), *Comics and the City: Urban Space in Print, Picture and Sequence* (London: Continuum, 2010), 32–44; and Jared Gardner, *Projections: Comics and the History of Twenty-First-Century Storytelling* (Stanford: Stanford University Press, 2012), 1–28.

18. For example Sidney Smith's 'The Gumps' (1917–59), Fontaine Fox's 'Toonerville Folks' (1918–55), Frank King's 'Gasoline Alley' (1918–), Harry J. Tuthill's 'Home Sweet Home' (1918–23; thereafter ran as 'The Bungle Family' until 1945), and Clare Briggs's 'Mr. and Mrs.' (1919–63). See Sabin, *Comics, Comix and Graphic Novels: A History of Comic Art*, (London: Phaidon, 1996), 24; Brian Walker, *The Comics before 1945* (New York: Harry N. Abrams, 2004), 124–35.

19. On the phenomenology and navigation of the superheroic city, see Scott Bukatman, *Matters of Gravity: Special Effects and Supermen in the 20th Century* (Durham, NC: Duke University Press, 2003), 188–211.

20. The original black-and-white twelve-panel strip was originally published in *CoEvolution Quarterly* 25 (Fall, 1979), 21–4, and appeared in Crumb's one-off *Snoid Comics* later that year. A colour version was later published as a poster by Kitchen Sink Press in 1981; when this went out of print Crumb produced the version with three additional speculative panels.

21. *A Life Force* (1988) and *Dropsie Avenue* (1995).

22. Jared Gardner, *Projections*, 153.

23. Probably the most significant thing about the 'Joe Blow' strip, which appeared in *Zap* #4 (1969), was the way it prompted the first concerted attempts to block the magazine's distribution. Several West Coast and New York-based booksellers were arrested for 'promoting obscenity'. Most of these cases led to nothing, but two New York booksellers, Charles Kirkpatrick and Peter Dargis, were successfully convicted after they were found selling *Zap* #4. By making anyone who sold comix a potential target for the authorities, these convictions had the effect of hampering the circulation of underground material, which contributed to the decline of comix in the early 1970s (See Gabilliet, *Of Comics and Men*, 81–2). Earlier attempts to satirise the domestic comedy can be found in *Mad* (1952–), which, according to Adam Gopnik and Kirk Varnedoe, offered an oppositional 'devaluation of American secular mythology' and realised 'comics as a place outside consensus culture' (*High and Low: Modern Art and, Popular Culture*, New York: Museum of Modern Art and Abrams, 1990: 212).

24. Griffith contributed a comic strip about his home town to a scholarly study of Levittown, Pennsylvania, Dianne Harris's *Second Suburb: Levittown, Pennsylvania* (Pittsburgh: University of Pittsburgh Press, 2010). Scenes of post-war Levittown, New York also feature in Griffith's recent memoir, *Invisible Ink: My Mother's Love Affair with a Famous Cartoonist* (Seattle: Fantagraphics, 2015).

25. Hatfield, *Alternative Comics*, 109. Hatfield notes, however, that these ongoing autobiographies offer comic-book readers the entirely familiar pleasures of seriality and character development. Ibid. 112. See also Joseph Witek, *Comic Books as History: The Narrative Art of Jack Jackson, Art Spiegelman, and Harvey*

Pekar (Jackson: University of Mississippi Press, 1989), and Andrew J. Kunka, *Autobiographical Comics* (London: Bloomsbury, 2017).

26. Quoted Ron Goulart (ed.), *The Encyclopedia of American Comics: From 1897 to the Present* (New York: Facts on File, 1990), 288.

27. See Hillary Chute, *Graphic Women*, and Trina Robbins, *The Great Women Cartoonists* (New York: Watson-Guptill, 2001), 107–19. Chute notes that Kominsky attracted considerable flak – including from feminist critics – for being self-deprecating and stylistically and thematically crude (ibid. 32); more broadly, graphic memoirs produced by women – like memoir in general – have sometimes been dismissed for showing too much.

28. On picturing embodied selves in graphic memoir, see Elisabeth El Refaie, *Autobiographical Comics: Life Writing in Pictures* (Jackson: University of Mississippi Press, 2012), 49–92.

29. Alison Bechdel, *Fun Home: A Family Tragicomic* (London: Jonathan Cape, 2006), 13. Subsequent page references given in parentheses.

30. See Hatfield, *Alternative Comics*, 108–27; El Refaie, *Autobiographical Comics*, 135–79.

31. In a useful analysis Baetens and Frey note that *Fun Home* is 'based throughout on an elementary page grid', which is adapted variously 'each time the visual rhetoric of the book makes this suitable'. Shifts from regular to less-regular page layouts mark dramatic developments in a paradoxically consistent manner. On the other hand, an 'exceptional, and exceptionally conventional' regular grid-like layout is reserved for a particular scene – the one which Bruce Bechdel confides to his daughter details from his sexual history while they are driving together in the shared darkness of the car – to 'underscore the exceptional status of this moment that will never come back'. Baetens and Frey, *The Graphic Novel*, 123, 126.

32. For this reason I would question Chute's belabouring the significance of the 'white space' between panels in *Fun Home*. Chute argues that the gutters constitute a place where 'time passes'; they articulate 'the irrecoverable break of history, the chasm between the present [. . .] and the past' (*Graphic Women*, 216). But one of the distinguishing features of Bechdel's graphic narrative is just how little white space there is on its pages: virtually all of the book's horizontal guttering is filled with her own retrospective narration. For me, the sense of time passing in these spaces has less to do with the interval between events depicted in different panels, or the 'chasm' between present and past, then it does with the act of narration itself.

33. Caitlin DeSilvey, Simon Naylor and Colin Sackett (eds), *Anticipatory History* (Axminster: Uniformbooks, 2010), 10.

34. Daniel Pauly, 'Anecdotes and the Shifting Baseline Syndrome of Fisheries', *Trends in Ecology and Evolution*, 10(10) (October 1995), 430.

35. One of the most foremost promoters is filmmaker and former marine biologist Randy Olsen, who in 2003 co-founded with coral-reef ecologist Jeremy Jackson the Shifting Baselines Ocean Media Project. This venture, which brought together several US-based conservation groups and scientific organisations, sought to educate the public about the wide-scale problem of shifting baselines.

The project's main platform was an interactive website, which hosted a number of short films whose purpose was to challenge the manner in which people had become comfortable with terms that register environmental degradation, such as 'jellyfish blooms'. Another central aim was advocacy for the establishment of Marine Protected Areas, which were understood to have significant educational potential as they approximated conditions prior to human exploitation. See 'Shifting Baselines: Common Sense for the Oceans'. Available at <http://www.shiftingbaselines.org/> (last accessed 11 March 2019).

36. For instance, 'Shifting Baselines and New Meridians: Water, Resources, Landscapes, and the Transformation of the American West', conference organised by the University of Colorado, Boulder's Natural Resource Law Center in June 2008; Jari Lyytimäki, 'Nature's Nocturnal Services: Light Pollution as a Non-Recognised Challenge for Ecosystem Services Research and Management', *Ecosystems Services* 3 (March 2013), e44-e48; Frans Vera, 'The Shifting Baseline Syndrome in Restoration Ecology', in Marcus Hall (ed.), *Restoration and History: The Search for a Usable Environmental Past* (London: Routledge, 2010), 98–110.

37. See Adam Rome, *The Bulldozer in the Countryside: Suburban Sprawl and the Rise of American Environmentalism* (Cambridge: Cambridge University Press, 2001) for an excellent overview of the development of anti-sprawl activism.

38. Ian McHarg, *Design with Nature* (Garden City, NY: The Natural History Press, 1969), 55.

39. The construction of The Woodlands was enabled by The Urban Growth and New Community Development Act of 1970, which provided financial assistance to developers willing to build environmentally sensitive cities. However, the ensuing federal programme failed to realise the ambitions of those who had campaigned for a new kind of community building. The new cities still had to compete in the marketplace with traditional developments, and financial incentives from the government did not ensure their profitability. The Woodlands may have been celebrated as a model of successful environmental planning, but of the thirteen beneficiaries of the new community programme, it was the only one not to end in insolvency. See George T. Morgan, Jr and John O. King, *The Woodlands: New Community Development, 1964–1983* (College Station: Texas A&M University Press, 1987), and Evan McKenzie, *Privatetopia: Homeowner Associations and the Rise of Residential Private Government* (New Haven: Yale University Press, 1994).

40. McHarg, *Design with Nature*, 125. Claims that McHarg actually coined the concept of the shifting baseline in *Design with Nature* abound online. However, the term is never used in McHarg's book.

41. Ibid. 104.

42. Ibid.

43. *Anticipatory History*, 10.

44. Ibid. 15.

45. Ibid. 65.

46. Caitlin DeSilvey, 'Making Sense of Transience: An Anticipatory History', *Cultural Geographies*, 19(1) (January 2012), 31–54, 35.

47. Ibid. 31.

48. Ibid. 48.

49. DeSilvey's approach is informed by the work of the human geographer Kevin Lynch, who argues for strategies for urban redevelopment and preservation that make 'visible the process of change'. Kevin Lynch, *What Time is this Place?* (Cambridge, MA: MIT Press, 1972), 57.

50. The sequence does, however, seem to correspond to one of the most famous of Zeno's Paradoxes, that of the arrow in flight. The arrow (or fletcher's) paradox runs as follows: at any given instant in time a flying arrow is not moving; given the fact that no motion takes place at any instant, and that time is comprised of an infinite succession of instants, motion is impossible. This discombobulating conclusion would seem to be confirmed by the fact that McGuire's arrow appears to make no progress across successive pages. One way of dealing with the paradox, however, is to argue that Zeno has disregarded speed, which of course is a relationship between time and distance. To imagine an object travelling at a particular speed at a given instant in time does not entail it is not moving, but merely that it *appears* to be motionless (since the dimensions that enable movement to be perceptible – time and distance – have been removed from the picture). The perception of motion requires a frame of reference; the motion of an object is always relative to something else. If it were possible to move in parallel with a flying arrow at the exact same speed, then it would appear motionless. The background, though, would appear blurred, as with McGuire's arrow. (The import of this is potentially vertiginous – it suggests the reader of *Here* does not, after all, occupy a fixed perspective.) Another way of responding to the paradox is to accept that time cannot meaningfully be broken down into instants, only intervals. Many of the ways we presume to capture instants in time – most obviously photography – actually represent intervals. Like photographs, comic-strip panels would be better said to constitute 'capsules' of time rather than instants (a fact made clear by the inclusion of elements such as motion lines and speech bubbles).

51. An e-book version of *Here* accompanied the release of the printed book. Obviously, my comments regarding the book's materiality do to not correspond with the electronic version in any significant way. However, the e-book facilitates other modes of interaction. When viewed on touchscreen tablets, viewers may directly select and shuffle the book's many frames, creating new arrangements and generating new associations. This incarnation would also seem to correspond more closely to one of the important inspirations of the original strip, Microsoft's Windows operating system for personal computers.

52. Leanne Shapton, 'Split Screens: An Interview with Richard McGuire', *The Paris Review*, 12 June 2015.

53. Ibid.

54. For example: Gardner, *Projections*, 171–2; Thierry Smolderen, An Interview with Richard McGuire', *Comic Art*, 8 (2006), 14–39; Françoise Mouly, 'A god among the gods', *Comic Art*, 8 (2006), 16–17.

55. Chris Ware, 'Richard McGuire and "Here": A Grateful Appreciation', *Comic Art*, 8 (2006), 4–7, 7, 5.

56. Ibid. 6.
57. Chris Ware, *Building Stories* (London: Jonathan Cape, 2012), no page numbers; all subsequent quotes are from this edition.
58. Scott McCloud, *Understanding Comics*, 115. Polyptychs are commonly, but by no means always, arranged as split panels. Equally, not all split panels are true polyptychs.
59. Hatfield, *Alternative Comics*, 51.
60. Pierre Fresnault-Deruelle, 'Du linéaire au tabulaire', *Communications* 24 (1976), 7–23. In *Alternative Comics*, Hatfield speaks instead of the tension between 'sequence' and 'surface'.
61. Hatfield, *Alternative Comics*, 53.
62. A much earlier depiction of such antics in comics can be found in Frank King's *Gasoline Alley* (1918–), from 1934 (reproduced in Robert C. Harvey, *Children of the Yellow Kid: The Evolution of the American Comic Strip*, Seattle: Fry Art Museum in association with The University of Washington Press, 1998, 43), in which the children Skeezix and Trixie are depicted clambering through the frame of a house under construction; the polyptych format is similar to Ware's composition and may well have provided a model.
63. Martin Dines, 'A Child in the Suburbs', in Christine Berberich, Neil Campbell and Robert Hudson (eds), *Affective Landscapes in Literature, Art and Everyday Life* (Farnham: Ashgate, 2015), 99–112.
64. Isaac Cates, 'Comics and the Grammar of Diagrams', in *The Comics of Chris Ware: Comics are a Way of Thinking*, ed. David M. Ball and Martha B. Kuhlman (Jackson: University of Mississippi Press, 2010), 114–29, 117.
65. Ware, 'Richard McGuire and "Here": A Grateful Appreciation', 5.
66. See for example Daniel Raeburn, *Chris Ware*, (New Haven, CT: Yale University Press, 2004), 26.
67. For example: Raeburn, *Chris Ware*; Gene Kannenburg, Jr, 'The Comics of Chris Ware', in Robin Varnum and Christina T. Gibbons (eds), *The Language of Comics: Work and Image* (Jackson: University of Mississippi Press, 2001), 174–97; Angela Szczepaniak, 'Brick by Brick: Chris Ware's Architecture of the Page', in Joyce Goggin and Dan Hassler-Forest (eds), *The Rise and Reason of Comics and Graphic Literature* (Jefferson, NC: McFarland, 2010), 87–101. However, *The Comics of Chris Ware: Comics are a Way of Thinking*, ed. David M. Ball and Martha B. Kuhlman Ball (Jackson: University of Mississippi Press, 2010) features essays on topics such as Ware's engagement with gentrification, and the manner in which memory is shaped by the habitation of buildings.
68. Gardner, *Projections*, 171.
69. Daniel Worden, 'On Modernism's Ruins: The Architecture of "Building Stories" and *Lost Buildings*', in *The Comics of Chris Ware*, 145–58, 145.
70. Gardner, *Projections*, 177.
71. Roger Webster, 'Introduction: Suburbia Inside Out', in Roger Webster (ed.), *Expanding Suburbia: Reviewing Suburban Narratives* (Oxford: Berghahn, 2000), 1–14, 2.
72. Robert A. Bell and Roy G. Hlavacek, Oak Park Landmarks Commission, Village

of Oak Park, National Register of Historic Places Inventory-Nomination: Frank Lloyd Wright–Prairie School of Architecture Historic District, State of Illinois, 27 March 1973.

73. See Charles E. Aguar and Berdeana Aguar, *Wrightscapes: Frank Lloyd Wright's Landscape Designs* (New York: McGraw-Hill, 2002), 6.

74. Ware has said that the disparate but interconnecting narrative structure of *Building Stories*, more than that of any other of his other comic strips, most closely resembles the way that he thinks. Raeburn, *Chris Ware*, 96.

75. On the other hand, Ware has stressed the importance of finding inspiration from other cultural forms (ibid.). A favourite saying of Ware's grandmother that appears as an epigraph to *Building Stories*, 'Don't forget to go out of the house every once in a while or you'll lose your source of pollination', seems to echo this sentiment, while also gesturing towards the narrative's preoccupation with bees and flowers and its attempts to tell a story that spans multiple sites.

76. *Building Stories* features one further sequence that involves future retrospection. Towards the end of the section that focuses on the abusive relationship between the townhouse's resident straight couple, a double-page splash features the dejected female partner about to board the 'L'. The skyline of Humboldt Park and distant buildings in downtown Chicago occupy the background. A turn of the page reveals an identically sized and positioned splash which depicts exactly the same view in the year 2156. This co-ordination of two impressions of the same site at radically different moments in time of course echoes McGuire's techniques in *Here*. And like McGuire's visions of the future, Ware's composition predicts environmental degradation: a digital display seems to indicate there has been a significant increase in temperature; even though it is a morning in May, the sky is an even sulphur-brown colour. And in the manner of McGuire's future archaeologists, Ware depicts the city's post-apocalyptic residents using advanced technology to muse on human society in the early twenty-first century. There is much about this sequence that deserves further commentary: it could be said, for instance, to be articulating an anticipatory history of heterosexuality. Clearly, though, a future Chicagoan's capture and scrutiny of 'some memory fragment from this area's consciousness cloud', as she puts it, constitutes one more self-reflexive gesture on the part of Ware: if some form of advanced technology might one day facilitate multiple meaningful connections across time and space, then *Building Stories* – with its array of juxtapositions, its complex patternings and symmetries – would seem to be providing something similar already. Thanks to Paul Williams for encouraging me to look again at this sequence.

Chapter 5: Devolved Authorship, Suburban Literacies and the Short Story Cycle

1. Kasia Boddy, *The American Short Story after 1950* (Edinburgh: Edinburgh University Press, 2010), 2.

2. Forrest Ingram's *Representative Short Story Cycles of the Twentieth Century: Studies in a Literary Genre* (The Hague: Mouton, 1971) is the first scholarly monograph

dedicated to the form and establishes a precedent for using the term cycle. Susan Garland Mann (*The Short Story Cycle*, Westport, CT: Greenwood, 1989), James Nagel (*The Contemporary American Short-Story Cycle*, Baton Rouge: Louisiana University Press, 2001) and Jennifer J. Smith (*The American Short Story Cycle*, Edinburgh: Edinburgh University Press, 2017) are among several who follow suit. Robert M. Luscher makes a case for sequence (in 'The Short Story Sequence', in Susan Lohafer and Jo Ellyn Clarey (eds), *Short Story Theory at a Crossroads*, Baton Rouge: Louisiana University Press, 1989, 148–67), as does J. Gerald Kennedy in his introduction to *Modern Short Story Sequences* (Cambridge: Cambridge University Press, 1995). Maggie Dunn and Ann Morris (*The Composite Novel*, New York: Twayne, 1995) controversially avoid any reference to the short story with their preferred term, 'composite novel'; Rolf Lundén (*The United Stories of America*, Amsterdam: Rodopi, 1999) retains composite but reinstalls short story. Lundén notes 'a plethora of terms' have abounded in addition to cycle, sequence and composite, most of which take either the novel or the short story collection as the basis of their identification. It is worth noting that few writers and fewer publishers employ any of these words as labels for their volumes; if an indication of a book's generic identity is required, 'novel' or 'stories' (and sometimes both in combination) are the terms most likely to be deployed.

3. See for example Nagel, *The Contemporary American Short-Story Cycle*, 12.
4. Smith, *The American Short Story Cycle*, 6.
5. See for instance Nagel, *The Contemporary American Short-Story Cycle*, 3–4; Kennedy, *Modern Short Story Sequences*, vii; Boddy, *The American Short Story after 1950*, 125.
6. William Dean Howells, *Suburban Sketches* (Stroud: Nonsuch, [1871] 2005), 13; subsequent page references given in parentheses.
7. Scott Donaldson, 'Cheever's Shady Hill: A Suburban Sequence', in *Modern American Short Story Sequences: Composite Fictions and Fictive Communities*, ed. J. Gerald Kennedy (Cambridge: Cambridge University Press, 1995), 133–50.
8. Cherry Kelly, *The Society of Friends* (Columbia: University of Missouri Press, 1999), 140.
9. Jeff Birkenstein, '"Should I stay or should I go?" American Restlessness and the Short Story Cycle', in Alfred Bendixon and James Nagel (eds), *A Companion to the American Short Story* (Hoboken, NJ: Wiley-Blackwell, 2010), 482–501, 496.
10. Cherry, *The Society of Friends*, 38.
11. Ibid. 171.
12. Birkenstein, 'Should I stay or should I go?', 496.
13. Smith, *The American Short Story Cycle*, 38.
14. Nagel, *The Contemporary American Short-Story Cycle*, 4–5.
15. Ibid. 255.
16. Rocio G. Davis, *Transcultural Reinventions: Asian American and Asian Canadian Short-story Cycles* (Toronto: TSAR, 2001), 10.
17. Elizabeth Ordoñez, cited by Davis, *Transcultural Reinventions*, 19.
18. Michael Fischer, cited by Davis, *Transcultural Reinventions*, 18.
19. See Kalita, S. Mitra, *Suburban Sahibs: Three Immigrant Families and their Passage from India to America* (New Brunswick, NJ: Rutgers University Press, 2003);

Wendy Cheng, *The Changs Next Door to the Diazes: Remapping Race in Suburban California* (Minneapolis: University of Minnesota Press, 2014); Willow S. Lung-Amam, *Trespassers?: Asian Americans and the Battle for Suburbia* (Oakland: University of California Press, 2017).

20. Jhumpa Lahiri, *Interpreter of Maladies* (London: Flamingo, 1999), 137.

21. Noelle Brada-Williams, 'Reading Jhumpa Lahiri's *Interpreter of Maladies* as a Short Story Cycle', *MELUS*, 29(3/4) (Fall/Winter, 2004), 451–64, 462.

22. Junot Díaz, *Drown* (London: Faber, 1996), 162. Subsequent page references given in parentheses.

23. See for example Lucia Suárez, *The Tears of Hispaniola: Haitian and Dominican Diaspora Memory* (Gainesville: University of Florida Press, 2006), 91.

24. David Cowart, *Trailing Clouds: Immigrant Fiction in Contemporary American Fiction* (Ithaca, NY: Cornell University Press, 2006), 204.

25. Kevin Lynch, *What Time is this Place?* (Cambridge, MA: MIT Press, 1972), 61–2.

26. Ibid. 62.

27. John Brinckerhoff Jackson, *Discovering the Vernacular Landscape* (New Haven, CT: Yale, 1984), 85.

28. John Brinckerhoff Jackson, 'The Domestication of the Garage', in John Brinckerhoff Jackson, *Landscape in Sight: Looking at America*, ed. Helen Lefkowitz Horowitz, (New Haven, CT: Yale University Press, 1997), 118–25, 124.

29. Pam Conrad, *Our House*, 10th anniversary edition (New York: Scholastic, 2005), 13. Subsequent page references given in parentheses.

30. Gaston Bachelard, *The Poetics of Space*, trans. Maria Jolas (Boston, MA: Beacon, [1964] 1994), 15.

31. Ibid. 9.

32. Lynn Spigel, *Welcome to the Dreamhouse: Popular Media and Postwar Suburbs* (Durham, NC: Duke University Press, 2001), 2.

33. Bachelard, *The Poetics of Space*, 26.

34. Ibid. 9, emphasis in original.

35. Ibid. 64.

36. Owain Jones, '"Endlessly revisited and forever gone": On Memory, Reverie and Emotional Imagination', *Children's Geographies*, 1(1) (2003), 24–31, 27.

37. Svetlana Boym, *The Future of Nostalgia* (New York: Basic, 2001), xviii.

38. Among the most widely disseminated were aerial photographs which documented the new suburbs' emergence – such as those of Lakewood, California by William Garnett, discussed in Chapter 3. These emphasised the mass-production processes involved; the uniformity and sterility of suburban life was implied by the absence of any obvious human habitation. By contrast, Brian Selznick's illustrations for the tenth anniversary edition of *Our House* typically feature the book's child protagonists framed by and engaged with their immediate environment. Indeed, one of the book's stories, 'Night Photograph', concludes with a child leaving off her ambitions to take a bird's-eye-view shot of her home.

39. John Barth, *The Development: Nine Stories* (Boston, MA: Houghton Mifflin Harcourt, 2008), 7. Subsequent page references given in parentheses.

40. Sven Birkerts, 'Lost in the Rest Home', *New York Times*, Sunday Book Review, 5 October 2008, 13.

41. Kathy Knapp, 'Richard Ford's Frank Bascombe Trilogy and the Post-9/11 Suburban Novel', *American Literary History*, 23(3) (Fall, 2011), 500–28, 503.

Conclusion: Built to Last? Staging Suburban Historicity in the Teardown Era

1. Bruce Norris, *Clybourne Park* (London: Nick Hern, 2010), 100.

2. Dolores Hayden, *Building Suburbia: Green Fields and Urban Growth, 1820–2000* (New York: Vintage, 2004), 244–5.

3. James Howard Kunstler, *The Geography of Nowhere: The Rise and Decline of America's Man-Made Landscape* (New York: Simon & Schuster, 1993), 245.

4. 'Census finds record low growth in outlying suburbs', *Daily Herald*, 4 April 2012. Available at <www.dailyherald.com/article/20120405/business/704059804/> (last accessed 11 March 2019).

5. Herbert Muschamp, *New York Times*, 'The Nation; Becoming Unstuck on the Suburbs', 19 October 1997, 4.

6. See Sugie Lee and Nancey Green Leigh, 'The Role of Inner Ring Suburbs in Metropolitan Smart Growth', *Journal of Planning Literature*, 19(3) (February 2005), 330–46; Paul Lukez, *Suburban Transformations* (New York: Princeton Architectural Press, 2007); Ellen Dunham-Jones and June Williamson, *Retrofitting Suburbia: Urban Design Solutions for Redesigning Suburbs* (Hoboken, NJ: Wiley, 2011).

7. See Jon C. Teaford, *The American Suburb: The Basics* (New York: Routledge, 2008), 55–7, and Willow S. Lung-Amam, *Trespassers?: Asian Americans and the Battle for Suburbia* (Oakland: University of California Press, 2017), 138–74.

8. *Levittown* was produced by Axis Company in association with What Man Theatre Company, and was first performed in New York City on 26 June 2006. *Clybourne Park* and *Detroit* both premiered at Chicago's Steppenwolf Theatre in 2010. Both subsequently premiered in New York off-Broadway at Playwright's Horizon: *Clybourne Park* on 21 February 2010, *Detroit* in the fall of 2012. *Detroit* won an Obie award for best play in 2013; the play was shortlisted for a Pulitzer Prize in 2011, but lost out to *Clybourne Park*, which also won the Lawrence Olivier Award for Best New Play in 2011 and the Tony award for Best Play in 2012.

9. Doreen Massey, 'Places and their Pasts', *History Workshop Journal*, 39 (Spring, 1995), 182–92, 185, emphases in original.

10. Camilo José Vergara, 'Downtown Detroit: "American Acropolis" or Vacant Land – What to do with the World's Third Largest Concentration of Pre-Depression Skyscrapers', *Metropolis*, 33, April 1995, 33–8.

11. Rebecca Kinney, 'The Naturalisation of Racism through Ruin Porn and Digital Memories', *Media Fields Journal*, 5 (Fall, 2012), 1–14. See also Dora Apel, *Beautiful Terrible Ruins: Detroit and the Anxiety of Decline* (New Brunswick, NJ: Rutgers University Press, 2015).

12. Several reviews of the production can be found on the Hilberry Theatre

Company's website. Available at <https://hilberry.wordpress.com/tag/lisa-damour/> (last accessed 11 March 2019).

13. See Jackson Bartlett, 'Raise Money, Raise Hell, or Leave: Contesting DIY Urbanism in the Black Outer City', unpublished PhD thesis, Northwestern University, 2017.

14. John Patrick O'Leary, 'Detroitism: What Does "Ruin Porn" Tell us about the Motor City?', *Guernica*, 15 January 2011.

15. Peter Moskowitz, *How to Kill a City: Gentrification, Inequality and the Fight for the Neighborhood* (New York: Nation Books, 2018), 83.

16. Patrick Sheehan, 'Revitalization by Gentrification', *Jacobin*, 11 April 2015. Available at <www.jacobinmag.com/2015/05/detroit-foreclosure-redlining-evictions/> (last accessed 11 March 2019).

17. In email correspondence.

18. Lisa D'Amour, *Detroit* (London: Faber, 2012), 77.

19. Hayden, *Building Suburbia*, 243.

20. Ibid. 242.

21. Marc Palmieri, *Levittown* (New York: Dramatists Play Service Inc., 2007), 7.

22. Ibid. 10.

23. Bruce Norris, *Clybourne Park*, 93, 46. Subsequent page references in parentheses.

24. Massey, 'Places and Their Pasts', 190.

25. Ibid. 191.

26. A demonym is a term used to describe a people or inhabitants of a place, for example: 'American', the German word 'Amerikaner' and the Russian word 'американец'. An exonym refers to demonyms or toponyms bestowed by those who are external to a population or place: 'Amerikaner' and 'американец' are exonyms; 'American' is an endonym.

27. Nagachan, *Ramblings of Wanderer: Random Thoughts and Adventures*, 'Rude Brusselites . . . Brusselians . . . Brussellers . . . whatever you call them!', 9 June 2010. Available at <https://nagachan.wordpress.com/2010/06/09/rude-brusselites-brusselians-brussellers-whatever-you-call-them/> (last accessed 11 March 2019).

INDEX